# I, CATHERINE

# I, CATHERINE

## Selected Writings of
## St Catherine of Siena

EDITED AND TRANSLATED BY
Kenelm Foster OP
and Mary John Ronayne OP

COLLINS
St James's Place, London
1980

William Collins Sons & Co Ltd
London Glasgow Sydney Auckland
Toronto Johannesburg

First published 1980
©Kenelm Foster 1980

ISBN 0 00 215351 3

Set in Baskerville by
Inforum Ltd, Portsmouth.

Made and printed in Great Britain by
T.J. Press Ltd., Padstow,
and bound by
Robert Hartnoll Ltd., Bodmin

To Sister Mary Catherine OP
and her Sisters at Carisbrooke

# CONTENTS

# INTRODUCTION

'A prophetess towered in the tumult, a virginal tongue told.'         G.M. Hopkins, *The Wreck of the Deutschland.*

The young woman who dictated the letters translated in this book was born, so far as we know, in 1347 at Siena in Tuscany, and died at Rome on 29 April 1380. Eighty one years later she was officially declared a saint by the humanist pope, Pius II, himself a Sienese. Sanctity, as the Church in such cases understands the term, is Christian virtue at a heroic degree and normally attested by extra-ordinary effects which, as held to be not accountable by the ordinary processes of nature, are called miracles. This is not the place for discussing miracles as such, nor indeed for much lingering over any external details of Catherine's brief intense life on earth; which in any case has attracted excellent biographers, especially as regards its later stages when Catherine was a conspicuous figure in the public life of her time. To study her letters is to be drawn deep into the history, both ecclesiastical and secu-lar, of late fourteenth century Italy. This is not, however, their principal importance. Incomparably more impor-tant is the doctrinal and spiritual message of these letters, I mean their writer's passionate insight into the central dogma of Christianity, the union of godhead and man-hood in Christ. For many this doctrine is pure fantasy and many others, while not denying it, give it only a desultory attention. For the Church of course it is every-thing, its entire *raison-d'être*. But to anyone, believer or not, who stops to reflect for two minutes, it must surely be clear that if that union *has* taken place, if our fellow-man Jesus *is* also God, then God is revealed as loving indeed and the New Testament affirmation 'God is love' [1] becomes a statement about our concrete human situation and one of the very utmost urgency. Now the whole importance of Catherine of Siena as a writer – the aspect of her that most concerns us here – lies in the exceptional clarity, force, sweetness and profundity of her utterances on this great matter.

In what follows I shall first sketch St Catherine's life (I) and then give a brief summary of her spiritual teaching (II). A final section will give a few details about the text of her writings and their more important editions (III).

\* \* \*

# I

She was born, then, probably in 1347, the twenty third of twenty five children of a fairly prosperous Sienese dyer, Jacopo Benincasa, and his wife Lapa. Their house was on the steep hill below San Domenico. A twin sister having died in infancy, Lapa for once had time, before her last pregnancy, to suckle Catherine herself and so to become, we are told, particularly fond of her – a fact that did not prevent her finding this child, as she grew up to adolescence, bewilderingly unmanageable.

Siena was still a self-governing republic though already overshadowed by the greater power of Florence to the north, as by now were all the Tuscan communes. Because of this Florentine predominance in the region, Tuscany as a whole was one of the five chief centres of power in Italy, the others being Milan and Venice, the States of the Church (lying north-east, east and south of Tuscany) and the Kingdom of Naples. Catherine never had much to do, directly, with the two northern states Milan and Venice, nor with the southern kingdom, despite her contacts by letter with the notorious Queen of Naples, Joanna (see letter 58). It was only with the affairs of Florence and the Holy See that Catherine became deeply involved.

Between 1305 and 1378 all the popes were Frenchmen, governing the Church from Avignon in Provence from 1309 to '67 and again from 1370 to '77. This long absence of the popes from Rome naturally affected their

Italian dominions, the history of which, during this period, falls broadly into two phases, before and after 1354. Before this date the picture is one of a general collapse of central authority. In every region nominally subject to the Holy See the cities set up local despots or succumbed to external ones. Rome itself fell a prey to the struggle for power of the great local families, a state of affairs only interrupted by the strange career (1347–54) of the patriotic idealist Cola di Rienzo. However in 1354 the able and energetic Spanish cardinal Albornoz was entrusted by Innocent VI with the task of restoring order in the States of the Church. Albornoz succeeded so well that in 1367 Urban V – warmly applauded by Petrarch – was able to bring the Curia back to Rome; only to return to Avignon, and die there, in 1370. The definitive return to Rome was effected by the next Pope, Gregory XI, in 1377, under strong pressure from St Catherine, as we shall see.

To return now to that dyer's house overlooked by the great Dominican church at Siena. To the Florentine Dante the Sienese seemed a vain and dreamy race,[2] but the Benincasa at any rate were practical bourgeois folk and in the swarming hurly-burly of her home Catherine grew up in full contact with human realities. She grew up quickly too in Christian piety and before she was twelve had vowed her virginity to Jesus – no other husband for her! – a step that brought her at once into sharp conflict with her family until Jacopo, convinced at last that this daughter of his was no ordinary girl, ordered Lapa and the rest to let her be. Catherine was allowed a room of her own and there she remained, praying day and night, only leaving it to go to church or help with the housework. At sixteen she got herself admitted, against stiff opposition because of her youth, into a Dominican lay sisterhood, the *Mantellate*. This did not make her a nun but it gave her the black and white Dominican habit and the great Order's protection. She continued to live at home but now in a still stricter seclusion which may have lasted three years and was only terminated when she received, as she believed, an order from Christ to come out of her solitude and begin to practise, in the world about her, his second commandment: 'Love your neighbour as yourself.'

It is worth pausing here to reflect briefly on Catherine's spiritual experience so far, and particularly on the 'preternatural' element in it. Of course we are largely in the dark as to what went on in her cell during these years of seclusion, but some gleams of light are not lacking, and we owe them to her closest friend, who was also her confessor, the Dominican Raymond of Capua (c. 1330–1399) who has left a fairly full account of Catherine's inner and outer life in youth and early womanhood. His *Legenda maior*³ is in fact our chief authority (apart from her writings) on the life of Catherine, especially in its earlier stages. One can of course question Raymond's testimony, but he knew Catherine very well, and most of her family too, her mother in particular; and if some of the miracles and visions he reports seem barely credible, he is always careful to identify, whenever a *miracle* is in question, the source or sources of his information – the evidence of his own senses or of those of persons he had consulted when preparing his book. I underline 'miracles' to distinguish them from 'visions', following Raymond in this, who usually reserves the term miracle for extraordinary happenings which might, in principle, have been witnessed by more than one person at a time; as distinct from 'visions' which are experienced only by those who see them. So when, says Raymond, it is a question of Catherine's 'visions' (with which he associates 'revelations') 'we have only her own word' for it.⁴ Lastly we have to take note of a third class of phenomena intermediary between miracle and vision (in the senses indicated) without being reducible to either. This is what Raymond calls Catherine's 'spirit of prophecy', under which he includes not only a power to see things 'at a distance', whether in time or space, but also that of reading other people's secret thoughts and intentions. Of Catherine's possession of this power Raymond gives some striking instances.

\* \* \*

Such, in outline, are the varieties of preternatural power attributed to Catherine by her earliest biographer; and they call for two observations. First, in a Christian perspective all such powers seem to come under the head of those 'charisms' enumerated by St Paul, in I Corinthians 12, as 'manifestation(s) of the Spirit for the common good'. Second, while such gifts may accompany holiness, they are not of its essence; which is constituted, simply and sufficiently, by what Paul in the next chapter of the same epistle calls the 'more excellent way', namely *agape* or charity, the love for God and one's neighbour (cf. Matthew 22:34 ff.). The other gifts 'do not make a saint, though they may help towards canonization. They are given for the sake of others, . . . as a means to an end . . . to draw attention to something else that really matters, the loving union of human beings with God'. Thus Thomas Gilby OP in his introduction to the English version of Raymond's book; but he knew very well, of course, that a craving for preternatural phenomena often tended in fact to blur the great distinction drawn by Paul, and that a good deal of this kind of confusion affected the cult of the saints in the late medieval Church. Catherine's own teaching is untouched by that confusion, but the same cannot be said of some of the devotion she inspired.

We have seen that Catherine came out of her seclusion – it was in or about 1367 – at the express command, as she believed, of Christ himself. This was only the last of a series of such communications, usually accompanied by a vision of him, that she received at this time. He would appear to her bodily senses, standing or moving about her room, sometimes alone, sometimes with Mary or one or other of the saints. The strongly visual element in her religion was never more active than at this time. More important is the intensity of her concentration on the figure of Jesus. If she is a Christian mystic, it is the adjective that has to be stressed: at the centre of her vision is always God *incarnate*; a fact which links her, as a mystical writer, with St Bernard rather than with, say, her English contemporary the author of the *Cloud of Unknowing*, or with the Augustine of the *Confessions*. In the *Confessions* and in the *Cloud* Christ is the precondition of the experiences described, not their direct object; they are theocentric rather than christocentric, while the reverse is true of Bernard's sermons and still more of Catherine's writings which to a very large extent are meditations on Christ crucified; a characteristic that led Paul VI, when he declared Catherine a Doctor of the Church in 1970, to speak of her deep affinity with St Paul. Paul and John in fact were her favourite New Testament authors.

\* \* \*

A noteworthy effect of her absorption with Jesus was the way (reminding one of St Teresa of Lisieux five centuries later) she did without normal 'spiritual direction'. True, she had her regular Dominican confessors, the Sienese Della Fonte at an early stage, and after 1374 Raymond of Capua, but only in a very qualified sense can they be said to have 'directed' her; indeed it was not long before Raymond, her senior by a good many years and a man of weight in his order, was calling her 'mother' and virtually submitting to *her* direction. Nor does he seem to have had any difficulty in accepting her account of the matter: 'You can take it as certain, Father, that I have never learned anything from men or women about the way of salvation, but only from the . . . sweet bridegroom of my soul, the Lord Jesus Christ, either in the form of an inspiration or from his speaking to me as I speak to you now, face to face.' [5] Two such communications are famous. The first came at an early stage and may well be the source of her later, very characteristic, teaching on self-knowledge. 'Do you know, daughter', Jesus said to her, 'who you are and who I am? . . . *You are she who is not, I am he who is.*' [6] The other communication is also recorded by Raymond. Jesus appeared to Catherine when she had been through a violent and prolonged erotic temptation. 'Where were you, Lord, all this while?' she asked him. 'I was in your heart', he replied.[7] In passing we may note that she seems never to have been tempted in her faith (as Teresa of Lisieux was) though she may well, in the dark days of the Schism, have been tempted to despair; and she must often, with her fiery temperament, have found patience a considerable strain, which no doubt is why she has so much to say about it. Raymond devotes a whole chapter to her patience.

Catherine's resolve, on leaving her long solitude, to serve Christ in her neighbour involved no challenge to current ideas as to work suitable for a woman, provided at least that the service was limited to corporal works of mercy. So for a time her originality appeared only in her very extraordinary tenderness to the sick in the Sienese hospitals, and to the poor everywhere but especially to those who came to beg at her father's door, and naturally came in greater numbers as the news of her reckless generosity got around. Some of the stories told of her at this time are like miniature epics of charity; feats of high courage no less than benevolence. Still, her charity so far (if we ignore some not too conspicuous miracles) was only extraordinary in degree, not in kind; it represented the sort of thing that Christian women had always done and were to go on doing; so that one might be tempted to pass on to enterprises more distinctive and original, to her in that day unfeminine apostolate of the word, to her interventions in the affairs of princes and prelates. But that would be to over-stress the preacher and the public figure at the cost of the saint, at the cost too of missing some of the youthful charm of that holiness which had now appeared in the streets and squares of Siena.

The slender figure in the white tunic and black mantle, going around on errands of mercy, began to be talked about. Some professed to be shocked by the freedom of her ways (she always, we are told, looked you in the eyes when she spoke); and her austerities, which she could hardly keep concealed, were criticized by the wise and prudent. But many were drawn to her, and not only by her cheerful goodness but also increasingly by her intelligence. She did not seek to be loved but to love; but her Dominican training had not been wasted and she was already clear in her young mind that the way to love lay through knowledge. This truth she had already tested in the matter of loving God; she now had to discover – for her a harder task – the lovableness of human beings. So, as usual, she turned to Christ and begged for the grace to 'perceive the beauty of all the souls she came into contact with, so that she would be the more prompt to work for their salvation';[8] and we may perhaps discern an answer to this prayer in her magnificent insight into that dignity of 'the being endowed with reason' which was to be a major theme of her letters. As T. Deman wrote in a fine essay: 'According to current views, what needs explaining is how man ever does what is right; but as Catherine sees it, what needs explaining is how he can ever go wrong.'[9] Catherine never grew accustomed to evil; and this because she had so accustomed herself to relate everything to God, the creative and creating Good. Evil had to be recognized, but it was always the desecration of a goodness *already* bestowed, which *need never have happened*; for sin is nowhere but in the will, and since the will cannot be coerced, no sin ever is or was *necessary*. Catherine is among the most vigorous assertors in the Catholic tradition of what Dante had called the soul's *innata libertate*; indeed on this matter of free will she and Dante speak with remarkably similar voices. Characteristic of both is an abhorrence of any suggestion that *moral* evil is unavoidable. Catherine had, however, this advantage over the great poet, that from girlhood she had spent herself on behalf of sinners and outcasts, had struggled with the demon of despair in the hearts of lepers and condemned criminals.

In 1368 her father died and in 1370 three brothers and her favourite sister-in-law migrated to Florence. Catherine felt these departures, for she was very much a woman, and an Italian one at that, as a chance remark she had once made about the children swarming in her mother's kitchen may serve to show: 'If decency allowed it, I would never stop kissing them.' [10] But meanwhile another 'family' had begun to form round her, the group of friends and disciples with whom her memory is connected; both men and women, priests and layfolk. The priests were mostly friars – Dominicans of course, but also Franciscans, and two Augustinians, one of them the English recluse with a Cambridge degree, William Flete. Some of the group were Catherine's seniors but the average age would not have been much over thirty. The Dominicans were on the young side (excepting Raymond of Capua, but he may not have known Catherine before 1373) and there were some young laymen, three of whom she was to use as her secretaries, dictating her letters to them. What held the motley company together was a common veneration for Catherine's manifest holiness. But mingling with this purely religious motive there must surely have been – if the distinction is admissible – an attachment to the woman in the saint. In a way this already appears in the fact that most of them called her 'mother' and she called them, whatever their age, her children (though in her letters to them she usually also said 'brother' or 'sister', as the case might be, or, when the man was a priest, 'father'). But the effect she had on men of her own age, or older, can hardly have been, in every case, originally simply 'maternal'. In her own way she must have been an attractive, if often formidable, woman. Consider this impression of her at this time, recorded by one of the Dominicans, Bartolomeo Dominici, many years later: 'She was young when I first knew her, and her face was sweet and gay (*il suo volto appariva dolce e gaio*) and I too was young and yet I never felt in her company the kind of embarrassment I would have felt in that of any other girl; indeed the more time I passed with her, the less was I troubled by human passions (*piú discorrevo con lei, e piú le passioni umane mi si spengevano nel cuore*).' [11]

This Bartolomeo became a close friend of Catherine, accompanying her on her journeys to Pisa (1375), Avignon (1376) and Rome (1378) and living to bear witness to her sanctity − with other Dominicans of the original group−at the offical inquiry into it set up by the bishop of Venice in 1411. He was a friar of some intellectual distinction and in general it was a mark of Catherine's influence that she attracted men of more than average culture and ability − priests like Bartolomeo himself and Raymond of Capua, the theologian Tantucci, William Flete and the celebrated spiritual writer Giovanni delle Celle; and among the laymen, Niccolò Soderini of Florence, the poet Neri de' Pagliaresi, the painter Andrea Vanni, the jurist Lorenzo del Pino. Catherine always had a flair for reaching men 'at the top' in every walk of life. 'It is not everyone', remarks M. de la Bedoyère, 'who before he reaches the thirties finds himself in familiar intercourse with popes and sovereigns, cardinals and generals, or who presumes to influence . . . their policies.' [12] It is true that obscure artisans, enclosed nuns, ordinary housewives and common criminals were among her correspondents; but among her closer friends and disciples there was from the beginning a certain preponderance of educated people of the middle and upper class. It is all very strange, of course. She was a woman, and young, and not of noble birth, and in the ordinary sense quite uneducated. The wonder is not that she aroused suspicion and hostility (as she did, especially in the early stages, at Siena, between 1368 and 1374) but that she aroused so little. Nor need this be explained simply by her sanctity. Medieval society, though stiff with legal and social restraints, was spiritually, in a sense, less restricted than modern society. The Church itself, in the relations between its members, found room for franker and more direct approaches than was customary after the Reformation. Moreover Catherine, as a Dominican tertiary, operated under the wing of a religious order of unsurpassed intellectual prestige and doctrinal authority. She could no more have done what she did as a simple laywoman than she could have done it as an enclosed nun; and her Dominican connection was a special and very great advantage. It also perfectly suited her candid, communicative nature. Possessed of a first-rate mind and also, as a Tuscan, of a subtle, vigorous and beautiful language, she took a spontaneous delight in knowledge and in its communication, finding in every act of understanding a glimmer of the 'sweet First Truth'. If, echoing Aquinas perhaps unconsciously, she called the intellect 'the noblest part of the soul', it was because she was in love with Christ, for her the only 'Master' and a fountain of endless wisdom precisely because, being the Logos incarnate, he rendered the Father's glory knowable (John 1:14, 18). And it was just here, in this concept of God-to-man communication, that she found the Dominican ideal which she made her own. For by definition Dominicans are preachers and in founding the Order St Dominic had taken as its model the apostolic preaching of St Paul, as defined in II Corinthians 4:5–6: 'For we preach not ourselves but Jesus Christ our Lord . . . For the same God who said "let light shine out of the darkness" has shone into our hearts to give the light of the knowledge of the glory of God in the face of Christ Jesus.' No words could better express the ideal and the practice of St Catherine.

There is evidence that Catherine was in Florence in the early summer of 1374. It seems likely that this her first journey outside Sienese territory had something to do with the simultaneous presence in Florence, at the General Chapter of the Dominican Order which met there that year at Pentecost, of the Master General, a Frenchman, and of Raymond of Capua, whom Catherine probably already knew. This is a plausible inference from a letter sent to Raymond two years' later by Gregory XI, in which the pope confirms an authority already (*olim*) conferred on Raymond by the Master General over Catherine and some other unnamed Sienese tertiaries. It is clear that the pope regarded Catherine as the leading spirit in this group. As for its activities, he designates them as propaganda for a crusade 'and other matters of interest to the Holy Roman Church.' [13]

By 1374–75, then, Catherine was already getting involved in higher Church affairs, and she was soon to be drawn, in fact, into direct relations with the central government of the Church, first in the context of its Italian policies – the conflict between Florence and the Holy See, 1375–78 – and then in that of the threat to the papal institution itself, represented by the Great Schism, which began in September 1378. In both matters Catherine played a not inconspicuous part, putting herself unreservedly at the service of 'Christ-on-earth', as she called the pope, but always intensely longing for peace. In the general disintegration of the medieval world, of *her* world, she was involved in an historical process far too complex for her to understand save in purely moral and religious terms. And yet her political naivety can be exaggerated. Some of her interventions had a real, if limited, effect; her efforts for peace between the papacy and Florence were not all wasted, and Gregory XI's decision to leave Avignon in September 1376 was precipitated by Catherine's pleadings, even if it had already been his intention, long before he knew her, to bring the Curia back to Rome. But these are questions that cannot be pursued here. It will be more to my purpose, before concluding this biographical sketch, to describe very briefly Catherine's basic attitude to the Church and to the situation in which it found itself in the last years of her life.

We have seen that since adolescence she had commit-

ted herself to an active life in the world; but this external
activity had to be nourished from an inward source, and
the more so as a circle of disciples formed around her,
eager for spiritual guidance, seeing in her not only an
example of rare virtue but a source of enlightenment. So
she became a teacher and preacher of 'the mystery of
Christ', finding, characteristically, her way to this
through the 'cell of self-knowledge'. And this alternation
of inward and outward, contemplation and discourse,
went on right to the end. But there was a gradual shift in
her teaching, I think, towards an increasing concern with
the Church. This was the effect mainly of the two succes-
sive events already mentioned, the papal-Florentine conflict (1375–July '78) and then the rebellion of the French
cardinals against Urban VI in the summer of 1378, which
led to the Great Schism. Catherine's passionate yet often
wonderfully lucid reactions to these disasters may be
studied in many of the letters in this volume. All that she
says in them springs from her theology of the Blood. For
her the indispensability of the Church consists precisely
in this, that it is the medium through which the blood
shed on the cross for the human race becomes not only
the *sign* of God's re-creating love for sinners but also the
vehicle of that love to this and that sinner individually.
The Church 'holds the keys of the Blood',[14] the Blood
reaches us 'through the ministers of holy Church'.[15]
Indeed the Church exists, for Catherine, only *in function
of* Christ's blood; but that was enough to prostrate her in
reverence before its meanest minister. Her mysticism is
extraordinarily 'ecclesial', a fact stressed by Paul VI in the
declaration cited above.

But it was not in Catherine's feminine nature to contemplate an ideal without at once wanting to get it realized in the world about her. So her Christian vision issues
into pleas for a general reform of the Church, usually
addressed to the two popes she knew, Gregory XI and
Urban VI; and in her letters to layfolk, especially those of
high rank and authority, into urgent reminders of the

respect they owed to the Church's ministers. Her protests against irreverence to the clergy became sharper as she became aware of the rising tide of anticlerical feeling in Italy, which the Florentines openly encouraged – exploiting the anti-French element in it – in their conflict with Gregory XI. But Catherine also knew very well that in many cases these anticlerical sentiments were thoroughly justified; and was not afraid to say so to Gregory himself. He however died in March 1378, and with the election on 8 April of Urban VI and the great division of the Church that ensued – beginning at the top among the cardinals, and spreading downwards into the laity, according as secular rulers took one side or the other in the quarrel – every other concern in Catherine's mind took second place to her zeal for the unity of the Church and the authority of Urban. Her first call now was to the clergy and it was essentially a call to obedience. But her greatest severity was reserved for those 'incarnate devils' the great prelates who had started the Schism or had, she thought, done nothing to prevent it spreading (see letter 47 below).

Thus we see Catherine, in the last five years of her life, confronting two major threats to the unity of Christendom: the division between clergy and laity, which found one expression in the papal-Florentine conflict (as it had already found another of a different kind, though in its own way a very Florentine one, in Boccaccio's *Decameron*); and then the schism in the clerical body itself, that greater disaster which was to bring Catherine, utterly exhausted, to a premature death. Two conflicts and two efforts at reconciliation, the second apparently a total failure; but there was another conflict, inherited and sacrosanct, which found Catherine the reverse of reconciliatory, the war with the enemy *outside*. As we saw in the letter from Gregory XI to Raymond, cited above, Catherine's ardour for a renewed crusade against the Moslems had been among the things that first brought her to the attention of the higher authorities in the Church while still in her nonage in Siena. Why the Avignon *curia* of the 1370s should have shown this interest in the idea of a crusade is a question that need not detain us here. Certainly it was a recurrent theme in Catherine's letters between 1373 and 1376, and more especially in those that she wrote from Pisa in 1375. Later, under the pressure of more urgent matters, she said less about the need for renewing the 'holy war' against the infidels, but she never seems to have doubted the rightness of such a war. As a woman of her time she thought it the plain duty of a Christian knight to be ready to draw his sword for the recovery of the holy places – which by right, she said, 'belong to us'. Nevertheless she could say of the Moslems, 'they are our brothers, redeemed by the blood of Christ just as we are' – a remarkable statement for that time.[16] And in a passage that seems to echo Romans 11:13–16 she looks forward to a rejuvenation of the Church, grown senile and sinful, by an inflow of converts from Islam.[17]

As the reader will recall, we left Catherine at Florence in the summer of 1374. Returning to Siena in the same year with Raymond of Capua, she found her city in the grip of the plague. Having laboured heroically among the sick and the dying, she moved south to Montepulciano, and then, early in 1375, with a number of friends and disciples, to Pisa. There she remained, on and off, for nearly a year. It was a year of much epistolary activity and of a considerable widening of her contacts and influence. As has been noted, many of her Pisan letters were aimed at spreading the idea of a crusade, but in the autumn, and on into 1376, she found herself increasingly engaged in the more urgent task of countering the anti-papal propaganda now emanating from Florence. In June 1375 the papal legate de Noellet had come to terms with Ghibelline Milan, thus leaving the notorious captain of mercenaries John Hawkwood free to invade Tuscany. Florence took alarm, scenting papal designs behind this threat; and began to organize an anti-papal league. Catherine, by now in touch with Gregory XI, was fighting on two fronts. Horrified by the anticlerical spirit now prevailing in Florence, she at the same time sympathized with the widespread Italian hostility to the pope's representatives (usually Frenchmen) in Italy. So she both pleads with Gregory on behalf of his rebel subjects and begs him to undertake a radical reform of the Church, beginning at the top; and in the meantime to come and deal on the spot with the misgovernment in his Italian dominions. In March Bologna fell to the anti-papal league and Gregory put Florence under an interdict. But there were influential Florentines who desired peace, some of them friends of Catherine; and they succeeded in getting her offer accepted to act as mediator between the city and the pope. In this capacity she went to Avignon in June, with the usual company of friends and disciples, including the one with most authority, Raymond of Capua. He served as her interpreter with the pope, translating her voluble Tuscan into Latin.

So far as the papal-Florentine conflict was concerned, this embassy was not a success; the war dragged on till July 1378. But Catherine's persistence did overcome the pope's hesitations about leaving Avignon; and he had done this, and arrived back in Rome by the end of January 1377. Meanwhile Catherine was back in Italy, and, after Christmas at Siena, moved south to the Val d'Orcia in the Sienese *contado*. Here, and in the wild country further west, she passed most of 1377, evangelizing the wretchedly poor countryfolk, helped always by friars from Siena. Her letters of this period, among which are some of her finest, are mostly on the themes she was to develop and expand in her great mystical treatise, traditionally called *Il Dialogo*, which she probably began to dictate to her secretaries in the winter of 1377–78, after returning from Val d'Orcia to Siena, and probably completed before she finally moved to Rome in November 1378. In the meantime she had been forced back into politics by an order from Gregory XI early in 1378. She was to return to Florence where it was hoped that her influence would tip the scales in favour of the Guelf party now working, against stiff opposition, for a final peace with the Holy See. Catherine obeyed and remained in Florence for about four months, narrowly escaping death at the hands of an anti-Guelf mob which took virtual control of the city on 22 June. Meanwhile Gregory had died and it was his successor Urban VI who finally made peace with the Florentines on 28 July.

This is not the place to go into the confused matter of the election to the See of Peter, on 8 April 1378, of the Archbishop of Bari, who became Urban VI. Catherine never doubted the validity of Urban's election though she may well have been tempted, in her heart, to regret it. Urban was upright and zealous, but irascible, rude, tactless and overbearing. Catherine had quickly read his character but was nevertheless overwhelmed with grief and horror when the majority of the cardinals went back on their oath to Urban, and on 20 September elected as their pope Robert of Geneva (Clement VII). Between these two elections Catherine, her work in Florence now finished, returned to Siena, her heart filled with misgivings by the rumours that reached her from Rome. Her first care was to warn Urban against his own temperament, her second to secure him good advisers. After the election of Clement VII, Urban let Catherine know, through Raymond, that he wanted her at Rome, but she refused to come without a direct command. When this came she went to Rome, arriving on 28 November. During the following terrible year, though her counsels of moderation were not all wasted on Urban himself, her general influence on the course of events was slight. The Schism spread across Europe following the lines of national frontier and rivalry; France, Scotland, Naples, and later Aragon were 'Clementine'; Italy, apart from the southern kingdom, England, Hungary and most of the Empire were for Urban. Catherine's own Dominican Order split along the same lines, the Master General, a Frenchman, becoming a schismatic. It was not long before the division became a military issue. In all this turmoil Catherine's voice is heard repeatedly pleading, arguing, denouncing; but her arguments for the validity of Urban's election involved her in disputes about factual details that lay outside her direct experience and could not be decided *a priori*. Her *forte* as teacher and preacher had always been her deep insight into the essential principles of Christian life; and her power as a Church reformer depended, now as always, on her ability to get these principles into the minds of men in authority in the Church, or to spread them as a leaven in the hearts of ordinary Christians. But in the conflict now raging, and with the Church divided from top to bottom, the first of these methods was, for the time being, virtually ruled out. Not entirely, however, the second one. Catherine still had her group of fervent disciples. There was Raymond who received, at Genoa, as a kind of spiritual testament, the last two letters translated in the present selection; and whom she expected – correctly as it turned out – to be elected General of the non-schismatic Dominicans at the General Chapter that was due to begin at Bologna in May 1380. And there was the rest of her 'family', many of whom were with her when she died, after much suffering, on 29 April. On 16 March she had been induced to call them all together and to give them a kind of summary, the gist of which has been preserved, of all that she had tried to teach them by word and example. Her book, the *Dialogo*, she had already bequeathed to Raymond.

* * *

## II

On 4 October 1970 Paul VI declared St Catherine a *Doctor Ecclesiae*, thus giving her a place among the Church's major theologians. The title itself has been given to relatively few of the saints, and so far to only two women, the other being Teresa of Avila. Of course these two great women are usually thought of as mystics rather than as theologians, but in Catholic usage the terms denote simply different ways of apprehending the same object, the God of the Christian faith, self-revealed in Jesus Christ. Theology, on this view, is mainly a skill in analyzing and expounding this Christian concept of God, whereas mysticism is an experienced contact with the reality to which it refers. Thus theology is chiefly intellectual, mysticism affective and experimental. But the *object* of both is the same, namely the living God whom Jesus has told us to love above all things (including our subtlest concepts) and who, having loved us first, can be trusted to love the mind that sincerely seeks him and to guide it into what St Paul called 'the depths of God' (I Corinthians 2:10). This is the guidance described by Catholic theology in terms of the gifts of the Holy Spirit, who is the spirit of love; above all the gift of wisdom, without which the cleverest theology remains arid and stunted.[18] In this sense all theology worthy of the name is in tendency 'mystical'. As for mystics in the more usual sense of the term, whether their contact with God will give rise to clearly articulated doctrine will depend, humanly speaking, on their natural gifts and circumstances.

Splendidly explicit as she always was about her love for God, Catherine must have had an inward experience of him that was hers alone. But the *image* from which her meditations commonly began was the familiar one presented by any crucifix. At whatever point we enter her mind we encounter Christ crucified, and in particular the thought of his blood. The blood shed on the cross became for her the supreme sign and pledge of divine love and the chief motive for ours. It summed up for her, both as a reality and a sign, all her understanding of Christianity.

Everything, for her, relates then to the cross; but to understand why this is so we have to distinguish, in Catherine's teaching, two other major topics: the need for self-knowledge and the doctrine of the soul as a created 'image' of the divine Trinity, Father, Son and Holy Spirit. I shall take the second of these three themes first; then the third; and conclude with that of the Incarnate Word on the cross.

## 1   *Self-knowledge*

The way to God, for Catherine, begins in the 'cell of self-knowledge'; this she never tires of repeating. But the point is sometimes imperfectly understood. Her insistence on the need for self-knowledge is not only, or even primarily, a way of saying that we must recognize ourselves to be sinners, and so acquire humility. Of course it is that; but Catherine always looks *through* the sin to the goodness which it thwarts and distorts – that is, to the soul's radical 'likeness' to the Creator whose image it bears. It was, in fact, a *double* illumination that Catherine had gained, in youth, through self-knowledge, and that she spent her life trying to communicate to others. In herself she had discovered both man and God; and each, again, under a double aspect. This is perhaps obscure, but the point should become clearer if we consider the human creature that she found in herself. She found it *morally* frail – full of self-love, greed, impatience, etc. – and she found a frailty in its very *being*. Presumably the former insight preceded the latter in time, being the more empirically evident one. And from it she derived, in the last resort, her fierce and very physical asceticism, her insistence on self-hatred as a concomitant of the love of Christ,[19] her ceaseless attack on that 'perverse self-love', often identified with sensuality, 'which is the root-cause of all our evils'.[20] But the other insight was a looking *past* sin to creatureliness as such, and so to the Creator this implied. A sense of the frailty of one's being may be no more than a sense of physical weakness, but it can also, in intelligences of the finer sort, contain an intuition of being as such; it can be incipiently metaphysical. And that it was so in Catherine I am led to believe by those words, already cited, in which she expressed this insight, and which she believed she had heard from Christ himself: 'Daughter, . . . you are she who is not, I am he who is.'[21]

Philosophy however, for obvious reasons, was not Catherine's vocation, and the doctrine of the creation of all things out of nothing quickly combined in her Christian intelligence with that which identified the Creator with the holy Trinity. Moreover the same faith which gave her this conception of God told her of a special likeness and affinity to God imprinted on the essence of man, as recorded in Genesis 1:26: 'Let us make man in our own image and likeness.' It followed that genuine self-knowledge must be some kind of discerning, in and through oneself, of the Father, the Son and the Spirit. This consequence Catherine eagerly drew, and she did so with what may be called a particularly Christian stress, inasmuch as the triune godhead whom she saw reflected in her soul was seen very specifically in relation to man, and to man not only as created in innocence but also as re-created after his lapse into sin. In other words, the discernment of the Trinity, through its 'image', which she claimed to have, included that of the whole divine plan and process with regard to man, as Christian faith represents this, the plan and process which she was accustomed to call simply 'the Truth', as in the following very typical passage: 'I do not see how we can relish . . . this truth if we do not know ourselves, for through genuine self-knowledge we discover that we are not, and we find our being in God, seeing that he has created us to his image and likeness . . . and we find moreover our re-creation inasmuch as God has re-created us . . . in the blood of his Son, the blood that shows us the truth of God the Father; whose truth is this, that he created us for the glory of his name and in order that we might have a share in his eternal beauty, being sanctified in him.' [22]

This text exemplifies the ease with which Catherine can pass from self-knowledge to the contemplation of God – albeit of God very much in relation to man. Hardly less noteworthy are some of her insights, drawn from the same source, into the human condition. Three of these may be singled out.

*a* Looking into herself Catherine was very aware of her propensity to love and to seek love; and in the light of the Christian idea of creation, and of her human experience, she thence drew out one of her sweetest and most pregnant generalizations: 'Because the soul is made in the image . . . of God, it is made of love and for love . . . and cannot live without love.' [23] And again: 'The human heart is drawn by nothing so much as by love, for man is made of love . . . both as to his soul and his body; for it was through love that God created man in his own image, and it is through love that a father and mother give of their own substance to the child whom they conceive and beget.' [24] But it is, of course, on the primal unmediated divine love creating the rational soul that Catherine most dwells; the love which has left its imprint indelibly in the soul; so that, as it was an infinite divine desire that brought man into existence, so man in turn, in his deepest self, is moved by an 'infinite desire' which makes it impossible for him 'to find peace in this life', since that desire aims at nothing less than 'union with the divine essence',[25] the 'sweet First Truth'.[26] 'The Deity', in short, 'is the soul's true object (*vero obietto dell'anima*)'.[27] Note that in these texts Catherine speaks of the soul's *nature*, not of any effect of 'grace' in the sense of a quality *super-added* to nature.

*b* An immediate consequence of the divine image in the soul is its *non*-subjection to anything but God. 'You alone', declares Catherine to God, 'are greater than we';[28] and what she has in mind above all is the freedom of the human will, the power of 'the creature endowed with reason' to decide 'freely and for itself' [29] – a power such that 'no devil or any other creature whatsoever can constrain the soul to a mortal sin against its will'. This last phrase – an echo perhaps of Romans 8:35 – recurs frequently, with slight variations, in the letters, and always in connection, implicitly at least, with the idea of creation. Characteristically, Catherine imagines God saying to the newly created Adam: 'Be it done as you will . . . I create you free, subject to nothing except me'; such being, she adds, the nobility (*eccellenza*) of man that 'all things are created to serve him, and he to have no master but God'.[30]

c It will be clear by now that Catherine took a special delight in the doctrine of creation. It is a trait that she shares with Dante; and as in his case so in hers, it goes with a strong sense of the radical goodness of human nature and indeed of all things considered in themselves. Evil manifests itself only as a disorder in desire. This disorder is sin, which Catherine identifies, in the last resort, as we have seen, with self-love, itself often characterized as sensuality. The task of self-knowledge is to unmask this self-love – to see it, and see it as perverse. Now all loving is perverse that is not, directly or indirectly, a love for God (which is always in fact a loving-in-return, since he has loved us first and all that is lovable in oneself, or in others, or in nature, is only so because of him).[31] The right order in loving – put negatively – is, do not love yourself for yourself, nor even God for yourself, but love yourself and everything else for God, and God for himself; in short, whatever you love, love it or him or her *in God*.[32] To flout this order is to try to enclose in the finite our natural desire for the Infinite [see above under *a*]; it is to act a lie against oneself and God. Such a perversion must be due to a darkening of the mind, a failure to *see* ourselves in our true relation to God. But what can account for this if not a prior misdirection of *desire* through absorption by, and in, the self and the sensible world? But does not this in turn entail some error of judgement? Further analysis would be needed to untie this knot, but we should not expect it from Catherine; enough for her to have seen – though she could not perfectly explain it – the interplay of error and self-love, of darkened mind and twisted desire, that is at the root of sin.[33]

## 2 *The creation of man as 'image' of the Trinity*

Catherine habitually thought of God as the three divine

Persons; but without giving particular attention to that *immanent* activity within the godhead posited by classical theology in its effort to give some account of the issuing of the Son from the Father, and of the Holy Spirit from both.[34] Catherine takes all that for granted, focussing her attention rather on the two great *external* actions of God which concern mankind: creation and redemption. As to creation, she mostly ignores (very unlike Dante here) the material world. Her focus is on the rational soul; but usually with at least implicit reference to the Genesis account of the creation of man in an original innocence. In her account of this creation two characteristic features may be noted here.

(i) She puts enormous emphasis on the *love*-motive in creation. She is never tired of repeating that we were loved before we began to exist. Gazing into himself, God fell in love with the beauty of his creature-to-be.[35] In the strongest possible sense of the term our creation is an act of sheer love. Man is God's darling. So much does she stress this point that she can speak of God as 'mad' or 'drunk' with love of his creature-to-be, and even – at the risk of scandalizing theologians – of his being 'compelled' by love to create man, though knowing full well that man would sin.[36]

(ii) The ultimate purpose of man's creation is that he may share in God's eternal joy. But this will only be the climax of a communication *already* established (but at risk of being lost by sin) in the original 'forming' of the soul to the image of the creating Trinity.[37] Catherine's treatment of this theme is a variant on the Augustinian tradition. A text from the *Dialogo* illustrates her procedure. She is commenting on Genesis 1:26: *Let us make man to our own image* – 'And this you did, most high eternal Trinity, so that man might participate in all of you (*in tutto te*). So you gave him memory, to remember your benefits; and by this he participates in your power, eternal Father. And you gave him intellect, to see and know your goodness, and so participate in the wisdom of the . . . Son. And you gave him will that he might love what with his understanding he saw and knew of your truth, and thus participate in the clemency of the Holy Spirit'.[38] This last term 'clemency', *clemenza*, raises questions which cannot be gone into here. It is often used by Catherine, instead of the more usual 'love', for the divine attribute 'appropriated', as theologians say, to the Holy Spirit. The appropriations of power to the Father and of wisdom to the Son are more traditional. Their reflections in the soul are the Augustinian triad of memory, understanding and will, united as a single image of the Creator.

### 3  Christ on the cross

The same love that moved God to create man in order that a creature might share in the uncreated divine life, moved him to recreate man when, by misusing his inborn freedom, he had in effect refused that destiny. It was one and the same love, only now even more ecstatically displayed; for not content with giving being to a creature bearing his image, God now, in the person of the Son, so identified himself with this creature as to share its very nature, human nature. This is the Incarnation – a love union of God with humanity aimed at *reconciliation*. And this reconciliation, considered from God's side, has three aspects corresponding to the three main evils involved in human sinfulness: disobedience, ignorance (especially of God's love) and the love of self in preference to God. Of these three evils the first is, in Christian tradition and for Catherine, the precondition of the others; for the state of spiritual blindness and disordered loving which is the general condition of sinful mankind, had its origin in an act of disobedience, the sin of Adam.

The remedying of these evils by the incarnate Word is seen by Catherine almost exclusively in terms of the Crucifixion.

Jesus' death on the cross was his supreme act of obedience to the Father (cf. Philippians 2:8, Romans 5:9). As such it reversed Adam's disobedience, cancelling, 'mak-

ing satisfaction' for, the offence to infinite Goodness
which that entailed (Romans 3:25; 5:19). But nothing
that Jesus did or suffered would have been of any avail
apart from the divine (not merely human) love – love for
the Father and for his fellow men – which drove him to
the cross. It is this infinite divine love, in the last resort,
that atones for the infinite *non*-love that is at the heart of
sin. Jesus' obedience was the expression of his redemp-
tive love. It was love, and not the nails, that held him fixed
to the cross.[39]

And this love, above all, is what the cross is a *sign* of,
what it *shows* to man's self-darkened understanding.
Here again Catherine is a pupil of St Paul (Romans 5:8;
8:31–2; Galatians 2:20), but she develops the idea that
God *reveals* himself on the cross with a persistence that is
all her own. She never tires of repeating that the blood of
Jesus is the medium through which we can now know 'the
truth of God the Father', that is, God's desire, from the
first, to give us his own glory and joy, in eternal life. For
her the Blood is the clue to the whole meaning of God in
relation to man (cf. Ephesians 1:9; Colossians 1:26); and
conversely, to the meaning of man. To 'lift the eye of the
intellect' to the Crucified is the first task of every Christian; and this not only for the ascetical reason that Christ
has shown that we have to suffer, and how we should
suffer, if we would be his disciples (I Peter 2:21).
Catherine accepts this reason, of course; but she sees in
the Blood much more than an example. She sees, or
strives continually to see, the *end* beyond all suffering and
discipleship; the end that will be the restoration in ourselves of the original unspoiled image of the Trinity, that
'pure tree of humanity' planted by God 'in the beginning'.[40] In this sense the Blood is the clue to a kind of
ultimate self-knowledge.[41]

This knowledge of God in and through Jesus is more
than merely natural or rational; it involves faith, the
starting point of Christian life. But what, for Catherine,
was the connection between this faith-knowledge and the

remedying of that disorder in desire which, as we have seen, was the third of the three great evils affecting mankind as fallen and sinful? In other words, how does Catherine view Christian life in relation to the *will*, to its rectification and sanctification? With my answer to this question I conclude this outline account of Catherine's teaching; and I would answer it as follows:

(i) Faith is a 'light' given to the soul at baptism so that it may come to know 'its true object, the . . . Deity'.[42]

(ii) The first step to that final vision is an understanding, in the light of faith, of God's love for man as revealed in Christ, especially in his Passion;[43] this understanding being distinct from the beatific vision of heaven inasmuch as its proper immediate object is God 'shown under the veil of humanity'.[44]

(iii) This understanding implies an act of love in the will turning the mind towards Christ. In this sense charity precedes faith and nourishes it.[45]

(iv) To know Christ is to desire to be rid of vice and to grow in virtue; which in turn brings vigorously into play, and the more the better, the 'natural light' of reason; the task of which, enlightened by faith, is to correct sensuality and bring the soul into a 'sweet and glorious order'.[46]

(v) As love follows knowledge (of the good), so the more Christ is known, the more he must be found lovable. This consequence is much stressed by Catherine – to the point, sometimes, of seeming to say that it is *only* ignorance of Christ that can account for sin.[47]

(vi) The love springing from faith has two main effects in the soul, one negative, the other positive. The negative effect is an annulling or 'stripping off' of self-love. The positive effect is a 'clothing' of the will in the will of God, so that it begins to seek God above all things, and nothing else except in and for him.[48] This is the 'bright garment' of charity,[49] the supreme virtue, a 'foretaste', *arra*, of eternal life.[50] But it is not enough to call charity a love for God; it is *love in return for love*, a love of love, a surrender, in fact, to the full force of him who IS Love (I John 4:8,

16) and who is now bringing his created image to its
ultimate point of resemblance to himself; communicat-
ing to it his own 'immortal riches',[51] and even his 'infinity',[52] and even, Catherine will say, making it 'god',[53]
another 'myself'.[54] And she can say all this without a hint
of pantheism because she is not speaking precisely of the
soul's *being* (which remains creaturely) but of its *powers*,
and especially of its power to love. To the soul's powers
God (their Creator in the first place) now gives himself
with the great twofold, divinizing gift; the gift, first, of
the incarnate Word enlightening the intellect; and then
of the Holy Spirit, God's love-gift *par excellence*,[55] whose
gift to us is nothing else than a share in the divine love
itself after which that Spirit is named.[56] At this point
Catherine's eloquence falters, her thought becomes less
clear. As a teacher she has much more to say about –
indeed she is usually much more concerned with – the
way to ultimate union with God than with the union itself.
But three things may be noted, to conclude, in what she
does say about it. First, the word 'peace', *pace*, expressing
the fulness of charity.[57] Second, that between God's love
for us and ours, however perfect, for him there is and
always must be this difference that his love for us is
absolutely *gratis, di grazia*, whereas ours for him is a love
we *owe*, it is *di debito*. Only in our neighbour-love can we
imitate *this* aspect of God's charity.[58] Third, Catherine
sees the Holy Spirit as the agent, as it were, of our final
union with God. The soul takes only charity with her into
eternal life;[59] charity the proper effect of the Third Person (Romans 5:5). And when in the vision described in
the famous letter on the execution of Niccolò di Toldo
she sees this young man's soul enter the heart of Jesus,
she adds that 'the hands of the Holy Spirit sealed him
in'.[60]

Catherine's teaching is intensely personal but its content of course is the common stock of Catholic belief as
she had imbibed this from childhood, at home and in
church, from sacred images and ritual and countless

sermons and instructions. She must have learned much also in conversation with the theologians of various traditions who became her friends. We know too, from Raymond (Life, pp. 96–7), that quite early she had learned to read the Psalms of the Divine Office in Latin, and this would have been her introduction to the Vulgate Bible. She was certainly familiar with the New Testament. No doubt she could also read Italian; she seems to have known the popular devotional theology of the Dominican Domenico Cavalca (1270–1342) who was also a translator of selections from the Church Fathers. Her writings, at all events, show some knowledge, however acquired, of works by St Augustine, Cassian, St Bernard and, to a lesser extent, St Thomas. But all this matter of Catherine's sources will presumably be discussed afresh by specialists in the coming centenary year, 1980. So there, for the present, we may leave it.[61]

\* \* \*

## III

St Catherine's writings are the book that has come to be known as the 'Dialogue' (*Il Dialogo della Divina Providenza*) and most, if not all, of the 382 letters traditionally ascribed to her. There are also transcriptions of 26 prayers, not written by her or dictated, but taken down, as she uttered them, by her disciples (critical edition by G. Cavallini, Rome, 1978). One or two of the surviving letters were written in the first place by Catherine herself,[62] and perhaps even parts of the 'Dialogue', but no autograph has survived and it is certain that the great bulk both of this work and of the letters was dictated to secretaries. The dictation of the 'Dialogue' can be dated to between December 1377 and the following autumn; and a complete fair copy was made, very probably before the end of 1382. This copy is preserved at Rome (ms. Casanatense 292) and serves as the basis of the best edition of the work, that by G. Cavallini, Rome, 1968. The

transmission of the text of the letters is a more compli-
cated matter, but for our purpose it will suffice to note
the following points.

1   Catherine began to dictate letters around 1370 and
continued to within two months of her death in April
1380.

2   Eight specimens of the original dictation have survived.

3   It is certain that small collections of letters were made
by her disciples during the decade following her death, at
the latest.

4   By about 1430 the larger collections had been made
on which all our printed editions are based. They can be
grouped into three 'families' each deriving from one or
other of three of Catherine's secretaries, Neri Pagliaresi,
Stefano Maconi and Fra Tommaso Caffarini.

5   The main motive behind these collections was the
preservation and diffusion of Catherine's spiritual teaching. The collectors ignore chronological sequence and
show little interest in the details of Catherine's day-to-day
life. This explains most, if not all, of the 'cuts' discernible
towards the end of many of the letters.

6   There seems to be no good reason to doubt the
authenticity of the great majority at least of the letters
ascribed to Catherine. This is the view of the three chief
scholars in the field, Fawtier (in his second volume,
1930), Motzo and Dupré Theseider. The chief editions
are those by Gigli, Tommaseo-Misciatelli and Dupré
Theseider (for details see the Bibliography below, and
the Translators' Preface).

KENELM FOSTER OP

[1] I John 4: 8, 16.
[2] *Inferno* XXIX, 121–2.
[3] English translation by G. Lamb, *The Life of St Catherine of Siena*; with an introduction by Thomas Gilby OP: London, Harvill Press, 1960.
[4] Raymond of Capua, *Life*, op. cit., p. 78.
[5] ibid., p. 72.
[6] ibid., p. 79.
[7] ibid., p. 94.
[8] ibid., p. 137.
[9] *Vie Spirituelle*, Supplément, Oct. 1934, p. 11.
[10] *Supplementum* (T. Caffarini's additions to Raymond's *Life*) transl. by A. Tantucci, I,II,12: Lucca, 1754.
[11] *Processo Castellano, Il (Fontes Vitae S. Cat. Sen. Hist.*, ed. Laurent & Valli, IX), Siena, 1942, p. 295.
[12] See *Catherine*, by M. de la Bedoyère (London, 1947), p. 35.
[13] See article by T.M. Centi, OP. in *S. Caterina tra i Dottori della Chiesa*, ed. T.S. Centi, OP., Florence, 1970, pp. 39–56.
[14] Cf. Dupré, letter XVII, p. 65.
[15] ibid., letter LXXXII, p. 334.
[16] Cf. Dupré, letter LII, p. 206.
[17] ibid., letter LXXIV, p. 304.
[18] Cf. St Thomas, *Summa theol.* 1a 2ae 68; 2a 2ae 45.
[19] e.g. letter 5 below.
[20] Dupré LXI.
[21] Raymond, *Life*, p. 79.
[22] Tommaseo 102.
[23] See letter 14 below.
[24] See letter 20 below.
[25] See Dupré XVIII.
[26] See Dupré XLV.
[27] *Orazioni* V, line 6.
[28] *Orazioni* VIII, line 175.
[29] See Dupré XVII.
[30] See letter 6 below.
[31] See Dupré XXXX.
[32] See letters 27, 39, 44 and others below.
[33] See letters 34 & 37 below.
[34] Cf. St Thomas, *Summa Theol.* 1a 27–31.
[35] See letter 2 below & passim.
[36] *Orazioni* IV, lines 95–117.
[37] *Orazioni* I, 1–16.
[38] See *Dialogue*, pp. 283–4 below.
[39] Cf. letters 3, 5, 16, 26 and others below.
[40] *Orazioni*, X, lines 1–11; cf. *Dialogue* ch. X.
[41] See the great passage in *Dialogue*, ch. CLXVII, beginning 'O

*Trinità eterna, fuoco e abisso di carità . . .* '

[42]  *Orazioni* V, 1–6; XVIII, 25–35, etc.
[43]  ibid., IV, 10–26; VIII, 56–62, and letter 42 & others below.
[44]  *Orazioni* XXI, 21–25; XV, 15–35; etc.
[45]  *Orazioni* VII, lines 62–79; VIII, 67–73; cf. letter 6 below, and *Dialogue*, ch. LI.
[46]  *Orazioni* VII, 92–102; cf. letter 59 below.
[47]  e.g. in letters 5, 17 & 34 below; cf. Dupré XL and LXI.
[48]  Cf. letters 27 & 28 below; *Orazioni* XXI *passim*.
[49]  See letter 42 below.
[50]  See letter 48 below.
[51]  *Orazioni* XXI, 90–95.
[52]  ibid. lines 104–9.
[53]  ibid., lines 117–20.
[54]  *Dialogue*, pp. 280–1 below.
[55]  Cf. St Thomas, *Summa theol*. la. 38.
[56]  *Dialogue*, ch. CLXVII; *Orazioni* XXII, lines 113–5; St Thomas, *Summa theol*. la 37.
[57]  *Dialogue* ch. LIV and letter 18 below.
[58]  *Dialogue*, ch. LXIV; *Orazioni* XXI, lines 80–89, and letters 38 & 44 below.
[59]  Cf. Tommaseo 345.
[60]  Letter 9 below.
[61]  For a provisional summary of the matter I may be allowed to refer to my article 'St Catherine's Teaching', in *Life of the Spirit*, XVI, no. 187 (1962), pp. 311–13.
[62]  See letter 272, Tommaseo-Misciatelli edition, IV, p. 215.

# TRANSLATORS' PREFACE

St. Catherine's letters were 'talked rather than written' (Vida Scudder), so much so that 'while the general trend of her discourse remains clear, in spite of the at times almost breathless multiplication of digressions and asides, her habit of relying on her memory alone rather than her eyes sometimes trapped her into leaving the structure of her original sentence hanging in mid-air' (Matilde Fiorilli). We have allowed this kind of broken syntax to speak for itself, except where some interpolation (indicated by the use of square brackets in the text) seemed unavoidable.

The first 29 letters in the present selection are translated from the text as critically edited by E. Dupré Theseider (see Bibliography). Two more, nos. 45 and 52, are from texts transcribed by E.G. Gardner in the Appendix to his monograph on St Catherine (1907). Unfortunately, Dupré Theseider published only one volume, containing 88 letters, of his projected critical edition. The translation of the remaining letters in the present selection – i.e. of those not edited either by Dupré Theseider or by Gardner – is based on the text given in the Tommaseo/Misciatelli edition, carefully compared with its more reliable predecessor (Gigli) and emended, where this seemed necessary, in the light of suggestions gleaned from the writings of Gardner, Fawtier, Dupré Theseider himself and others. We gratefully acknowledge our debt to these scholars, and also to Professoressa Giuliana Cavallini, Directress of the *Centro Nazionale di Studi Cateriniani* in Rome, for much help in clarifying obscure passages; and our further debt to the late editor's son, Prof. Franco Dupré Theseider and to his collaborator and successor, Prof. Enzo Petrucci, for graciously allowing us access to his unpublished papers.

Some further points.

(1)   Though 'unlettered' in the strict sense, Catherine was so steeped in the Scriptures (see Introduction, p.39) that she tended to talk in scriptural language, often unconsciously and occasionally out of context. For all her direct quotations we have used the RSV, 'tailored' as necessary to suit Catherine's often fairly free rendering of the Vulgate; all or most of the many other scriptural texts she alludes to or uses in various ways have been identified in the footnotes.

(2)   We regret not having been able to include in this selection any of St Catherine's characteristic and revealing prayers, the text of which is now available in Cavallini's fine critical edition (see Bibliography).

(3)   While this selection is the fruit of a close and happy collaboration between us at all stages and covering every aspect of the work, Sr M. John has been principally responsible for the historical and biographical material given in the footnotes.

\*      \*      \*

Of the many people who have helped in many ways to make this selection possible, we wish to thank especially the Co-ordinating Committee of the Dominican Association; Dominican and other librarians, particularly at the Newport Branch of the Isle of Wight County Library; above all, the members of the community here at Carisbrooke. We acknowledge, too, our special debt to Father Cornelius Ernst OP who welcomed the idea and helped to determine its shape but has not lived to see it implemented; and to Wendy Field who helped considerably in the translation.

*St Dominic's Priory,*                    KENELM FOSTER OP
*Carisbrooke*                             MARY JOHN (Ronayne) OP
September 1979

# SELECTED BIBLIOGRAPHY

(Showing abbreviations used
for works cited frequently in the text)

*A*  *St. Catherine's Writings*

  a  *The Letters*

DUPRE — *Epistolario di S. Caterina da Siena,* a cura di Eugenio Dupré Theseider, Istituto Storico Italiano, Rome, 1940. Vol. I only.

TOMMASEO — *Le Lettere di S. Caterina da Siena* con note di Niccolò Tommaseo, a cura di Piero Misciatelli, 3rd edition, Siena, 1922.

GIGLI — *L'Opere di S. Caterina da Siena nuovamente pubblicate da Girolamo Gigli, colle annotazioni del P. Federigo Burlamacchi,* Vol. II, Lucca, 1721; Vol. III, Siena, 1713.

CAVALLINI — *La Verità dell'Amore.* Scelta di scritti cateriniani a cura di Giuliana Cavallini, Rome, 1978.

SCUDDER — *St Catherine of Siena as seen in her Letters.* Translated and edited with Introduction by Vida D. Scudder, London, 1905.

  b  *The Dialogue*

DIALOGO — *Il Dialogo della Divina*

*Provvidenzia di S. Caterina da Siena*, a cura di Giuliana Cavallini (Edizioni Cateriniane [Testi Cateriniani – I]), Rome, 1968.

FIORILLI    *Libro della Divina Dottrina di S. Caterina da Siena*, a cura di Matilde Fiorilli, Bari, 1922.

THOROLD    *The Dialogue of the Seraphic Virgin Catherine of Siena*, translated (and abridged) by Algar Thorold, London, 1907. Paperback edition: Rockford, Ill., 1974.

c    *The Prayers*

ORAZIONI    *Le Orazioni di S. Caterina da Siena*, a cura di Giuliana Cavallini (Edizioni Cateriniane [Testi Cateriniani – IV]), Rome, 1978.

## B    *Biographical sources*

a    RAYMOND    Raymond (Blessed) of Capua, OP, *Life of St Catherine of Siena*, translated by G. Lamb from G. Tinagli OP's Italian version (1934) of the Latin original, London, 1960.

PROCESSO    *Fontes Vitae S. Caterinae Senensis Hist. IX: Il Processo Castellano*, a cura di M.-H Laurent, Milan, 1942.

b    DRANE    Drane, A.T., *The History of St Catherine of Siena and her Companions*, London, 1880.

GARDNER    Gardner, E.G., *St Catherine of Siena,* London 1907.

FAWTIER    Fawtier, Robert, *Sainte Catherine de Sienne, Essai de critique des sources,* Paris, 1921 (Vol. I); 1930 (Vol. II). (Explicit references are to Vol. II only).

CURTAYNE    Curtayne, Alice, *St Catherine of Siena,* London, 1929.

PAPÀSOGLI    Papàsogli, Giorgio, *Sangue e fuoco sul ponte di Dio,* Rome, 1971.

C    *Other works consulted*

   a    *Theological studies*

GRION    Grion, Alvaro, OP, *Santa Caterina da Siena: Dottrina e Fonti,* Brescia, 1953 (reviewed by G. D'Urso in *Sapienza*, Naples, 3–5, 1954, pp. 364–69).

CENTI    Centi, T.S., OP, *S. Caterina tra i dottori della Chiesa. Miscellanea a collaborazione,* Florence, 1970.

FOSTER    Foster, K., OP, 'The Spirit of St Catherine', in *Life of the Spirit,* April 1961, and 'St Catherine's Teaching', ibid., February 1962.

   b    *General background*

DUPRÉ THESEIDER, E., *I Papi ad Avignone e la questione romana,* Florence, 1939.

HUIZINGA, J., *The Waning of the Middle Ages,* London (Penguin) 1965.

MEERSSEMAN, G.G. (in coll. with Pacini, G.P.), *Ordo Fraternitatis. Confraternite e pietà dei laici nel medioevo.* (3 vols.), Rome, 1977.

MOLLAT, G., *The Popes at Avignon*, ET London, 1963.

POWER, EILEEN, *Medieval Women* (edited by M.M. Postan), Cambridge, 1975.

ULLMANN, W., *The Origins of the Great Schism*, London, 1948.

# KEY EVENTS IN
# CATHERINE'S LIFE

c. 1347      Birth in Siena.

c. 1354      Vow of virginity.

1363      Received into Order of Penance (*Mantellate*).

1363-66(7) Lived in seclusion. Mystical marriage.

1367-70     Corporal works of mercy. The 'family' of disciples begins to form.

1373-74     First political moves and letters (e.g. to Bernabò Visconti of Milan and his wife – Dupré XVII & XVIII).

1374      Visit to Florence. Raymond of Capua becomes Catherine's director. Plague in Siena.

1375      Visit to Pisa. Receives the Stigmata. Execution of Niccolò di Toldo in Siena. Preaching of the crusade. Florence organizes anti-papal league. War begins.

1376      Florence placed under interdict. Catherine goes to Avignon; pleads for reform of Church and return of Pope to Rome.

1377      (January) Gregory XI enters Rome. Catherine and her disciples in Val d' Orcia.

1378      Pope sends Catherine to Florence. 27 March: death of Gregory XI. 8 April: election of Urban VI. June: Riots in Florence. Catherine in danger. 28 July: Papacy and Florence sign peace treaty.

20 September: election of antipope
Clement VII.

December: Urban VI summons Catherine
to Rome.

1379      29 April: Urbanist victory at Marino and
recovery of Castel S. Angelo.

1380      29 April: Catherine dies in Rome.

# GROUP 1

## *Early Letters*

LETTER 1   (Dupré III; Tommaseo 41; Gigli 105)
*To:*   *Fra Tommaso della Fonte OP, a cousin of Catherine and her first confessor.*

*Date:*   Before May 1374, while Fra Tommaso was recuperating at S. Quirico d'Orcia, near Siena.

In the name of Jesus Christ crucified.[1]

Beloved father of our souls, greetings in Christ Jesus from Caterina and Alexa[2] and all your other daughters, who wish to see you as well as God wills in soul and body.

I, Catherine, unprofitable servant of Jesus Christ, am the most unworthy of all your daughters because I do not hunger much for the honour of God and have not kept very much in mind his repeatedly telling me to live as dead to my own perverse will, so I have not duly submitted my will to the yoke of holy obedience to the extent that I could and should have done. What a wretch I am not to have run with all my might to embrace the cross of my sweet spouse, Christ crucified, choosing, in my negligence and ignorance, to sit down and rest instead. But now I am sorry and acknowledge my fault to God and to you, father, and I implore you to absolve me and to bless me and all the others.

And now, father, let me ask you to fulfil my desire, which is to see you united to and transformed into God – something that cannot happen unless we are united to his will. O sweet eternal will of God, you have taught us how to find you! If we were to ask our sweet and loving Saviour[3] and most merciful Father: 'How are we to find it?' he would reply: 'If you want to find and experience the fruit of my will, dwell always in the cell of your soul.' Now the cell is a well containing earth and water. We can take the earth to be our own poverty, the recognition that of ourselves we are nothing, and so we acknowledge that our being comes to us from God.

O ineffable and burning Charity, I see that we have found the earth, but there is living water too, that is, true knowledge of his blessed will, that wants only our sanctification[4]. Let us then plunge into the well, where we cannot but know ourselves and hence also the goodness of God. The recognition that *we* are not makes us humble, and so we are able to pass into the flaming burning open heart [of Christ], like an unshuttered window that stands ever open[5]. When we gaze in with the eye of free will God has given us, we see clearly that he wants only our sanctification. O sweet and blessed Love, open out, open out our memory so that we can take into ourselves and cling to God's great goodness, and understand it too – for through understanding we love, and through loving we are united and transformed into the Love that is mother[6] of charity, having already passed through, yet never ceasing to pass through, the gateway of Christ crucified, as he promised his disciples: 'I will come and make my home with you'[7].

This is what I want, [father]: to see you in such a home and transformed in such a way. I want this for you in particular, and then for everybody. I beg you to remain nailed fast to the cross.

You wrote saying you had visited the body of St Agnes[8] and I was greatly comforted to know that you have recommended us to her, and to her daughters[9]. As for your saying that you don't want to come back and don't know why, there could be two reasons for this: one is that when a soul is closely united and transformed into God it forgets self and creatures; the other is when a person finds himself somewhere that helps him to be recollected. If these apply to you, I am greatly consoled, for my soul desires nothing else for you. Indeed, I have sometimes thought, and think, that my own wretchedness and ignorance are responsible for the delay [in bringing it about]. I think, too, that God in his ineffable charity wants to punish and correct my iniquities, and this he does in his great love that I may know myself.

It seems you are proposing to go somewhere else. It did not seem to me that you ought to do this now; however be it done according to God's will, and yours. May God grant you to choose what is best in this, and to make whatever you do serve God's honour and your own salvation. Praised be Jesus Christ crucified[10].

I recommend our Caterina to your prayers. Alexa too urges you particularly to pray to God for her and to bless her on behalf of Christ crucified. Pray to God for crazy Giovanna too.[11]

Catherine, servant and slave redeemed with the blood of the Son of God.[12]

Forgive me for any presumption in what I have said. May God set you on fire with love. Sweet Jesus. Sweet Jesus. Jesus, sweet Jesus.[10]

---

[1]  This or a similar invocation, often including an appeal to 'sweet Mary', appears at the head of each letter in the mss.

[2]  a. *Caterina* di Ghetto, one of Catherine's early disciples.
b. *Alexa* (or Alessa) Saraceni, a widow of noble birth who had given all her possessions to the poor and joined the Order of Penance (known as *Mantellate* from their black cloak) to which Catherine herself belonged, as did Caterina di Ghetto and several other early and devoted disciples. Cf. Gardner, p.52 and Raymond, pp.66–68.

[3]  Lit. 'young man'.

[4]  I Thess. 4:3 – this text recurs like a refrain throughout Catherine's letters.

[5]  In Catherine's day, most windows were arched or square openings fitted with shutters but without glass.

[6]  This idea seems to come from St Bernard: ' . . . it is rightly said, charity is God, and the gift of God. Thus charity gives charity; substantial charity produces the quality of charity.

Where it signifies the giver, it takes the name of substance; where it means the gift, it is called a quality.' *On Loving God*, XIII, 36, in *The Works of Bernard of Clairvaux*, Treatises II; Cistercian Fathers Series no. 13, Cistercian Publications, Consortium Press, 1974. Cf. also *The Letters of St Bernard of Clairvaux* (ET London 1953) pp.10 & 26.

[7] John 14:23

[8] *Agnese* Segni of Montepulciano (1268–1317). This foundress of a Dominican monastery called after her was renowned for her sanctity and miracles. She had been popularly styled 'Saint' long before she was officially canonized in 1726. Catherine always had a great devotion to her; the early biographers record a variety of wonders connected with her visits to the shrine; cf. Raymond, pp.292–297.

[9] The nuns at the monastery.

[10] The endings of these early letters vary considerably as compared with the more or less set formulae Catherine later adopted.

[11] Probably *Giovanna* di Capo, another early and faithful disciple; the epithet suggests that she acted as the secretary on this occasion.

[12] This is one of the few letters bearing Catherine's formal signature.

LETTER 2   (Dupré V; Tommaseo 204; Gigli 109).

*To:*   *Fra Bartolomeo Dominici OP, Catherine's second confessor, while he and Fra Simone OP of Cortona[1] were on a Lenten preaching assignment in Asciano, not far from Siena.*

*Date*:   March 1372 or April 1373.

To you, dearest brother in Christ Jesus, I, Catherine, servant and slave of the servants of God, write to encourage you in the precious blood of the Son of God, desiring[2] to see you so plunged and drowned in Christ Jesus as to lose all thought of self.

But I cannot see this happening unless you raise the eye of understanding (of true desire) above yourself to meet the look of ineffable divine charity with which God gazed – and still gazes – upon his creature even before he created it. When he looked into himself, he fell so much in love that out of sheer love he created us. He wanted us to enjoy and to share in the good that was in himself, but was thwarted in this by Adam's sin. So, constrained by the fire of divine charity, God sent the sweet incarnate Word, his Son, to buy man back and release him from bondage. The Son rushed to give himself to the shame of the cross, and to associate with malefactors, public sinners, and outcasts of all kinds (you cannot set a law or limit on charity: it is oblivious of self and quite un-selfseeking).[3] Because the first man fell from the height of grace through love for himself, God had to do things the other way round. That is why he sent the spotless Lamb who, in his boundless and ineffable charity, sought not himself but only the Father's honour and our salvation. O sweet and loving Knight-at-arms, you care not whether you live, die or suffer dishonour. Indeed, on the cross you grapple with the death of sin, and death prevails over the life of your body, while your death destroyed ours.

Love, you see, is the explanation of all this. His eye was fixed entirely on his Father's honour and on accomplishing in us the Father's will, namely that we should enjoy God, the end for which he created us.

Beloved son, I want *you* to be conformed to this Word who is our rule, and to the saints who have followed him, for then you will become one with him and have a share in his generosity, instead of being narrow and constricted. I say again that unless a soul raises itself up and opens its eye to focus it on the boundless goodness and love God shows for his creature, it can never attain this great generosity but will always remain so constricted that it will have no room either for self or for neighbour. That is why I urged you, and desire you, to be plunged and drowned in him, with your attention fixed on the loving eye of his Charity. Then you will be able to love perfectly what he loves and hate what he hates. Oh, raise up your

puny heart and narrow, troubled conscience. Give no
house room to the wicked demon who is out to prevent
the doing of so much good. *He* does not want to be driven
out but *I* want you, with perfect courage and manly zeal,
to see that the law of the Spirit is quite different from that
of men. Model yourself on that tender lover, Paul. Be a
vessel of love[4] carrying and proclaiming the name of
Jesus. I feel sure that Paul met the gaze from that Eye and
lost himself in it, becoming so utterly free and open that
he longed to be himself accursed and cut off from God
for the sake of his brethren.[5] Paul was in love with what
God had fallen in love with; he saw that charity does not
offend others and is not itself put out in any way.[6] Moses,
too, was concerned about God's honour, which is why he
wanted to be blotted out of the book of life rather than that
his people should die.[7] Therefore I both constrain you
and, in Christ Jesus, *want* you to be firm in uprooting vice
and planting virtue, following – as I said – in the footsteps
of the First Truth and his saints (who did just that) and
not setting any bound or limit on a desire that should be
boundless. Accept the fact that you are living among a
faithless wicked bunch of outcasts! This being so, your
association with them cannot but be prompted by love. I
assure you that for this very reason your activity will be
prompted by charity (in other words, concern for their
salvation) and not by what they are in themselves.
Indeed, if your association with them were prompted by
self-love or by any spiritual or material pleasure uncon-
nected with hunger for their good that you derived from
them, then you would have cause both to flee and to fear
their company. So banish all narrow-minded resentment,
and trust more in others than in yourself. And if the devil
still goes on troubling your conscience, tell him to argue
this and everything else out with *me*: a mother has to
answer for her children! So be up and doing, for there is
no cause so difficult, no stronghold so impregnable that it
cannot be broken down (and you built up) by Charity.

Bless my son Fra Simone for me and tell him to run

with the baton of holy desire, by which I mean the cross. Let me know how you both are and how God's honour is progressing.

Alessa *grassotta*[8a] says that you are praying for her and please will you go on doing so – and for me, too, your time-waster, Cecca.[8b]

Pray, too, for Lisa.[8c]

Abide in peace and in the love of God.

---

[1]   An early and ardent disciple.

[2]   Cf. Luke 22:15. The Vulgate form of this text 'With desire I have desired' lies behind this frequently recurring opening thought in Catherine's letters.

[3]   Cf I. Corinthians 13:5

[4]   Lit. 'dilection' cf. Acts 9:15 A.V. and Douay.

[5]   Romans 9:3.

[6]   I Cor. 13:4–7.

[7]   Exodus 32:32 & cf. Dialogue, p. 283.

[8a]   Lit. 'Fatty Alex', but *grassotta* is kinder and more affectionate than the English equivalent. Cf. letter 1, note 2b.

[8b]   *Cecca* (Francesca) Gori, another early and faithful disciple. Again, the epithet suggests the identity of the secretary.

[8c]   *Lisa* is probably the wife of Catherine's brother, Bartolommeo. All three women frequently accompanied Catherine on her travels and often acted as her secretary.

## LETTER 3   (Dupré XI; Tommaseo 107; Gigli 238).

*To:*   *Luigi Gallerani, a Sienese nobleman who was in Asciano on what was probably official business for the Republic of Siena.*

*Date:*   Not long after letter 2.

To you, my very dear brother in Christ Jesus, I, Catherine, servant and slave of the servants of God, write to encourage you in the precious blood of the Son of God, desiring to see you advancing like a brave knight; not retreating to avoid being hit, but keeping steadily on, for, as you know, only perseverance (and not the mere fact of having begun) wins the prize.[1]

And if you grow weary of standing fast on the field of battle, then, beloved brother in Christ Jesus, seize hold of the holy standard of the cross, a strong pillar on which rests the Lamb who was slain for us. It is so strong that it takes away all our weakness and so strengthens a man's heart that no devil or creature can force him to move unless he himself chooses. And no wonder! It was the strength of love that kept the Lamb bound and nailed to the wood of the cross. Up then, I beg you, and bind your own self there so that you will be quite unable to turn back; up there you'll find the source of all virtue; there, too, you will find the God-Man, through the union of the divine and human nature, and also the abundance of divine charity with which he snatched the human race, his bride, from the hands of the devil who had made an adulteress of her.

O Jesus, sweetest Love, unarmed and nailed fast to the cross you overcame all our enemies!

He came as our peace, to reconcile man with God, as St Paul has told us: 'I am Christ's messenger and ambassador to you. I beseech you, beloved brothers, to be reconciled to one another and to make peace with him who came as our mediator to reconcile man to God.'[2]

Sweet Jesus, you are indeed our peace, and tranquillity, and serenity of conscience, and there can be no bitterness or sadness or poverty in any soul where you dwell by grace.

It stands to reason that such a soul possesses perfect joy and all riches, for God is supreme joy; that it is not bitter or dejected, for he is the supreme riches that never fail and no thief can ever steal.[3] So I beg you with all my heart to be up and doing for the little time that is left to you, since to live well and virtuously is in itself a great consolation. That is why I said I wanted you to be a real knight, not backing out of the solemn resolution you have made, but rather armed with truly solid virtues and leaning on the pillar of the cross which will protect you from being bitten[4] or tormented by the devil or any other creature who tries to keep you from virtue. Pay no heed and put no faith in the counsels of anyone who tries to deflect you from your purpose; rather, go often to confession and associate with the kind of people who will help you to live in the grace of God. No more now.

Bathe your memory in his Blood.

Greetings from Fra Bartolomeo and Neri.[5] Please convey their greetings and mine to Messer Biringhieri.[6] Abide in the holy peace of God.

---

[1]   Cf. Matthew 10:22

[2]   Cf. II Cor. 5:20 and I Tim.2:5.

[3]   Matthew 6:20

[4]   Cf. Numbers 21:9 and John 3:14.

[5a]   *Fra Bartolomeo* Dominici OP; cf. letter 2.

[5b]   *Neri* Pagliaresi, a young Sienese nobleman and poet, one of Catherine's early and most faithful disciples. He became a constant companion and regular secretary, being one of the three to whom she dictated the *Dialogue*, and frequently acted as her ambassador on difficult assignments. After her death he became a hermit. We owe one of the early collections of her letters to his loving industry.

[6]   The parish priest of Asciano with whom Catherine was in correspondence.

LETTER 4   (Dupré XIV; Tommaseo 18; Gigli 250).

*To:*   *Benincasa, Catherine's eldest brother.*

*Date:*   Possibly during the winter of 1373–74 when the dyeworks that Benincasa and two of his brothers had set up in Florence was in difficulties.

Dearest brother in Christ Jesus,

I, Catherine, an unprofitable servant, comfort and bless you, and also urge you to practise that sweet and holy patience without which we cannot please God. So that you will, in fact, reap the benefit of all your trouble, I beg you to take a firm grip on this weapon of patience. You may be finding it difficult to cope with all your problems, so let me suggest three things which may help you to be a bit more patient. First of all, I want you to reflect on how short life is; you are not sure even about tomorrow. Indeed, we can say that we haven't got either the troubles we have endured in the past or the ones that lie ahead of us; all we have is the one moment we are living through now. Surely we should be patient since the time *is* so short! Secondly, bear in mind the fruit to be gained from all the toil, for St Paul says that there is no comparison between our present trials and the fruit and reward of eternal glory.[1] Thirdly, think about the evil consequences of giving in to anger and impatience. We then have these evil things with us here, and eternal punishment hereafter.

So I beg you, dearest brother, to endure your trials patiently. Let me also remind you of the need to make amends for your ingratitude and lack of feeling. I mean your debt to your mother, whom you have a God-given duty to honour. I have watched your ingratitude increasing to the point that not only have you not supported her as you should have done (let's grant that you are excused for this because you were not able) – but even if you had been able I am not sure that you would have done so, for you've been mean even with words. What ingratitude! You forget her labour in bringing you into the world, the milk with which she fed you, and all the trouble she had in rearing you and the others. You may want to say that she didn't look after us, but I say that isn't true. Her great care and concern for you and your brother[2] have cost her dearly. And even if it were true, *you* are still the one who is under an obligation to her, not she to you. She did not get her flesh from you, but gave you hers.

I beg you to correct this and your other faults – and to forgive my bluntness. Only my love for you and concern for your soul make me say these things. Don't forget to go to confession – and the rest of your family, too. No more now . . . [lacuna in ms.][3] Abide in the sweet and holy love of God. Sweet Jesus. Jesus, Love.

---

[1]  Cf. Romans 8:18.
[2]  Their mother, Monna Lapa, seems to have been somewhat demanding and impatient. Catherine's own letters to her are gently chiding but here she defends her mother loyally. The third brother, Stefano, died some time before October 1373.
[3]  Here, as in many of the other letters, the more intimate personal details and messages that almost certainly followed at this point have been deleted by the early editors.

LETTER 5   (Dupré XXIII; Tommaseo 101; Gigli 27).

*To:   Cardinal Iacopo Orsini, official 'protector' of the Sienese Republic at the papal court in Avignon.*[1]
*Date:* End of 1374

Beloved and most dear father in Christ Jesus,
I, Catherine, servant and slave of the servants of Jesus Christ, write to you in his precious blood, desiring to see you bound in that same bond of burning divine Charity which moved God to draw us out of himself (that is, out of his infinite Wisdom), so that we might share in, and enjoy, the bliss of his own supreme Goodness; the bond that bound and tied God into our human nature when man lost grace through sin. It made a graft in us: life was grafted into death so that we, who were dead, have come to life again through being united to him. God was grafted into man so that the God-Man could run like a lover to meet the shameful death of the cross, the tree to

which the incarnate Word wished to be grafted, and to which he was held not by cross or by nails, but by Love. Nothing else could hold the God-Man.

He is the Master who has taken his chair to teach the true doctrine, following which no soul can be overtaken by darkness.[2] He is also the Way leading to this school, that is, if we follow his example. He has said: 'I am the way, the truth and the life'.[3] And he really is, father, for whoever follows this teaching – by insults, anguish and mockery, by suffering, contempt and trials, by true and holy poverty, by meek and humble submission to and patient endurance of injury – learning the way from this Master (for he both made it and kept to it by doing all these things himself) – returns good for evil to everyone, as he taught us to do. See his patience in the face of our past and continuing misdeeds. He seems to be pretending not to see (though when we come to die, he will show us he had seen, for then every sin will be punished and every good deed rewarded). And how patiently he disregards the abuse hurled at him! On the cross he hears the cries of the Jews, some shouting 'Crucify him', others challenging him to come down. But his cry is: 'Father, forgive them'.[4] Ignoring their taunts, he hangs there to the end.

Then we have his cry of joy: *'Consummatum est'*,[5] which may sound like a cry of anguish, but was in fact one of joy from the soul of the incarnate Word, God's Son, utterly consumed in the fire of divine Charity. It was as though sweet Jesus were saying: 'I have accomplished everything that has been written about me; I have satisfied my anguished yearning to redeem the human race, so now I rejoice and exult that this suffering is at an end; that I have now – as I longed to do – performed the task laid on me by my Father'.[6]

Sweet Master, you have indeed shown us the way and expounded to us your teaching. You spoke truly when you said that you were the way, the truth and the life. No one who follows your way and your teaching will have death in himself; rather, he will receive in himself ever-lasting life, which no devil or creature or injury inflicted on him can take from him without his consent.

Shame, shame on our human pride, self-indulgence and self-love, in spite of God's great goodness, the count-less graces and benefits he showers on us out of his bounty and not as our due.[7] Foolish man seems neither to see nor to feel the heat of a love so fierce that, were we made of stone, it would by now have shattered us. Alas, I, poor wretch, can see only one explanation. We just will not raise up the eye of knowledge to consider the tree of the cross where such heat of love, such sweet and persua-sive doctrine, rich in life-giving fruit, is made manifest; where is displayed, too, the generosity which tore open his body so that he might bathe and baptize us in his Blood – the baptism we can and should make use of every day with great love and continual remembrance. For, as the baptism of water cleanses us from original sin and gives us grace, so his Blood washes away all the sins and acts of impatience we ourselves commit. It swallows up every injury (so that we do not remember, let alone seek to revenge it) and we receive the fullness of grace which leads us along the right way, as I have said. I am sure that if the soul really sees this, it cannot but want to destroy and drown entirely its own perverse sense-appetite – always a rebel against the soul itself and its Creator – and, forgetful of self, be on fire with love for the honour of God and the salvation of souls. Like a man in love, it will have no time for thought of self, but will be totally absorbed in the object of its love. Such is the power of love that lover and beloved are one in heart and mind; what one loves, the other loves – nothing else would be perfect love. I have often noticed that when we really love or want something (whether something useful or something that brings us joy or pleasure), we do not care what insult, injury or trouble we have to endure in order to acquire it, being so intent on getting what we want that we scarcely even notice the effort involved.

[Begging the Cardinal to be a sweet-smelling flower in the garden of the Church (cf. letters 32, 47 & 51) and conformed in all things to Christ crucified, Catherine urges him to do his utmost to prevail on the Pope to return to Italy without further delay.]

---

[1]   Catherine may first have met this great Roman aristocrat when he visited Siena (where he was given a civic welcome) on his way to Avignon in September 1371. It is worth noting that the Florentines too, tried to influence Pope Gregory through him. Cf. Gardner, pp. 159 and 184.
[2]   John 12:35.
[3]   John 14:6.
[4]   Luke 23:34.
[5]   'It is finished' – John 19:30.
[6]   Cf. John 17:4.
[7]   Romans 4:4–5, another of Catherine's favourite texts.

LETTER 6   (Dupré XXIV; Tommaseo 69; Gigli 243).

*To:*   *Sano di Maco, a Sienese wool merchant and member of a pious association known as the 'Company of the Virgin Mary'.*
*Date:* Spring 1375, shortly after Catherine's arrival in Pisa.

Beloved brother in Christ Jesus,
I, Catherine, servant and slave of the servants of Jesus Christ, write to encourage you in the precious blood of the Son of God, desiring to see in you the persevering faith of the Canaanite woman[1] whose faith was so strong that she merited to have the devil driven out of her daughter. And not only that! Wishing to show how her faith pleased him, God[2] attributed the victory to her, saying: 'Be it done to your daughter as you desire.' What

a high and glorious virtue faith is, revealing the fire of divine charity in a soul – for a man has faith and hope only in what he loves.

Each of these virtues follows from the others, for there is no love without faith and no faith without hope. They constitute three pillars holding together and supporting the fortress of our soul so that no wind of temptation, no word of abuse, no flattery, no love for earthly things – not even wife and children – can bring it down. In the midst of all these things, it will stand fast on its three pillars.[3]

Then we shall do what the Canaanite woman did. Seeing Christ going into our soul, our true and holy longing will make us turn to him with deep contrition and regret for sin and say: 'Lord, release my daughter (that is, my soul), for the devil is tormenting her with all sorts of temptations and unruly thoughts.' And if we stand fast and keep a firm grip on our will so that it does not give way or tend to love anything apart from God, humbling ourselves and considering ourselves unworthy of peace and quiet; if while we wait with faith, and in the patient confidence that we can do all things through Christ crucified, we repeat with St Paul: 'I can do all things – not of myself but through Christ crucified who is in me and strengthens me',[4] then we shall hear that gentle voice: 'Let your daughter (that is, your soul) be healed as you desire'. Thus does God, in his infinite goodness, reveal to the soul the treasure of free will he has given it, for no devil or any creature can force it to commit a mortal sin without its consent.

Dearest son in Christ Jesus, realize with faith and true perseverance that these words are addressed to us until we die. I will tell you something. When God created man, he said to him: 'Be it done according to your will',[5] that is, 'I make you free, subject only to myself'. O infinitely precious Fire of Love! You show forth the nobility of your creature, creating all things to serve him and him to serve you. And yet we, miserable creatures, go and love the world and all its luxury and splendour, so that our soul loses its sovereignty and is degraded to the service of sin, with the devil as its master. And a dangerous master at that, since his one aim is to encompass man's death. I don't think we want to serve that kind of master. No, *we* must be souls in love with God, recognizing always that we slaves have been ransomed by the blood of the Lamb. Remember, a slave is not free to sell himself or to serve any other master. Remember too, that the ransom money was not paid in gold or even in the sweet coin of love but in Blood.[6]

Oh, let our hearts and souls burst with love! Let them hasten to serve and fear our good sweet Jesus, acknowledging that he has rescued us from prison and from bondage to the devil who had us in his power. He went bail and surety for us, and tore up the deed of bond.[7] When? When he became a servant by assuming our humanity. Alas, even that was not enough for us until he had paid the debt incurred on our behalf. Again, when? On the wood of the most holy cross when he gave up his life in order to restore to us the life of grace we had lost. O sweet and measureless Charity! You destroyed the deed of bond between man and the devil, tearing it up on the wood of the cross. It had been drawn up on parchment of lambskin, the skin of the spotless Lamb who tore up the bond and enrolled us into himself instead. So let our souls take comfort. We have been enrolled and the deed of bond destroyed, so that our enemy and adversary now has no hold over us.

Let us run, then, my son, embracing virtue with true and holy desire, mindful always of the gentle Lamb who was slain with such burning love. No more now.[9]

Bear in mind that, like the Canaanite, in this life we can have only the crumbs – which are the graces we receive – as they fall from the Lord's table. But when we come to eternal life where we shall taste God and see him face to face, then we shall partake of the food on the table. So never shirk the toil. I will send you crumbs, and food too, as to a son; you do battle and preach like a man.

We are all well by God's grace. His honour is more in evidence from day to day. We have not yet left Gherardo's house,[8] but will do so when the time ordained by God comes. I will let you know when as soon as I can.

Abide in the sweet and holy love of God.[9]

---

[1]  See Matthew 15:22–28. This was the gospel read at Mass on the first Thursday in Lent.

[2]  God, here, means God the Son, the incarnate Word.

[3]  Cf. Matthew 7:24–27

[4]  Cf. Philippians 4:13.

[5]  Catherine makes a daring application of Mary's words of consent to the Incarnation; cf. Luke 1:38.

[6]  Cf. I Peter 1:18–19.

[7]  Cf. Colossians 2:13–14

[8]  *Gherardo* Buonconti, a prominent citizen of Pisa who acted as Catherine's host during her visit and remained thereafter a devoted disciple, as did several of his brothers.

[9]  Catherine's letters are falling into a set pattern. Where the phrases 'No more now' and 'Abide in the sweet and holy love of God', etc. are juxtaposed, we can nearly always assume that the early editors have deleted what may have been a substantial portion of the original letter, corresponding to such practical, homely and affectionately teasing advice and comment as we see her giving here.

LETTER 7    (Dupré XXVII; Tommaseo 146; Gigli 115)

*To:*    *Fra Bartolomeo Dominici OP,*[1] *while he was assigned to the Dominican Studium in Florence.*

*Date:*  Spring 1375, from Pisa.

Beloved father (out of reverence for the most blessed Sacrament) and son in Christ Jesus.

I, Catherine, servant and slave of the servants of Jesus Christ, write to strengthen you in the precious blood of the Son of God, desiring to see you wholly consumed in the fire of his charity, for I know that this burns up all thought of self. And this I want for you. By means of this burning charity, I invite you to enter into a calm deep sea. I have just discovered this again – not that the sea is new, though it is new to me, as I feel it in my soul[2] – in the words: 'God is love.'[3] As a mirror reflects a man's face and the sun lights up the world, so these words light up in my soul the fact that all its operations are simply love, for it is made of nothing but love, which is why he says: 'I am God, Love.' This throws a light on the inestimable mystery of the incarnate Word who, out of sheer love, was given to us with a humility that shames my pride. It teaches us to look not only at what he did for us but at the glowing love of the Word given to us, telling *us* to behave like a lover who, when a beloved friend comes bringing a present, does not look at the gift in his hands but opens the eyes of his love and fixes them on the heart and affection of his friend. This, then, is what God wants from us when, in his supreme, eternal, ever-blessed goodness, he visits our soul. When he comes with his prodigal gifts, let your memory open at once to receive what the understanding knows in the divine Charity; then the will rises with most ardent desire, receiving and beholding the burning heart of sweet good Jesus, the Giver. Thus you will find yourself smothered and clothed with fire and with the gift of the blood of God's Son, and be free from all pain and discomfort. It was this that took away the disciples' pain when they had to leave Mary and one another, though to spread God's word they bore it gladly. Run, run, run.

I cannot answer your questions about Benincasa's affairs as I am not in Siena. Please thank Messer Nicolaio[4] for his kindness to them all.

A thousand thousand greetings from Alexa (and from me, your poor Cecca[5]). May God be with you always. Amen. Jesus. Jesus.

Catherine, servant of the servants of God.[6]

[1]   Cf. letter 2.
[2]   Catherine is unlikely to have seen the sea before this visit to Pisa.
[3]   I John 4:8.
[4a]  for *Benincasa*, cf. letter 4.
[4b]  An unknown benefactor.
[5]   Cf. letter 1, note 2 and letter 2, note 8.
[6]   Once again, as in letter 1, we have Catherine's formal signature.

## LETTER 8   (Dupré XXX; Tommaseo 140; Gigli 220).

*To:   John Hawkwood, leader of a notorious band of mercenary soldiers.*[1]

*Date:*   27 June 1375, or thereabouts.

Beloved brothers in Christ Jesus,
I, Catherine, servant and slave of the servants of Jesus Christ, write to you in his precious blood, desiring to see you being true sons and warriors of Christ to the extent of desiring to lay down your lives a thousand times, if need be, in the service of the sweet good Jesus and so of making reparation for all the iniquities we have committed against our Saviour.[2]

My dear brother in Christ Jesus, it would be a fine thing if you would withdraw a little into yourself and reflect on all the trials and hardships you have had to endure in the devil's pay and service. I want you now to make a change and to enrol instead in the service and cross of Christ crucified – you and all your men – and so become Christ's Company, ready to march out against the infidel dogs who are in possession of our Holy Place where the sweet First Truth lived and suffered and died for us.[3] Since God (and our holy Father too) has decreed a campaign against the infidels, and since you enjoy war and fighting so much, I now plead earnestly with you in Christ Jesus to stop making war against Christians (for that is an offence against God) and to go and fight the infidels instead. How cruel that we, who are Christians, members bound together in the body of holy Church, should be persecuting one another. We must not do this. Indeed, we must give up all thought of doing any such thing.

I am truly astonished that you who – so they tell me – have already promised to go and die for Christ on the crusade[4] should now be wanting to make war in these parts. This is not the holy state of mind God requires of you, if you are to go to such a holy and venerable place. It seems to me that you ought now to be setting about practising virtue until the time comes for you and your companions to set out to give your lives for Christ and in this way prove yourself a brave man and true knight.

Fra Raimondo (who is father and son to me)[5] will be visiting you and will give you this letter. You can rely on all that he says, for he is a true and faithful servant of God and will not tell you anything or advise you in any way contrary to the honour of God and the salvation and glory of your soul. I will say no more.

I beg you, dearest brother, to remember that life is short.

Catherine, unprofitable servant, etc. [lacuna in original].[6]

Abide in the sweet and holy love of God. Sweet Jesus. Jesus, Love.

---

[1] Following the signing of a peace treaty in June 1375 between the scheming Bernabò Visconti of Milan and the tyrannical and incompetent Cardinal de Noellet, papal legate in Italy and governor of Bologna, Hawkwood and his men had been dismissed from the Church's service. It was this, coupled with the evil government and iniquitous policy of the papal representatives, that precipitated open rupture between Florence and the Church and the formation of the anti-papal league, inasmuch as the presence, and the depredations, of Hawkwood's men on the Tuscan frontiers induced first Florence and then Pisa and

Siena to buy them off – and then to retaliate by imposing heavy taxes on the clergy as a means of recovering from the Church much of the money they felt its pastors had wrongly made them pay. Cf. Gardner, pp.142–144, & also letter 24, note 4.

[2]   Catherine invariably associates herself with even the worst of sinners.

[3]   Catherine's desire to see the long-promised crusade become an accomplished fact prompts her to make her own shrewd if not very realistic proposal to the war-loving adventurer; cf. Introduction, pp.24–5.

[4]   Lit. 'on the holy passage.'

[5]   *Fra Raimondo* delle Vigne, OP, of Capua, Catherine's confessor, director, and close friend (cf. Introduction; letter 9, note 1, and passim) who, at Catherine's instigation, went to see Hawkwood at his camp near Pisa bearing this letter as a credential.

[6]   Cf. letter 4, note 3.

## LETTER 9   (Dupré XXXI; Tommaseo 273; Gigli 97).

*To:*   *Fra Raimondo of Capua, OP.*[1]

*Date:*   Probably June 1375 (though Gardner (p.210) suggests a date two years later), from Siena.

Beloved father and dearest son in Christ Jesus, I, Catherine, servant and slave of the servants of Christ, write and recommend myself to you in the precious blood of the Son of God, desiring to see you plunged and drowned in that sweet blood, all aglow with his burning charity. Yes, this I desire for you, and for Nanni and Giacomo.[2] I see no other way for us to come to those basic virtues we all need, my son. Nor can your soul acquire them otherwise, that soul which has become my food (and not a moment passes without my partaking of this food at the table of the sweet Lamb who bled to death with such burning love). As I say, unless you are drowned in his blood, you can never acquire the little virtue of true humility born of self-hatred which, in turn, is born of love, for a soul comes out of it with perfect purity, as iron is taken dross-free from the furnace. So, lock yourself into the open side of the Son of God, that fragrant storehouse[3] where even sin becomes fragrant. There the sweet bride reclines on the bed of blood and fire, and the secret of the heart of God's Son is laid bare.

O pierced Wine-cask, with the wine you offer you intoxicate every loving desire; you fill the understanding with joy and light and so flood every memory that endeavours to find you as to leave it incapable of remembering, understanding or loving anything other than yourself, good sweet Jesus, Blood and Fire, ineffable Love!

So that my soul may indeed exult to see you drowned in this way, I want you, like one who draws water in a bucket, that is, in your boundless desire, to pour the water over your brethren who are all members with us in the one body, the sweet Bride. And be sure you keep at it, whatever trick the devil may play (and I know you have been and will be troubled in this way), until we actually see their sweet and loving desires flowing like blood.

Come, father, this is no time for sleep. The news is such that I simply cannot rest. Already I have taken a man's head in my very hands, and been so deeply moved that my heart can hardly conceive it or my tongue relate it and I am sure no eye has seen or ear heard the like.[4]

God's will was at work (as it had been in the mystery of what went before) but I will not go into all the details as it would take too long. Well! I went to see the person you know about[5] and my visit helped him so much that he went to confession and made a good preparation. He made me promise, for the love of God, to be with him at the end. I gave him my word, and kept it. So, early that morning before the bell rang,[6] I went to him and he was much consoled. I took him to hear Mass and he received holy communion, which he had never done before. His own will was conformed and subject to God's, but he was still fearful that he might not be strong when it came to the point. However God, in his boundless and burning goodness, deceived him, as it were, by instilling into him such love and affection for *me* (in God) that he did not know how to be without *Him*. He kept saying: 'Stay with me and don't leave me; then I shall be all right and die happy' – and all the time he leaned his head on my breast. I was aware of sudden joy, of the odour of his blood in some way mingled with that of my own, which I hope to shed for sweet Jesus my bridegroom. As my own yearning increased and I sensed his fear, I said to him: 'Courage, dearest brother. We shall soon be at the wedding. *You* will be going to it bathed in the sweet blood of God's Son and with the sweet name of Jesus [on your lips]. Don't let it slip from your mind for an instant. I shall be waiting for you at the place of execution.' Think of it, father (and son). At that, his heart lost all fear, the sadness on his face turned to joy and he kept rejoicing and exulting and saying: 'How have I been given so much grace that my soul's delight will be waiting for me at the blessed place of my execution?' (He had reached the point of being able to call the place 'blessed'!) Then he said: 'I shall go with joy and courage and the time in between will seem like a thousand years, thinking that you will be there waiting for me.' He said such lovely things that one could almost burst at the goodness of God.

So I waited for him at the place of execution. All the time I waited I was praying and sensing the presence of Mary and of Catherine, virgin and martyr. Before he arrived, I lay down and placed my own head on the block, but I did not quite have what I wanted. So I begged, indeed forced Mary to get me the grace I wanted, which was that I might give him light and peace of heart at the moment of death, and then see him going to God. I was so absorbed in the assurance I received that my prayer would be granted that I saw no one in the crowd around me.

At last he arrived, as meek as a lamb. When he saw me, he began to laugh and wanted me to make the sign of the

Cross over him. I did so and then said: 'Down with you to the wedding, brother! You will soon be in the life that never ends.' He laid himself down with great meekness; then I stretched out his neck and bent over him, speaking to him of the blood of the Lamb. His lips murmured only 'Jesus' and 'Catherine', and he was still murmuring when I received his head into my hands, while my eyes were fixed on the divine Goodness as I said: '*I will*'.

Then I saw the God-Man as one sees the light of the sun. His side was open to receive into his own the blood that had just been shed; a fire of holy desire, which his grace had poured into and concealed in that soul, was now received into the fire of his own divine Charity. After receiving the blood and the desire, he received the soul itself and plunged it into the mercy-filled storehouse of his open side. Thus did the First Truth show that his reception was due entirely to God's grace and mercy and to nothing else. How indescribably moving it was to see God's goodness; to see the gentleness and love with which he waited to welcome that soul – with the eyes of his mercy fixed on it – as it left the body and was plunged into his open side, bathed in its own blood that now possessed merit through the blood of God's Son. When he had been thus received by God in his almighty power[7], the Son, who is wisdom and incarnate Word, gave him a share in the crucified love with which, in obedience to the Father, he himself had endured his own painful and shameful death for the benefit of all mankind. Then the hands of the Holy Spirit sealed him into that open side.

But he did such a lovely thing – one last gesture that would melt a thousand hearts (and no wonder, seeing that he was already experiencing the divine sweetness). He looked back, like a bride who pauses on the bridegroom's threshold to look back and bow her thanks to her escort.

When he had gone, my own soul was serenely at peace, and so impregnated with the scent of blood that I could not bear to remove the blood itself that had splashed onto me. Alas, poor me, I can say no more. I was so envious, seeing myself left behind.

The first stone really does seem to have been laid, so don't be surprised if I lay on you only my longing to see you, too, plunged into the blood and fire flowing from the side of God's Son. No more carelessness, my beloved children, for the blood has begun to flow and receive life.[8]

---

[1]  A learned, cautious and experienced Dominican who had already been Prior of the Minerva in Rome and chaplain to the Dominican nuns at Montepulciano for some years when he was assigned as Lector to the Studium in Siena shortly before (or, possibly, after) the General Chapter of 1374. At this chapter, he was officially appointed confessor and director to Catherine and her *Mantellate* companions. See T.M. Centi, 'Un processo inventato di sana pianta', in *S. Caterina tra i dottori della Chiesa*, ed. T.S. Centi OP, Florence, 1970.

[2]  Unidentifiable.

[3]  Cf. letter 18, note 5.

[4]  Cf. I Corinthians 2:9, yet another text that rings like a refrain through Catherine's letters.

[5]  The person in question seems to have been a young Perugian nobleman, Niccolò di Toldo, who had been condemned to death in Siena for speaking disrespectfully of the Sienese government.

[6]  The curfew bell – it was illegal to be on the streets before it rang.

[7]  Italian: *per potentia fu potente di poterlo fare* – an almost untranslatable play on the words *potentia/potente* (power/powerful) and *potere* (to be able).

[8]  Not clear. Catherine may mean Christ's blood, flowing from the fountain (cf. par.2) in the form of sweet and holy desire, and receiving back into it the re-awakened spiritual life of all over whom it flows.

LETTER 10    (Dupré XXXV;  Tommaseo 66;
Gigli 125).

*To:*    *Bro. William of Flete, an Augustinian hermit.*[1]
*Date:*  Probably July 1375, from Pisa.


Beloved father and dearest son in Christ Jesus,
Your unworthy Catherine, servant and slave of the
servants of Jesus Christ, writes to you in the precious
blood of the Son of God, my desire being that God's
words to Abraham: 'Leave your home and your country'[2]
be addressed to us too. The obedient Abraham did not
resist the summons. God said: 'Follow me', and he followed. What bliss when we too shall hear the sweet summons to depart from the country of our poor wretched
bodies!
A man must rise up and follow the First Truth who is
calling him in two ways. First, we must turn away from the
home of our earthly sensual feelings, our love for our
own selves; and then from our country, namely by
detaching ourselves from all earthly love and following
the Lamb who was slain on the wood of the most holy
cross. This Lamb calls to us and invites us to follow him
along the way of insults, suffering, and reproach, which
are utterly sweet and wholesome to a soul whose taste has
been trained for such things. To such a state has God
drawn us in his infinite goodness and mercy. What
further summons does the soul await, now that it has
heard and responded to the first one by abandoning vice
and pursuing the virtues which enable it to savour God by
grace in this life? Do you know, father, what it longs to
hear? That sweet summons in the canticle: 'Come,
beloved bride.'[3] At once is fulfilled between soul and
body that saying of Christ to his disciples: 'Let the children come to me, for to them belongs the kingdom of
heaven.'[4] This is God's way with his servants when he
takes them from this wretched life and leads them to a
place of rest, saying to our [body of] flesh which has been

the soul's servant and disciple: 'Let this soul come to me, for to it belongs the kingdom of heaven.'

O boundless, sweetest, burning Charity! You say this, no more no less, as if the soul had served you of its own accord, whereas in fact you are yourself the doer and giver of every service we render to you. You are he who is and without you we are not, as the apostle said 'We have not the power to think aright unless it be given to us from above.'[5] So your giving is sheer grace and in no way due to us.[6] Your boundless love does it all, for you choose to reward in us what is your own. Hence, when a soul sees such burning love, it is so taken out of itself that it loses all self-awareness, seeing and feeling everything in its Creator. This is the summons my soul longs for us both to hear.

But I hardly think I would be so very pleased then, father, unless I had first heard that other summons which all God's servants long to hear: 'Go out, children, from your countries and your homes; follow me; come and offer your bodies in sacrifice.'[7] When I think, father, of God granting us such a grace – to hear this summons and be allowed to give our lives for the unbounded love[8] of the Lamb – the very thought seems to make my soul want to leave my body bit by bit. Let us run, then, brothers and children in Christ Jesus, let us expand our sweet and loving desires, begging and constraining the divine Goodness to make us worthy quickly. No negligence, then, but be up and doing, always urging on yourself and others.

The time of waiting seems shorter when people show themselves willing. I want you to know that our brother Jacomo[9] whom we sent to the Judge of Arborea[10] with a letter about the crusade has sent a kind answer saying that he is ready to come himself and to provide, for two years, ten galleys with one thousand horsemen, three thousand foot-soldiers and six hundred crossbowmen. The Genoese, too, are all agog, undertaking to place themselves and their property at the Judge's disposal.

Clearly, God is seeing to his own honour in this and all the rest.

No more now, except that I would ask you to see that arrangements are made as soon as possible for this young man – whose name is Mateo Forestani[11] and whom I recommend to you – to be received as a religious. Do all you can to develop real solid virtue in him, and in particular to mortify in him his attitude to the world and his own will. I thought it best that he should not undertake another journey, which might have served more to unsettle his mind than anything else.

Fra Nofrio[12] told me that Fra Stefano[12] was ill and that once again this has affected you as you feared there would be no one to attend to your needs. Have no fear; trust that when God takes one from us, he gives us another. Comfort and bless Fra Antonio[12] a hundred thousand times in Christ Jesus. Abide in the sweet and holy love of God. Jesus, Jesus, Jesus.

---

[1]  This rather intolerant Englishman had withdrawn from Cambridge in 1359 to live as a hermit at the monastery of Lecceto, near Siena. Catherine and her disciples often called him 'the Bachelor' because of his academic degree (cf. *Dictionnaire de Spiritualité*, Fasc. XLII–XLIII, cc. 1204–1208 Paris, 1967).

[2]  Genesis 12:1, which Catherine has combined with Luke 5:27 and other NT parallels.

[3]  Song of Songs 2:13.

[4]  Mark 10:14.

[5]  Cf. II Corinthians 3:5.

[6]  Romans 4:4–5.

[7]  Catherine interprets the Genesis 12 text as an invitation to join the Crusade.

[8]  Original here has *nome* (name). Tommaseo's emendation *amore* (love), upheld by Dupré, seems more likely.

[9]  or 'fra Jacomo'; in either case this person is unidentifiable.

[10]  Mariano d'Oristano, overlord of Sardinia (or his son Ugo, if the letter was written after Mariano's death on 10 August 1375).

[11]  Contemporary chronicles refer frequently to this person,

who seems to have had much to do with the Misericordia Hospital of which Catherine's devoted disciple Matteo di Cenni (cf. letter 39, note 2a) was rector.

[12] Other Augustinian hermits, of whom *Fra Antonio* (cf. letter 51) at least belonged to Catherine's inner circle.

LETTER 11   (Dupré XXXVII; Tommaseo 136; Gigli 36).

*To:*   *Messer Angelo Ricasoli, Bishop of Florence.*
*Date:*   Probably July 1375, from Pisa.

Venerable and most dear father in Christ Jesus, I, Catherine, servant and slave of the servants of Jesus Christ, write and recommend myself to you in the precious blood of the Son of God, desiring to see you nailed fast by holy desire to the wood of the sacred and venerable cross where we shall find the spotless Lamb, roasted in the sweet fire of Charity. On this tree we find the source of all virtue, for charity is the fruitful tree which served as both cross and nail holding God's Son fast, where no cross or fetter could have done so. Here we find the Lamb that was slain devouring his Father's honour and our salvation, for his love was so great that he could not express it by means of his physical agony alone.

O inestimable, sweet and lovely Charity, in your insatiable hunger and thirst for our salvation you cry out that you thirst.[1] The agony you were enduring certainly made your physical thirst on the cross extreme, but your thirst for our salvation was even greater. Alas! Alas! Will no one offer you a drink? The bitter draught of countless sins? That, yes! But a willing service with pure and loving hearts? Very few indeed are ready to offer *that*.

Dearest and venerable father, I beg you to shake yourself out of the sleep of negligence (when the sun is actually rising is no time to be asleep) and give him the drink he begs from you so meekly. You may say: 'I have nothing to give him, child.' But I have already explained that I long for you to be nailed fast to the cross, where we find the Lamb that was slain with his blood gushing out, for he has made himself, for us, a wine cask, the wine itself, and the cellarer. Thus we see that his humanity is the cask that concealed the divine nature, and that the fiery hands of the Cellarer, the Holy Spirit, tapped the cask on the wood of the cross. And that sweet Wine, Wisdom, the incarnate Word, deceived and overcame the devil's malice, catching him with the hook of our humanity. So we cannot say he has not given us to drink, that is to accept [and offer back to him] the wine of his burning desire for our salvation.[2]

I beg you, father, like a good shepherd, to lay down your life for your subjects and your sheep. Open the eye of your understanding [and] fix it on God's hunger for the food of souls; then your own soul will be so filled with the fire of holy desire that you would give your life for them a thousand times over, if possible. Be the kind of man who eats and savours souls,[3] as this is the food God calls for. And I implore the supreme eternal Truth in his grace and mercy to grant that I may see you opening your veins and your whole body – for God's honour and for the sake of this blessed food – as he was opened for us. Then shall my soul be blessed, sweet and venerable father.

May I add, father, that Fra Raimondo[4] has not performed the obedience you laid on him because he has been very busy and unable to get away; he had to wait for several noblemen in connection with the crusade,[5] and still has a great deal to do. He will get away as soon as he can and be at your service. Forgive him, and my own presumption. Abide in the holy love of God.

---

[1]    John 19:28.
[2]    With Dupré, we accept the *lectio difficilior*; an authoritative

variant reads as follows: 'So we cannot say we have nothing to give him; rather we ought to accept the wine of his burning desire for our salvation and return it to him by way of our neighbour.' – a characteristic theme developed by Catherine in a number of letters, e.g. nos. 32, 48 & passim.

³    To hunger for souls and then 'eat' or 'savour' them is a favourite metaphor of Catherine's; cf. in particular letter 36, but also letters 13, 31, 37 and passim.

⁴    of Capua OP; cf. letter 9, note 1, and passim.

⁵    Cf. letter 8, note 4.

LETTER 12    (Dupré XLIV; Tommaseo 43; Gigli 240).

*To:*    *Ser Cristofano Guidini, a Sienese notary, from Pisa.*

*Date:*    Some time before Ser Cristofano's marriage, on 28 October 1375.[1]

Dearest brother and son in Christ Jesus,
I, Catherine, servant and slave of the servants of Christ, write to you in the precious blood of the Son of God, desiring to see you a loyal son, always persevering and carrying out the task entrusted to you by our true Father in heaven when he says: 'Whoever does not abandon mother and father and sisters and brothers and himself is not worthy of me.'[2] So he would seem to want us to abandon them. But it does not look as if you intend to do what he says, under the pretext of having a conscience about leaving her.[3] This conscience comes more from the devil than from God, in order to debar you from the perfect state to which the Holy Spirit seems to have been calling you. You may say to me: 'But God commands me to obey them.' That is true, so long as they do not keep you back from God's way; but if they debar us from that, we must step over them and follow our true Father, bearing the standard of the most holy cross, suppressing and destroying our own perverse wills.

Alas, dearest brother in Christ Jesus, I am indeed sorry that you are hanging back from entering into this holy state. It seems to me that you ought to have more of a conscience about *not* leaving her than about leaving her. However, since that is how it is, I beg the supreme and eternal Truth to lay his sacred hand on your head and to direct you into whichever state is most pleasing to him. Whatever your state in life and in all your occupations, I implore you to keep your eyes fixed on God, seeking always his honour and the salvation of his creatures. And never forget the price, the blood of the Lamb, that has been paid for us with such burning love.[4]

As for the choice, I must say I am very reluctant to get mixed up in something that concerns seculars rather than me. However, considering the situation of all three – and each is good – I cannot disagree with your choice. If you feel you do not mind the fact that she has already had a husband, then go ahead and marry her, since you *will* get mixed up in the perverse and wicked world. Otherwise, choose the daughter of Francesco Ventura da Camporeggi.[5] No more now.

I pray that the supreme and eternal Charity will grant you whatever will be most to his honour and your own salvation. May he pour out on both of you the fullness of his grace and his supreme and eternal blessing. Abide in the blessed love of God.

---

[1]   Ser Cristofano, who was devoted to Catherine and sometimes acted as her secretary, has recorded that, under her influence, he had resolved to be a religious but his mother prevailed on him to change his mind while Catherine was away in Pisa. He wrote to tell her of his decision and to ask her advice in choosing a wife from three possible 'candidates', one of whom was a young widow.

[2]   Cf. Matthew 10:37.

[3]   His mother.

[4]   Cf. I Peter 1, 18–19.

⁵   This girl may have been related to Pietro di Ventura, one of
Catherine's most faithful disciples (cf. letters 37 and 49).


## LETTER 13    (Dupré LI; Tommaseo 109; Gigli 41).

*To:*    *Berengario, Abbot of San Pietro, Lézat, (Pamiers,*
        *Ariège), several times papal nuncio in Italy.*
*Date:*   After 17th May 1375.¹

Venerable spiritual father in Christ Jesus,
    I, Catherine, your unworthy servant and daughter,
servant and slave of the servants of Jesus Christ, recommend myself, and write, to you in the precious blood of
God's Son, desiring to see you a true priest, and a
member attached² to the body of holy Church.
    O venerable and dearest father in Christ Jesus, what
bliss for your own soul, and mine, when I shall see us both
bound² in the fire of that divine Charity that gives her
milk to suckle and nourish her children. It seems to me
that this milk can only be had in the way a child draws
milk and nourishment from its mother's breast. So too, as
you know, our soul cannot have life except through
Christ crucified. As the First Truth said: 'No one can go
to the Father except through me;'³ and in another place
he said: 'I am the way, the truth and the life, and whoever
goes by my way will not walk in darkness but in the light'.⁴
O inestimable and sweetest Charity, which is your way,
the one you chose with so much love? Not, I see, the way
of honour, luxury and human glory; nor of self-love, for
charity seeks not self⁵ but God's honour and the salvation
of creatures. And his life was nothing but mockery and
insults, reproaches and treachery, culminating in the
shameful death of the cross. His saints followed after him
along this way, as befits members bound into and made
one with their sweet head, Christ Jesus who, in his

loving-kindness, nourishes and gives life to each one of his members.

And if we ask: 'How am I to follow my sweet Head and bind myself to him?' the answer is that you can only bind a man with bonds; he can only become one with fire by throwing himself right in and being completely enveloped in it. This is the bond of love which binds the soul to Christ. Such a sweet bond, for it bound God's Son to the wood of the most holy cross!' Once a man, thus bound,[2] is enveloped in the fire of divine Charity, it produces in his soul the effects of material fire, which gives heat and light and transforms everything into itself.

O sweet and captivating Fire, generating heat and driving out the icy chill of vice, sin and self-love!

The heat warms and sets alight the dry wood of our will which then bursts into flame and expands with sweet and loving desire, loving what God loves and hating what he hates. And as the soul [begins to] see how immeasurably it is loved, and that the Lamb was slain for its sake on the wood of the cross, [this,] I say, is the fire setting it alight and driving out every vestige of darkness, so that once this venerable fire is aglow, the understanding is made to swell and expand. Once this, too, has been bathed in light, it is able to discern God's will for it, and desires only to follow in the steps of Christ crucified, for it sees clearly that it cannot travel by any other road; its one wish is to delight in the shame and degradation that were his. Then, through the flesh of Christ crucified, it sucks the milk of divine sweetness, a sweet light in which there is no interior darkness or pain (whatever superficial trials and tribulations may occur) because by the light from the fire it sees clearly that everything, except vice and sin, comes from God. It sees that God wants only our sanctification[6] and that, to bring it about by his grace, he came right down to man's level and made him one with himself. His humility uproots our pride; he is the guide we ought all to follow.

The enlightened understanding sees all this as it gazes

into the divine charity and goodness of God. And where does it find this? Within, in knowledge of its own self, for it sees that it has no being of itself: it has its being from God, by his grace and love and not as its due.[7] The instant your understanding grasps such immense goodness, a living spring of grace will gush forth in it, an oil-vein of profound humility making impossible any fall, or upsurge, into pride, whatever position of honour or renown one may hold. Like a good shepherd, your soul will tread the path the Master trod, as did the sweet and holy Gregory[8] and his successors. Being the greatest, they were the least; their wish was not to be served but to serve others in their spiritual and temporal needs, and this more by the example of their lives than by their words.

When the understanding has received the light from the fire in the way I have said, it is transformed into it so that the two become one: thus, the memory becomes one with Christ crucified, retaining nothing, delighting in nothing, thinking of nothing but the Beloved, for the memory is flooded in an instant with the ineffable love it sees poured out on itself and on all mankind, and the person becomes so great a lover of both God and his neighbour that he would give his life for him a hundred thousand times over. And no personal advantage is sought in all this. Seeing how supremely God loves his creatures, he too delights in loving what God loves. So we can say that now he is indeed fire, giving out heat and light and transforming everything into himself. The three powers of the soul are at one in this fire: the memory treasuring all God's benefits; the understanding knowing his goodness and his will (as I have said) and the will so expanding with love that it cannot love or even desire anything apart from God. All the soul's movements are centred on God, and it has eyes only for him; its one concern is to do what is most pleasing to its Creator because it realizes that no sacrifice is so pleasing to him as an insatiable hunger for souls. This is the kind of zeal and hunger for souls that he requires of you, father, in particular, and of others in your position. This is the way of Christ crucified, who will always give us the light of his grace. Any other road will only take us deeper and deeper into darkness and, in the end, to everlasting death.

My dear father, your letter gave me great comfort and joy – to think that you should remember a poor wretch like me! I have understood what you said in it.[9] I answer the first of the three queries you put to me by saying that our sweet Christ-on-earth[10] (I believe and see this in the sight of God), that there are two things in particular defiling the bride of Christ that [he] should remove.[11] One is too much attachment to and concern about one's own relatives, a thing that especially needs to be mortified once and for all. The other is excessive softness due to excessive leniency. Alas, alas, this is why the limbs of the body are rotting: lack of due correction.

Moreover, Christ singles out as evil three vices in particular: lust, avarice, and an overweening pride which is queening it in Christ's bride, in her very prelates, who think of nothing but pleasure, status and wealth. They actually stand by and allow devils from hell to carry off the souls committed to their care because they themselves have become wolves, trafficking in divine grace. The strong hand of justice is needed to bring them to order; excessive leniency is, in fact, the greatest cruelty – but in correcting, let there be justice and mercy.

I tell you, father, that I hope, by God's goodness and through the petitions and promptings his servants keep presenting to him,[12] that at least a start will be made in eliminating this fault of over-attachment to relatives. I do not say that Christ's bride is not also suffering persecution, but I believe she will continue to flower, as she must. To put things right everything will have to be demolished, right down to the foundations.[13] I want you to understand the destruction [I speak of] in this sense, not in any other.

As to what you say about God being abundantly merciful to you on account of your sins, you know that God does not will the death of the sinner, but that he be converted and live.[14] I, your unworthy daughter, have taken, and will take, the burden of your sins upon myself and with yours and mine together we shall burn in the fire of most sweet Charity, where they are consumed; hope, then, and firmly believe that they *have* been pardoned by divine grace. So now set about living well and virtuously, keeping his crucified love for you planted in your heart and choosing to die rather than offend your Creator, or shut your eyes to your subjects' doing so.

The other thing [is] that when I urged you to shoulder your burden in holy Church, I was not referring only to your being burdened in temporal matters (though these are good); but more especially to your working together with the holy Father, doing all you can to rid the shepherds of the wolves and incarnate demons in their midst. They are interested only in good food, elegant houses and fine horses. Alas, that what Christ purchased on the wood of the cross should be spent with harlots! I beg you, though you die for it, to urge the holy Father to put a stop to such iniquity; also, when the time comes to make shepherds and cardinals, let them not be appointed through flattery, for money, or for simony. Beg him, insofar as you can, to look for and be guided by virtue and a good and holy reputation in the candidate. Let nobility weigh no more with him than lowly birth, for it is virtue that makes a man noble and pleasing to God. This is the burden, father, that I asked you then, and again now, to take upon yourself; granted that your other labours are praiseworthy, but this is quite the best. I will say no more now.

Forgive my presumption. I recommend myself to you one hundred thousand times in Christ sweet Jesus.

Please bear Messer Antonio's affairs in mind.[15] If you see the archbishop there, greet him as warmly as possible from me.[16] Abide in the holy love of Christ Jesus. Jesus, Jesus.

¹ In April 1375, Gregory XI sent the Abbot to mediate in the long-standing dispute between the Salimbeni family and the Republic of Siena. He probably met Catherine when he passed through Pisa on his way to Siena, where he was given a civic welcome on 17 May.

² Ital. *legato*. Dupré discounts the suggestion that Catherine is here using the word to mean 'legate' as well as 'bound, linked, attached to,' etc.

³ John 14:6a.

⁴ Catherine here runs two texts together: John 14:6b and 8:12.

⁵ I Cor. 13:5.

⁶ I Thessalonians 4:3.

⁷ Romans 4:4–5

⁸ St Gregory the Great, 540–604 AD., who first applied the formula *servus servorum Dei* (servant of the servants of God) to himself as Pope.

⁹ Italian: *intesi*, which could mean either 'I have heard' or 'I have understood'. The phrase seems to suggest that Catherine had her letters read to her, as she also dictated most, if not all, of those she herself wrote.

¹⁰ Catherine's favourite way of referring to the Pope.

¹¹ The text here is unsatisfactory, due partly to the kind of broken syntax referred to in the translators' preface.

¹² the Pope.

¹³ Cf. Jeremiah 1:10.

¹⁴ Ezekiel 33:11.

¹⁵ Unidentifiable.

¹⁶ Possibly Archbishop Angelo Ricasoli of Florence (cf. letters 11 & 32). 'There' is probably Florence, but could be Avignon, in which case the letter is unlikely to have been written much before the end of 1375.


## LETTER 14   (Dupré LII; Gardner I).

*To:*   *Messer Bartolomeo Smeducci, lord of San Severino, in the Marches of Ancona.*

*Date:*  Second half of 1375.

[Writing to this young ruler whose growing reputation for valour was giving him an importance out of proportion to the forces at his disposal,[1] Catherine urges him to face the world, the flesh and the devil fearlessly, for they have all been overcome by Christ.]

I want your security to be in Christ sweet Jesus. He has clothed us in the strongest of all clothing: in the garment of love fastened with the clasp of free will (so that you can do it up and undo it as you choose). If a man wants to throw off this garment of charity, he can; and if he wants to keep it on, he can do that too. Reflect, dearest father, that the very first garment we had was love. By love alone were we created to the image and likeness of God – and so man cannot exist without love, for of love he is made. Everything he has in soul and body is his through love, for, by God's grace, the father and mother give being, that is the substance of his flesh, to their son through love alone. This is why a son is so indebted to his father; moreover, through the filial love to which nature inclines him – if he is a true son – he cannot endure his father's being injured or insulted in any way. Of course, self-love may cause a man to quarrel with his father but, if so, his blindness is making him go against his own nature.

[Catherine applies this idea to our relationship with God. By its very nature a soul loves God and seeks to avenge offences against him, and so readily strikes out at the world, the devil and its own fleshly sensitive nature with the sword of hatred (of sin) and love (of virtue). By contrast, a soul that yields to the poison of loving self in such a way as to make a god of its own flesh, interests and ambitions, not only fails to avenge the outrages offered to the Father but, since Christ died because of sin, itself encompasses his death.]

I don't want this to happen to you, but I do want you to follow the promptings of the noble soul God has given you; with love and free will put on the garment I spoke of and fasten it up so that no devil or creature can strip it from you. Clothed thus, armed with virtue and with the sword of hatred and love in hand, you will lose all servile fear and be master of the city of your soul. You will never cower away from the blows of any trial or tribulation you may have to endure, nor will you look back (that is, go back to the vomit of your mortal sins) once you have set out on the path of virtue.[2] I don't want that! Rather, true perseverance right to the end. Crowns and accolades of glory are not for beginners, only for those who persevere. Coward indeed is the man who embarks on something and does not see it through. And well-merited the discomfiture if a knight on the battlefield were to turn and run just as he was on the point of winning!

Courage, then, my friend. No more carelessness; no more looking back longingly at the foolish wretchedness of the world. Its fickle delights are gone with the wind. Do not rely on your youthful vigour or on worldly renown. A man is alive today and dead tomorrow; well today and ill tomorrow; master today and servant tomorrow. What folly for a man to be attached to such things, relying on the unreliable, waiting for a time that will never come, while at the same time fleeing from the one thing he can have and keep for his own, namely grace. He can have as much grace as he likes whenever he likes – not through any merit of his own, of course, but by the gracious gift of the Holy Spirit who gave us our free will.

O inestimable, sweetest Charity, who prompted you to do it? Love alone. Jesus, sweetest Love, to make this soul strong and rid it of the weakness it had incurred by sin, you built a wall round it by mixing mortar and copious quantities of that blood of yours which blends and moulds the soul into conformity with the sweet will and love of God. As lime mixed with water is put between stones to bind them securely together, so between his creature and himself God has put the blood of his only-begotten Son made into mortar with the living lime of blazing charity – there is no blood without fire and no fire without blood, for that Blood was shed with the burning love of God for all mankind. Thanks to this wall, the soul is so strong that no wind could bring it down unless the soul itself chooses to topple it, using the 'pick' of mortal sin!

['Is anyone so obdurate that the realization of God's love for us leaves him unmoved?' asks Catherine. She then invites Smeducci to show his love for God and make up for his sinful past by being ready to give 'blood for Blood' in the crusade.]

I beg you, for the love of Christ crucified, to respond with joy and eager longing to the invitation to this glorious wedding-feast, with its promise of sweetness, joy and every delight. At this feast we leave all uncleanness behind; released from sin and suffering, we dine at the table of the Lamb, where the Lamb himself is both our food and our servant.[3] The Father, you see, is our table, bearing everything that is – except sin, which is not in him. The Word, God's Son, has made himself our food, roasted in the blazing fire of charity, while the servant at table is that very charity, the Holy Spirit, who gave and gives us God with his own hands. He is all the time serving us with every spiritual and temporal grace and gift. How foolish if you, or anyone else, were to hold back from such delight. In my view, every man should get himself there somehow – on his hands and knees if he can't walk upright – so that we can demonstrate our love by giving him our lives for the love of life, and also by using our body to make reparation for our sins and failings, as we used it to offend him.

This will be the sweet and holy vengeance we shall take on ourselves. Once our sensual nature and fragile bodies have been overcome, we shall have won the battle. Reason and our soul will then be free, the lady of the manor, and possess God, the supreme eternal Good. Let us wait no longer, dearest father.

Follow in the steps of Christ crucified.

Bathe yourself in the blood of Christ crucified.

Hide in the wounds of Christ crucified.

Fix the eyes of your soul on Christ crucified, and so dwell always in love and filial fear, fearing sin but not suffering. I'll say no more.

Forgive my presumption; let love and longing be my excuse, and my distress at seeing how blindly and obstinately we run into the wretchedness of mortal sin.

Abide in the sweet and holy love of God. Sweet Jesus. Jesus, Love.

---

¹  Gardner, p.139.
²  Cf. Proverbs 26:11 and II Peter 2:22.
³  Catherine frequently uses a series of trios as an image of the blessed Trinity; cf. letters 16 & 18, and also letter 11, where she applies the metaphor somewhat differently.

LETTER 15   (Dupré LIV; Tommaseo 185; Gigli 1).

*To:*   *Pope Gregory XI*

*Date:*   This first extant letter from Catherine to Gregory was written from Siena some time between mid-December 1375 and mid-March 1376 — most probably in January.

Beloved and reverend Father in Christ Jesus,

Your wretched and unworthy daughter Catherine, servant and slave of the servants of Jesus Christ, writes to you in his precious blood, desiring to see you a fruitful tree, laden with sweet and wholesome fruit and set in fruitful soil (out of the ground it would dry up and bear no fruit!), that is, the soil of true self-knowledge. A soul that knows its own self is humble, for it sees nothing to be proud of; the sweet fruit of glowing charity is nourished within it as it knows in itself God's boundless goodness; knows, too, its own nothingness and attributes all it has to the One who is. Such a soul seems to be *forced* to love what God loves and hate what he hates.

O true and precious knowledge, bearing the weapon of hatred (wielded by the hand of holy desire) to seize and kill the worm of self-love which would otherwise gnaw away at the root of our tree so that it could not possibly bear fruit![1] Any fruit on it would wither and its leaves shrivel up, and all because wicked pride, the root cause of all evil, is at work in any man, be he prelate or subject, who loves himself.

Any man who loves himself (I mean for his own sake and not for God's) cannot but do evil; virtue is quite dead in him. He is like a woman whose children are stillborn; very much so, for he is without the life of charity that seeks only the praise and glory of God's name.

And if that man is a prelate? He too does evil, if love of self and his fear of incurring the displeasure of mere creatures (a fear that springs from self-love and self-seeking) cause holy justice to die within him. Though he sees those under him doing wrong, he pretends not to, and does not reprimand them. And even if he does, his show of reproof is so half-hearted that it is useless, serving only to plaster over the evil. He is all the time afraid of displeasing people and setting them against him, and all because he loves himself. Sometimes, men like this *do* want to put things right, but without upsetting anybody. I tell you, this is the greatest cruelty of all. If a wound needs to be cauterized and the badness cut out of it, yet nothing but ointment is put on it, not only will it not heal but it will fester so completely that, in many cases, death will be the result. Alas, alas, *dolcissimo babbo mio*,[2] this is why your subjects are corrupt, full of impurity and iniquity. Alas indeed – and I say it with tears – how very dangerous is that worm I spoke of. Not only does it bring death to the shepherd; through it all the others, too, fall sick and die! Why does he persist, then, in applying ointment? To keep himself out of trouble. The patient does not object if he is given only ointment; he does not mind or bear any ill will, as his own will in the matter has not been crossed. He was hoping for ointment and ointment he's been given. Poor foolish men! Blind the patient who fails to recognize his need, and blind the shepherd-physician, concerned only for his own comfort and self-interest, who, to avoid losing these, refrains from using either the knife of justice or the fire of glowing charity. Both bear out Christ's words: 'If the blind lead the blind, they both fall into the pit.[3] Doctor and patient finish up together in hell.

[Catherine elaborates this theme, but ends on a note of encouragement:]

Even if you have not been very faithful in the past, begin now to follow Christ, whose vicar you are, in real earnest. And do not be afraid ... Attend to things spiritual, appointing good shepherds and good rulers in the cities under your jurisdiction – for it is the bad ones who have provoked rebellion.[4] Above all, delay no longer in returning to Rome and proclaiming the crusade.

[She then urges Gregory to take special pains to retain the loyalty of Lucca and Pisa, whose citizens are under strong pressure to join the anti-papal league; comments briefly on his creation of unsatisfactory men as cardinals, and begs him to appoint a good and virtuous man as vicar of the Dominican Order if, as rumour has it, he intends to promote the Master General. She concludes with a request for the Pope's blessing and a humble apology for presuming to write.]

---

[1]   Cf. Jonah 4:7.
[2]   This phrase means literally 'sweetest daddy mine'. It was Catherine's favourite form of address for this apparently rather hesitant, over-sensitive Pope into whom she sought untiringly to instil the faith in God and confidence in his own powers he so badly needed.

³ Matthew 15:14.
⁴ Cf. letter 8, note 1.


LETTER 16    (Dupré LV; Tommaseo 181; Gigli 40).

*To:*     *Messer Nicola da Osimo, papal secretary.*
*Date:*   Contemporary with letter 15, i.e. probably January 1376.

Beloved and dearest father in Christ Jesus,
    I, Catherine, servant and slave of the servants of Jesus Christ, write to you in his precious blood, desiring to see you an unshakeable stone laid on the sweet cornerstone Christ Jesus . . .

    [A brief reflection on the parable of the houses built on sand and on rock follows – see Matthew 7:24–27.]

So my soul longs to see us all laid on the living Cornerstone.
    Dearest father, can we be better or more pleasurably employed than in building our soul? It's a delightful task, for we have stone, master and servant to hand, the very labourer we need.¹ What a sweet builder the eternal Father is, storehouse of infinite wisdom, knowledge and goodness. He is our God, the One who is; all that has being comes from him. He is a master who knows our every need and wants only our sanctification.² Whatever he gives man or allows to happen to him (whether temptation by the devil, trials and temptations of various kinds occasioned by other human beings, being exposed to injury or insult, or any other tribulation that may come our way), he gives or allows for our good, either to cleanse us from our sins or to make us grow in perfection and grace. Sweet indeed is our Master Builder, so skilled in building and laying according to our need. More than

that! Seeing that water alone would not do to moisten the lime when laying the stone of real solid virtue, he gave us the blood of his only-begotten Son. You know that, before the Son of God came, virtue, of itself, could not avail to restore to man the life he had lost through sin. Oh, father, let us contemplate the inestimable charity of this Master. Perceiving that the water of the holy prophets had not life enough to give us life, he drew from himself and proferred to us the incarnate Word, his only Son, entrusting to him his own power and authority[3] and setting him in our building[4] as the corner-stone without which we cannot live. And so sweet is this Son (for he is united to the Father and one with him) that in his sweetness every bitter thing is made sweet. In him is pure living lime, with no admixture of earth or sand.

Sweet Fire of Love, as our servant and labourer, you have given us the bountiful and most merciful Holy Spirit, Love itself, whose mighty hand kept the Word nailed and fastened to the cross. It was he who crushed that precious body to extract from it enough blood to give us life and bind the stones together. Now *every* virtue, when laid on Christ and soaked in his blood, avails and gives us life. Oh, let our hearts split open with love on perceiving that the blood has done what the water could not. Could anyone ask more? Could anyone choose to sprawl in gutters in search of some sad disordered wordly pleasure? Let these stony hearts of ours melt with the heat!

So the Father – what it is to see him! – with his wisdom, power and goodness, has made himself our Master Builder (it is the master builder who does the work, that is, he exercises his innate power when he evokes what is to be done from his memory, knows it through his understanding and implements it with the 'hands' of his will), creating and building our soul to his own image and likeness. We lost grace through sin, but he came in our nature, made himself one with it, indeed grafted himself into it. He has given us everything, for he gave us his essence when he gave us his Son, whom he also made a master, as we said, by conferring on him his own power. He made him a corner-stone, too – St Paul tells us that Christ is our corner-stone[5] – and the labourer at work on the building, that is, the inestimable charity and love with which he gave his life and mixed the mortar with his own blood, so that we lack nothing. Let us rejoice and exult to have so sweet a Master, Corner-stone and Labourer. He has walled us about with his Blood and made our wall so strong that no devil or creature, no hail, storm or wind, can cause the building to move without our consent.

Let memory bestir itself and treasure so great a gift, while understanding and knowledge gaze upon Love and its goodness in seeking and desiring only our sanctification[6] – for Christ saw himself not with eyes of self-love but of God's honour and our salvation. Once the memory has taken all this in and the understanding has understood and 'known' it, there must not be – I hardly think there could be – any holding back of the will from running eagerly, spurred on by the heat of charity, to love what God loves and hate what he hates. Nothing will ever disturb it then, or shake its holy resolution, for it will abide in true patience through having been laid on Christ, the living corner-stone. And that is why I said I wanted you to be a stone laid on that Stone, and I beg you, for the love of Christ crucified, to keep on growing and persevering in your holy resolution. Do not move or relax your vigilance, no matter what opposition you may encounter. Be for me an unshakeable stone built into the body of holy Church, seeking always God's honour and her glory and renewal.

[After begging her correspondent to urge the holy Father to return to Italy soon and to proclaim the crusade in spite of the outbreak of rebellion in the papal states, Catherine refers to the possibility of the Master General of the Dominican Order being 'promoted'. She names a possible vicar, whom she asks

Messer Nicola to recommend to Gregory, adding that she has already urged the Pope to consult his secretary on the matter.]

---

¹   Cf. letter 14 note 3.
²   I Thessalonians 4:3.
³   Cf. Matthew 28:18 & Luke 9:1.
⁴   Ephesians 2:20 & I Peter 2:4.
⁵   In Italian *pietra* can mean both 'stone' and 'rock'; here Catherine is probably thinking of I Cor. 10:4 without adverting to the context.
⁶   Again, I Thessalonians 4:3.

LETTER 17   (Dupré LVIII; Tommaseo 164; Gigli 348).

*To:   Melina Barbani of Lucca.*¹
*Date:*   Early 1376.

Daughter in Christ Jesus,
I, Catherine, servant and slave of the servants of Jesus Christ, write to you to comfort and strengthen you in his precious blood, my desire being to see you so totally transformed into divine Charity that nothing and no one will separate you from it.

You know, my beloved daughter, that if two things are to be joined into one, there must be nothing in between, otherwise the join will not be perfect. Realize that this is how God wants our soul to be: with no love of self or of any other creature in between, for God loves us with nothing in between. Freely and abundantly he loved us, as his own free gift and not as our due,² loving without being loved. No *man* can love like that. His must always be a love in return, a love that is owed in return for being given a share in the gifts and goodness of God. Hence, we have to love in this second way, but at least let our love be so pure and free that we love nothing *apart* from God, whether creatures or created things, on the spiritual or the temporal plane. If you say to me: 'How can I acquire such a love?' I answer that we cannot have it or draw it from anywhere except its spring and source, the First Truth. At this spring you will find the dignity and beauty of your own soul; you will see the Word, the Lamb that was slain, who gave himself as your food and your ransom, prompted only by the fire of his love and not by any service rendered to him by man, from whom he received nothing but offence! So I say that when a soul that hungers and thirsts for virtue looks into this spring, it drinks at once without either seeing or loving itself or anything else for its own sake. It sees everything in the wellspring of God's goodness, loving all it loves through him, and without him nothing. How could any soul that has seen God's boundless goodness keep itself from loving? To this the sweet First Truth would seem to have been calling us when he uttered his heartfelt cry in the temple: 'Whoever is thirsty, let him come to me and drink, for I am the source of living water.'[3] Notice, daughter, that [only] the thirsty are invited. He does not say: 'If you are not thirsty' but 'Anyone who *is* thirsty'. God, then, is urging us to bring the vessel of our free will, with thirst and a desire to love. So let us go to the fount of the sweet goodness of God, as I said. In it we shall find knowledge of ourselves and of God; and when we plunge our drinking vessels into it we shall draw out the water of divine grace which suffices to bring us to eternal life.[4]

Reflect, though, that we cannot make any headway if we have a weight to carry, so I don't want you to be clothed with your love for me or for any other creature, but only with your love for God. I say this because of what was in your letter about your distress at my departure. I want you to learn a lesson from the sweet First Truth, whose tender love for his mother and his disciples did not stop him running to meet the shameful death of the cross, as a lover runs to meet his beloved, leaving Mary and the disciples behind in spite of his boundless love for them. In the same way, after the disciples had received the Holy Spirit, they too went off in all directions for the honour of God and the salvation of creatures, because they were not concerned with their own feelings; indeed, as befits men with an insatiable hunger for souls, they refused consolation for themselves for the praise and glory of God. You can be sure that they would willingly have stayed with Mary in their time of trouble, for they all loved her dearly; but instead they all left her, precisely because they were loving neither themselves, their neighbour, nor even God for their own sakes. Him they loved because he was so supremely good and worthy of love; created things, their neighbour and themselves, they loved only in God.

This, then, is how I want you and the others to love. Look at me only in order to give the honour due to God directly to him and the service to your neighbour. Naturally, we do not like to see someone we love going away; but this need not distress us if our love is really genuine, rooted in God's honour and more concerned with the salvation of souls than with ourselves. So let me see no more laments, as this would be a barrier preventing you from being really united with and transformed into Christ. It is because I think God wants us to give ourselves freely just as he did that I said I wanted you (and all the others whom I love so dearly) to be one with and transformed into God by love, with nothing in between, except, of course, divine charity, which is the one sweet and glorious medium that makes things one instead of keeping them apart.

And he really does seem to do what a mason building a wall does: gathers a great many stones and fits them together and so turns them, through the mortar he uses, into both stones and a wall. Without the mortar, the stones would fall down and be more scattered and broken than before. Now realize that our soul has to gather all creatures together in this way and be made one with them by love and longing for their salvation, so that they may share in the blood of the Lamb. Then the wall holds together: many creatures, yet one. Saint Paul would seem to have been summoning us to this when he said that many compete for the trophy but only one wins it[5] – the one who has used this medium of divine charity. But you might say to me what the disciples said to Christ when he said: 'A little while and you shall not see me, and a little while and you shall see me.'[6] 'What is he going to do?' they said. 'What does he mean "a little while and you shall not see me, and a little while and you shall see me?"' You too could say: 'First you say God wants no medium, yet now you say we are to use a medium?' I will explain. The medium you are to use is the fire of divine Charity, the one medium that is not one, because it becomes one with the object, like wood that is put on a fire. Would you say the wood on a fire was wood? No, it has turned into fire. But if you introduce the medium of your own self-love, this would certainly keep you away from God even though, in itself, it is absolutely nothing (for sin is nothing, and all our sins spring from self-love and from pleasures and delights apart from God). As [love for God] proceeds from charity and gives life to all virtue, so from self-love proceeds all vice, killing the soul and destroying all the virtues. And that is why I said that God does not want a medium and that love not rooted in the one true medium cannot last.

Run, then, my dearest daughters; let us sleep no longer. I felt for you in your distress, so suggest this remedy: love God without any medium. And if you must have a poor wretch like me as a medium, let me teach you where to find me so as not to be separated from this true Love. Go with that sweet lover Magdalen to the sweet and venerable cross. There you will find the Lamb (and me), where you can [freely] feed, nourish and fulfil all your desires. In this way only do I want you to seek me, and every created thing. Let this be your banner and your refreshment. And don't think that because I myself have gone from you, my love for you and concern for your salvation have gone too. They are more with you, not less, now that I am away from you. Don't you know that after the Master had gone, his disciples had a deeper awareness and knowledge of him than before? You see, they had loved his humanity so much that they did not look beyond it. But once they were deprived of his presence, they began to understand and appreciate his goodness. And that is why the First Truth said: 'It is necessary for me to go, otherwise the Paraclete will not come to you.'[7] So I, now, say: 'It was necessary for me to leave you, so that you could begin to seek God in truth and not through any medium.' I assure you, you will be better off than before when you have entered into yourselves and reflected on the words and the teaching you have been given, for by God's grace you will thus receive the fullness of grace. I will write no more as I have no time.

This letter is mainly for you, Melina, and then for Caterina and Monna Giovanna, Monna Chiara and Monna Bartolomea, Monna Lagina and Monna Colomba.[8] Support one another and abide in the sweet and holy love of God.

---

[1] One of a group of disciples who had gathered round Catherine when she stayed for a while in Lucca on her way home from Pisa to Siena.

[2] Romans 4:4–5.

[3] John 7:37.

[4] John 4:14.

[5] I Corinthians 9:24.

[6] John 16:16–18.

[7] John 16:7.

[8] Some of Catherine's disciples in Lucca. Her letters to several of them are extant.

LETTER 18    (Dupré LXII; Tommaseo 75; Gigli 146).

*To:*    *The Abbess and Nuns of the Augustinian Monastery of*
         *S. Gaggio (or Caio), near Florence.*[1]
*Date:*  March 1376.


         Dearest mother and daughters in Christ sweet
Jesus,
    I, Catherine, servant and slave of the servants of Jesus
Christ, write to you in his precious blood, desiring to see
you hidden and locked away in the side of Christ
crucified; otherwise, the mere fact of your being locked
inside walls counts for nothing except, perhaps, as a
judgement. As your bodies are physically enclosed, so let
your desires and affections be kept under lock and key,
turned away from the pride and pleasures of the world to
follow Christ Jesus, your loving bridegroom. I feel sure
that, as lovers of the eternal Bridegroom, you will follow
in his footsteps.
    You know, don't you, the way he went? The way of
voluntary poverty and obedience. Out of humility, his
supreme Highness descended to the lowness of our
humanity; in his humility and ineffable love for us he
handed his humanity over to the shameful death on the
cross by choosing the way of torture, scourging, anguish
and abuse. Such is the humility you must imitate. And
remember, it can only be had by means of true thorough
self-knowledge, and by reflecting on the deep humility
and meekness of the Lamb, slain with such burning love.
So then, he chose the way of true poverty, for he was so
poor that he had nowhere to lay his head,[2] and when he
was born his mother Mary had just enough cloth to wrap
her son in![3] So you, his brides, must follow this same way
of poverty. Indeed, you have promised to do so, and I beg
you, for the love of Christ crucified, to keep that promise
until death. Otherwise, you would no longer be brides
but adulteresses, loving something apart from God – for
it is because she loves another man more than her hus-

band that a bride is said to be an adulteress. And how does a bride show her love? By obeying her husband. Hence, after poverty and humility comes obedience, for the more a bride chooses to be poor in spirit and the more completely she renounces worldly wealth and position, the humbler she will be; the humbler she is, the more perfect her obedience. A proud person is never obedient, for pride makes one unwilling to submit to any creature. So I want you all to be humble, with your hearts and affections stripped until death – you, Lady Abbess, obeying the Rule and you, her subjects, obeying the Rule and your Abbess.

Learn, oh learn how from the sweet good Jesus, your bridegroom, who was obedient unto death.[4] Reflect that without obedience you could have no share in the blood of the Lamb. What is a religious without the yoke of obedience? A dead woman, a devil incarnate no less, not keeping but transgressing the Rule. She is under sentence of death, for she has transgressed God's holy commandments, and the promise she made at her profession. Beloved sisters and daughters in Christ sweet Jesus, let no such disgrace befall you. I want you all to try not to trangress the Rule in the slightest. You long for happiness with your Bridegroom? Then destroy your own perverse will; never rebel against the requirements of true obedience. Reflect that one who is truly obedient never questions the will of his superior but bows his head at once and does what he has been told to do. Let yourselves be capitvated by true solid virtue like that. You long for peace and quiet? Then strip off your own will, which is causing all the trouble. Put on instead the sweet abiding will of God, and so be sure of eternal life and of being called earthly angels even in this.

Model yourselves on the sweet First Truth. But this you cannot do unless you open the eye of knowledge to gaze into the fire of divine Charity lit by God in every rational creature. Remember, mother and daughters, that you have a greater obligation than others to do this because

God, in addition to loving you as he loves all men, has singled you out by taking you away from the ugliness, the dark and fetid vice and squalor of the world, and setting you apart to be his very own. So you must never be casual about him, but try always to discover all the things, places and ways which will enable you to please him most. If you ask me the way, I will tell you to go *his* way, the way of abuse, suffering, torture and scourging. And how are you to go? By way of true humility, and of burning charity and ineffable love, the love with which we turn away from worldly wealth and status and so come, as I said, from humility to obedience, and thence to peace, for, by eliminating the root cause, our own will, obedience soothes away all pain and gives all delight.

Moreover, to enable the soul to attain this perfection, Christ has made his body into a staircase, with great steps. See, his feet are nailed fast to the cross; they constitute the first step because, to begin with, the soul's desire has to be stripped of self-will, for as the feet carry the body, so desire carries the soul. Reflect that no soul will ever acquire virtue without climbing this first step. Once you have done that, you come to real, deep humility. Climb the next step without delay and you reach the open side of God's Son. Within, you will find the fathomless furnace of divine Charity. Yes, on this second step of the open side, there is a little shop,[5] full of fragrant spices. Therein you will find the God-Man; therein, too, the soul becomes so satiated and inebriated as to become oblivious of self for, like a man intoxicated with wine, it will have eyes only for the Blood spilt with such burning love. With eager longing it presses on upwards and reaches the last step, the mouth, where it reposes in peace and quiet, savouring the peace of obedience. Like a man who falls asleep after drinking heavily and so is oblivious of both pain and pleasure, the bride of Christ, brimming over with love, sleeps in the peace of her Bridegroom. Her own feelings are so deeply asleep that she remains unruffled when assailed by tribulation and rises above undue delight in wordly prosperity; for she stripped herself of all desire of that kind back on the first step. Here [on the third] she is conformed to Christ crucified and made one with him.

Run, then, with brave hearts, for you know where, and how, to go to reach the place where you will find a bed to rest on, a table to fill you with delight, and food to sate your desire – for he is our table, our food and our servant.[6] You would indeed be deserving of rebuke if, through your own fault, you failed to seek this repose and foolishly kept away from this food. I want you, indeed I beg you, on behalf of Christ crucified, to warm yourselves by bathing in Christ's blood. Also, so that you are indeed made one with him, let there be no shying away from toil, for the toil is slight and the fruit is great. I'll leave it at that.

[Catherine then sympathises with the nuns on the death of their abbess, urging them not to grieve but rather rejoice that she is now eating the food of life at the table of eternal life. The ending to the second letter is no longer extant.]

---

1   An almost identical letter was sent to the abbess and nuns of the Benedictine Monastery of Monte San Savino, near Siena.
2   Matthew 8:20.
3   Cf. Luke 2:7. But this medieval idea of Christ's abject poverty is not borne out by the gospel texts.
4   Philippians 2:8.
5   Italian *bottega* – a modest artisan-type shop specializing in a limited range of goods (e.g. spices), still common in Italy.
6   Cf. letter 14, note 3.

LETTER 19   (Dupré LXIII; Tommaseo 206; Gigli 5).

*To:*   *Gregory XI*

*Date:*   Towards end of March 1376.[1]

Most holy, sweet and dearest father in Christ sweet Jesus,

Your wretched and unworthy daughter Catherine, servant and slave of the servants of Jesus Christ, writes to you in his precious blood. With desire I have desired[2] to see in you such fullness of divine grace that you may thereby be the means and the instrument for bringing peace to the whole world. And so I urge you, dearest father, to exercise the power and authority that are yours with all diligence and a most earnest desire for peace, the honour of God and the salvation of souls. And if you say to me, father: 'The world is so very torn and troubled. How can *I* bring about peace?', I answer, on behalf of Christ crucified, 'You need to exercise your power in three main areas: first, in the garden which is the Church let you (who are in charge) pull out all the stinking flowers, full of filth and greed and swollen with pride' – that is, all the bad shepherds and rulers[3] who are poisoning and polluting the garden. O please, dear father gardener, use your power. Dig up those flowers. Throw them out where they can no longer wield authority. Compel them to learn how to govern themselves by a good and holy life. Plant fragrant flowers in the garden for us: shepherds and rulers who will be true servants of Jesus Christ crucified, concerned only for the honour of God and the salvation of souls, men who will be true fathers of the poor.

Alas, what a spectacle! To see the very men who should be mirrors of voluntary poverty, humble lambs distributing the Church's wealth to the poor, more involved in the empty pleasures, pomp and power of the world than if they belonged to it a thousand times over! Indeed, many seculars put them to shame by their good and holy lives.

It really looks as if the supreme eternal Goodness is compelling us by force to do what we have not done through love; is allowing the Bride's luxuries and power to be taken from her, as if to show that he wills holy Church to go back to being poor, meek and humble, as in those blessed early days when her one concern was the honour of God and the salvation of souls, spiritual and not temporal things. Ever since she has attended more to the temporal than to the spiritual, things have gone from bad to worse. So you see, God in his supreme justice is allowing her to suffer and be persecuted.

But take heart, father, and have no fear, whatever happens or may happen, for God is doing this to make the Church perfect once more; to ensure that lambs will once again graze in this garden instead of wolves who devour the honour due to God by stealing it and appropriating it to themselves. Take heart in Christ sweet Jesus, for I trust that his help, the fullness of divine grace, will soon support and sustain you. If you act as I have said, you will come from war to great peace, from persecution to great unity not by human means but by the practice of virtue – and so prevail over the devils we see – wicked men – and the ones we don't, though they are ever on the watch.

But remember, sweet father, that you would be unlikely to achieve this unless you also do the other two things that make up the three – namely your return,[4] and then that you raise the standard of the most holy cross.[5] Your holy desire must not falter whatever you may see or hear in the way of scandal, or cities in revolt. Rather, let such things be as fuel on the fire of your holy desire to accomplish these things. In any case, do not postpone your coming. Pay no heed to the devil; he knows he stands to lose and is doing his utmost to put obstacles in your way and rob you of what is yours, by making you lose love and charity and preventing your coming. I tell you, father in Christ Jesus, to come, soon, like a meek lamb. Respond to the Holy Spirit who is calling you. Come,

come, come, I say, and do not wait for time which does not wait for you. Then you will do as the Lamb who was slain did, whose vicar you are. Unarmed he destroyed our enemies, for he came as a meek lamb, the virtue of love being his only weapon, his one aim being the protection of spiritual things and the restoring of grace to man who had lost it through sin.

Alas, sweet father, with such gentleness I beg you, nay I say to you from Christ crucified, to come and overthrow our enemies. Put no faith in the devil's counsellors who may try to block your good and holy resolution. Show the manliness I expect from you – no more cowardice! Answer God's call to you to come and take possession of the place of the glorious shepherd Saint Peter, whose vicar you still are, and then to raise the standard of the holy cross for, as by the cross we were delivered (as *Pavoloccio* said[6]) so when this standard – which I see as the solace and refuge of Christians – is raised, we shall be delivered from war, disputes and iniquities and the infidel people from their infidelity. In this way you will come, and then you will see holy Church reformed[7] through the appointment of good pastors; you will restore to her the colour of glowing charity she has lost – so much blood has been sucked out of her by wicked gluttons that she has gone pale all over. But take courage and come, father. Do not keep the servants of God waiting any longer, for they are in torment with their desire. And ı, poor wretch, can wait no longer. Though alive, I feel I am dying of anguish, when I see God so vilified. But do not abandon peaceful measures because of what has happened in Bologna; just come, for I tell you that these raging wolves will put their heads in your lap as meek as lambs and will beg for mercy.

Father, I will say no more. I beg you to grant an audience and to listen to what Fra Raimondo and those with him have to say, for they come from Christ crucified and from me; they are true servants of God and sons of holy Church. Pardon my own ignorance, father, and in your gracious kindness forgive me for the love and sorrow that make me speak. Grant me your blessing.

Abide in the sweet and holy love of God. Sweet Jesus,. Jesus, Love.

---

¹   Bologna had joined the anti-papal league on 21 March 1376, thereby greatly magnifying the threat it posed to Gregory's position. This letter, which is in some sense a credential, was delivered to Gregory by Fra Raimondo, who went ahead of Catherine to Avignon.
²   Catherine's use of Luke 22:15 (see letter 2, note 2) is here explicit.
³   These 'rulers' are probably ecclesiastics appointed to rule cities and towns in the papal states; cf. letter 8, note 1.
⁴   to Rome.
⁵   i.e. proclaim the crusade.
⁶   A favourite term of endearment – meaning almost 'dear little Paul' – used by Catherine for the great apostle. For the scriptural reference, cf. John 3:15 or possibly Galatians 5:1.
⁷   Text reads *'nformatione'*. We accept the variant reading *'riformatione'* here.

LETTER 20   (Dupré LXIV; Tommaseo 196; Gigli 4).

*To:*   *Gregory XI*

*Date:*   Early April, probably from Siena.

Most holy and reverend father in Christ sweet Jesus,

I, Catherine, your wretched and unworthy daughter, servant and slave of the servants of Jesus Christ, write to you in his precious blood, desiring to see you a good shepherd, for I consider, *babbo mio dolce*,¹ that the infernal wolf is carrying off your sheep and there is no one to rescue them. I turn to you, then, our father and shepherd, begging you on behalf of Christ crucified to learn from him who with such burning love submitted to the shameful death of the most holy cross in order to wrest the lost sheep of mankind from the hold the demons had got, and retained, over it through man's revolt against God,

But then God's infinite Goodness passes by and sees the silly sheep's plight, its damnation and ruin; sees, too, that anger and war will not extricate it. So, in spite of having been itself offended by the sheep – for by his act of rebellion in disobeying God man merited eternal punishment – the supreme eternal Wisdom wills not to do this. Instead, he finds a delightful way, the sweetest and most loving way possible – for he sees no more powerful way of enticing the heart of man than by love, since man is made of love and this seems to be why he loves so much: he is made of nothing but love in soul and body. In love God created him to his own image and likeness; in love his father and mother gave him his [bodily] substance when they begot and conceived their child. Seeing, then, that man is so apt for love, God forthwith throws him the hook of love by giving us the Word, his only-begotten Son, assuming our humanity in order to bring about the great peace.[2]

But justice demands that the offence offered to God be avenged. So along come divine Mercy and ineffable Charity; having clothed his Son in our humanity, that is in the stuff of Adam that had perpetrated the offence, [God] now condemns him to death, to satisfy both justice and mercy.[3] His death thus placates the Father's wrath, justice being satisfied through exacting retribution from the person of the Son, and mercy through wresting mankind from the grip of demons. This Word fought hand to hand on the wood of the most holy cross, death grappling with life and life with death. Thus, by his death he destroyed ours; consuming his own bodily life, he gave us life. With love, then, he enticed us; with his benignity he so conquered our malice as to have enticed every heart, for he could not have shown greater love, as he himself

said, than to give his life for his friend.[4] And if he com-
mends the love that gives its life for a friend, what are we
to say of the burning consummate Love that gives its life
for an enemy?[5] For through sin we had become God's
enemies.

O sweet and loving Word, by love you have found the
lost sheep, by death you have given it life and brought it
back to the fold by restoring to it the grace it had lost!

Sweet and most holy *babbo*,[1] I see no other means or
remedy whereby you can recover your rebellious sheep
who have left the fold of holy Church by refusing obedience and allegiance to you, father. Speaking therefore on
behalf of Christ crucified, I beg you – indeed I urge you –
to do me this favour: overcome their malice by your own
goodness. We are yours, father, and I well know that they
all realize they have done wrong. Granted that there may
be no excuse for doing wrong, nevertheless, considering
all the suffering, injustice and iniquity they have had to
endure at the hands of bad shepherds and rulers[6], they
seemed to have no alternative. The stinking lives of bad
rulers (whom you yourself know to be devils incarnate)
made them so afraid that, like Pilate who killed Christ
through fear of losing his position, they turned against
you rather than lose their dignity. So I beg you to have
mercy on them, father, and ignore the pride and waywardness of your children. Instead, with the bait of love
and your own gracious goodness, employing only such
gentle discipline and mild reproof as shall seem good to
your Holiness, restore peace to us, your wretched children, who have offended you.[7] From Christ in heaven I
say to you, sweet Christ-on-earth, that if you do this
without a storm or tempest they will all be truly sorry for
their behaviour and will come and put their heads in your
lap. Then you shall rejoice and we shall rejoice, for by
love you will have restored the lost sheep to the fold of
holy Church.

That done, *babbo mio dolce*,[1] you will be able to carry out
your holy purpose and God's will – the crusade. In God's

name, I call on you to do it soon and without delay. They will all rally lovingly round you, for they are ready to give their lives for Christ.

Alas! – God, sweet Love – raise the standard of the holy cross *soon*, father, and you will see the wolves turning into lambs. Peace, peace, peace, so that war does not delay the great day. And if you should want revenge and strict justice, wreak it on me, miserable wretch. Hand me over to whatever pain and torment you please, even death. I truly believe that many of the faults, the serious difficulties and the discord are due to the stench of my sins. On me, then, your wretched daughter, take what revenge you like.

Alas, my father, I am dying of sorrow and cannot die. Come, oh come, and stop pulling against the will of God who is summoning you. Your famished sheep are waiting for you to come and take possession of the place of your predecessor and champion, the apostle Peter. You, as Christ's vicar, ought to reside again in your proper place. Come then, come without further delay. Take courage and have no fear whatever happens, for God will be with you.

I humbly beg your blessing on myself and all my children[8] and implore you to forgive my presumption. I will say no more. Sweet Jesus. Jesus, Love.

---

[1]   See letter 15, note 2.

[2]   Cf. II Cor. 5:20 and I Tim. 2:5.

[3]   For this whole passage, cf. *Dialogue*, pp284 & 287 and Dante, *Paradiso*, VII.

[4]   John 15:13.

[5]   Cf. Romans 5:8.

[6]   See letter 19, note 3.

[7]   Catherine had yet to hear that Gregory had already issued a fierce decree of interdict and excommunication against Florence on 31 March 1375; see Gardner, pp. 163–4 for the economic consequences of this step.

8   As Catherine was *mamma* to her disciples, so they were all her 'children' (and/or 'family') regardless of age. Cf. letters 2, 37, etc.

LETTER 21   (Dupré LXV; Tommaseo 219; Gigli 87).

*To:*   *Fra Raimondo of Capua, OP; Maestro Giovanni Tan-tucci; Fra Felice of Massa, OP, and others, in Avignon.*[1]

*Date:*   Early April, 1376.

My beloved children in Christ Jesus,

With eager longing I, your wretched mother, have longed and still long[2] to see you nailed heart and soul to the cross; to see you all made one in the bond which bound and grafted God to man and man to God. My soul longs to see your hearts and affections so grafted into the incarnate Word, sweet Jesus, that no devil or creature can ever part you from him. I know that once you are bound to Jesus and on fire with him not all hell's demons with all their wiles could ever part you from so sweet a union. Since this bond is so strong and so very necessary, I want you never to stop putting the wood of self-knowledge onto the fire of holy desire, for it is this that feeds the fire of divine charity that comes with knowledge of the inestimable Charity of God.[3] The soul then becomes one with its neighbours too, and the more wood of self-knowledge it puts on the fire, the hotter burns its love for Christ and its neighbour. So hide yourselves away in self-knowledge, and don't wander outside yourselves, lest *Malatasca*[4] should get you with fanciful imaginings about one another and so deprive you of the union of divine charity. Hence I desire and command you all to be subject to one another, learning to bear one another's faults from the sweet First Truth who chose to become the least of all and humbly bore all our iniquities and faults.[5] Children, I want you to do the same.

Love one another. Again and again I say it! Rejoice and exult, for summer is coming. I know this for, on the night of 1 April, God showed me his secrets more than usual – such marvels that my soul seemed to leave my body and receive such delight, such fullness of knowledge as no tongue can tell of[6] – explaining and making clear to me every aspect of the mystery of the persecution the Church is now undergoing and of the renewal and exaltation that is to come. He told me that what is happening now is permitted in order to make the Church once more what she should be, and pointed to two sayings in the gospel: 'It is necessary that there should be scandal in the world, but woe to the man by whom it comes'[7] –as if to say: 'I am allowing this time of persecution in order to dig out and clear away the thorns with which my Bride is overgrown, but I will not allow the evil plotting of men. You know what I do, don't you? I do what I did when, in the world, I made a whip of cords and drove out all those who were buying and selling, for I would not allow my Father's house to be made a den of thieves.[8] In the same way, I now use creatures as my whip to drive out that filthy troop of greedy, money-grubbing, swollen-headed shopkeepers, who are buying and selling the graces and gifts of the Holy Spirit.' So you see, the suffering and persecution are the whip God is using to drive them away from their disordered, shameful lives.

The fire of holy desire grew within me as I gazed, and I saw Christians and pagans flooding into the side of Christ, and myself with my love and desire in their midst, going with them into Christ sweet Jesus, accompanied by my holy father Dominic, the beloved John,[9] and every single one of my children. Then he placed a cross on my shoulder and an olive branch in my hand as if desiring me to hold it out to Christians and pagans alike – indeed he told me to do this. 'Say to them: "I bring you news of great joy," '[10] he said. Then my soul was fuller than ever and found itself immersed in the divine Essence, together with those who are truly blessed, so great was its state of union and love. Such was my delight that the past anguish of seeing the offence offered to God quite disappeared. In fact, 'O happy and blessed fault'[11] burst from me. Then sweet Jesus smiled at me and said: 'Blessed? Sin, which is nothing? What do you suppose Gregory meant when he said: "Happy and blessed fault"? What do you think is happy and blessed in it, as Gregory says?' I replied as he made me reply: 'Well do I see and know, sweet Lord, that sin is not worthy of blessedness and therefore is neither blessed nor happy; but the fruit that comes from sin is. This, I think, is what Gregory meant: that on account of Adam's sin God gave us the word of his only-begotten Son, and the Word gave us his blood; by giving his life, he gave us back grace with such burning love. So sin *is* blessed, not because of the sin but because of the fruit and gift that has come forth and we have received from it.' Yes, that *is* how it is. And so, from the sin of wicked Christians in persecuting the Bride of Christ proceeded exaltation, light and fragrance of virtue in the Bride. Such was her beauty that there seemed to be no comparison between the sin committed and the immense goodness and kindness of God made manifest in the Bride. Then I rejoiced and exulted and felt so certain about this future glory that I seemed already to possess and be savouring it. And then, like Simeon, I said: *'Nunc dimittis servum tuum Domine'* etc.[12] and beheld such mysteries that no tongue could describe them, no heart conceive them nor eye see them.[13]

What tongue could recount the wonderful things of God? Not mine, poor wretch that I am. So I choose to keep silent; to devote myself solely to seeking God's honour, the salvation of souls, and the renewal and exaltation of holy Church; and, by the grace and strength of the Holy Spirit, to persevere thus until death. This desire made me and will make me call out with great love and compassion to our Christ-on-earth, to you, father, and to all my dear children, as it made me press for and be granted your petition.

Rejoice, then; rejoice and exult. O sweet God, Love, fulfil soon the desires of your servants. I'll say no more and I've said nothing! In my anguish I am dying of desire. Have pity on me. Beg the good God in heaven and Christ-on-earth to hurry. Abide in the sweet and holy love of God.

Drown yourselves in the blood of Christ crucified, and flinch at nothing; rather, take fresh courage. Rejoice, rejoice at sweet toil. Love, love, *love* one another. Sweet Jesus. Good Jesus. Jesus, Love. Jesus, Jesus.

---

[1a]  *Fra Giovanni Tantucci*, an Augustinian hermit and Master in Sacred Theology – hence the designation 'Master'. From hostile critic and denigrator, he had become one of Catherine's most devoted disciples; see Gardner, pp. 92–96.

[1b]  Little more is known of *Fra Felice* than that he was a member of Catherine's circle.

[2]  Catherine again uses Luke 22:15 with full emphasis.

[3]  Cf. letter 1, note 6.

[4]  Lit. 'bad sack' – a nickname Catherine seems to have invented for the devil, perhaps suggested by the sack carried in her day by begging friars or hermits. (Raymond, p. 115.)

[5]  Cf. Galatians 6:2 and Isaiah 53:4–5.

[6]  I Cor. 2:9.

[7]  Matthew 18:7.

[8]  Cf. John 2:14–16 and parallels.

[9]  Ital. *Giovanni singulare*, which Dupré takes to mean 'singularly beloved'. Catherine had a very special affection for the beloved disciple. Cf. letter 57, note 12.

[10]  Luke 2:10.

[11]  from the *Exsultet*, an Easter Vigil chant, attributed in Catherine's day to St Gregory the Great.

[12]  'Lord, now lettest thou thy servant depart in peace,' etc. – Luke 2:29.

[13]  Again, cf. I Cor. 2:9.

LETTER 22   (Dupré LXX; Tommaseo 211. Gigli 88).

*To:*   *Fra Raimondo of Capua, OP, in Avignon.*

*Date:*   ? May 1376, from Siena, or perhaps from Florence
which Catherine probably visited on her way to
Avignon, where she arrived on 18 June.[1]

Reverend father in Christ Jesus,

I, Catherine, servant and slave of the servants of Jesus
Christ, write to you in his precious blood, desiring to see
you and the others clothed in the wedding garment that
covers all our iniquities and nakedness.[2] It serves as
armour[3], too, preventing the blows of our adversary, the
devil, from striking home[4] so that one is strengthened
rather than weakened by every blow of enticement or
temptation from the devil, from creatures or from one's
own flesh struggling to rebel against the spirit.[5] I tell you,
not only are such blows not harmful; they will be precious
stones and pearls adorning this garment of glowing charity.

But what if a soul did not endure trials and temptations
whenever and however God permits them to come its
way? Such a soul's virtue would be untried, since virtue is
tried by its opposite. How is purity tested and acquired?
By the pull of its opposite, impurity. A man who is
already impure needs no tempting with thoughts of
impurity; but when it is clear that a man will not consent
to such things, and has been cleansed of all stain by his
true and holy desire to serve his Creator, then the devil,
the world and the flesh *will* trouble him. Each vice, then,
is driven out by its corresponding virtue.

See [how], through pride, we acquire humility. When a
man sees he is being tempted to pride, he humbles himself at once, acknowledging his sinfulness and pride as he
could not have done without that particular temptation.
Having humbled himself and seen himself [as he really
is], he learns to despise himself in such a way as to welcome and rejoice over any suffering or injury he may
have to endure. Like a gallant knight, he does not shrink

from being hit, but considers himself unworthy of what seems to him to be – and in fact is – a very great grace: that of enduring suffering, trials and temptations for the sake of Christ crucified. And all because of the hatred he now has for himself and the love he has conceived for virtue. So you see, we must not run away or complain when all is in darkness, for out of darkness comes light.

Sweet loving God, how sweet is your doctrine that virtue is acquired by its opposite!

Through impatience we acquire patience. When a soul is aware of its own impatience it learns to endure patiently the injuries inflicted on it, being impatient only with the act of impatience, more grieved at being grieved than at anything else. Thus, by the pull of opposites a soul grows towards perfection without even noticing, finding it has become perfect through countless storms and temptations. The port of perfection can be gained in no other way. So tell yourself that a soul cannot acquire or even desire virtue without also enduring conflicting desires, trials and temptations with true and holy patience for the love of Christ crucified. We must rejoice, then, and be glad at times of battle, temptation and darkness, for these will bear fruit in joy and virtue.

Alas, son given to me by that sweet mother Mary,[6] I don't want you to fall into tedium or confusion, however troubled in mind you may be. No, I want you to hold onto the good holy and truly faithful will that I know God in his mercy has given you. I know you would rather die than offend him mortally, and so from the darkness I look for self-knowledge, not confusion; from your good will a recognition of God's infinite goodness and inestimable charity. Realize that in his love he preserves this will for good within you and does not let it run away by consenting to or hankering after devilish thoughts. Again, in his love he allows you and me and his other servants to suffer harassment and illusions from the devil, from creatures, and from our own flesh, simply in order to rouse us from our negligence and bring us to

real earnestness, to true humility and burning charity –
the humility that is born of knowledge of self, the charity
that springs from knowledge of God's goodness, wherein
the soul is inebriated and consumed with love.

Rejoice, father, and exult. Take courage and have no
servile fear, or any fear, whatever you see happening or
likely to happen. Yes, take courage, for perfection is
within your reach. Give the devil his answer by telling him
that you did not exercise that virtue through me, since it
was not in me.[7] You exercised it through the grace of the
infinite love and mercy of God. By the power of Christ
crucified, then, you can do all things.[8] Do everything with
a keen sense of faith, and don't be surprised if you see
things going in a way that seems contrary to what you had
intended. Take courage, I say and repeat , for the sweet
First Truth has promised to fulfil in you your own desire,
and mine.

Pour out your being by burning desire with the Lamb
who was slain and poured his life out for us.

Rest in the cross – with Christ crucified.

Delight – in Christ crucified; delight in suffering.

Be a glutton for abuse – for Christ crucified.

Let your heart and soul be grafted into the tree of the
most holy cross – with Christ crucified.

Make his wounds your home.

And forgive me, who am the real cause of all your
suffering and imperfection. If I were indeed an instrument of virtue, you and all the others would experience
the fragrance of it. I do not say this to sadden you – for
when you are sad, I am too – but so that you and the
others will pity me in my wretchedness. I have every hope
and confidence that, by his grace, the Holy Spirit will do
away with everything that is contrary to God's will.

Think of it. I, poor wretch, am in the body yet find
myself, by desire, continually out of it. Alas, sweet good
Jesus, I am dying and cannot die. I am bursting and
cannot burst with my longing for the renewal of holy
Church, the honour of God, and the salvation of every

creature; and to see yourself and the others clothed with purity and utterly consumed in his burning Charity.

Tell Christ-on-earth not to keep me waiting any longer. When I see this come about, I'll sing with dear old Simeon: '*Nunc dimittis servum tuum, Domine, secundum verbum tuum in pace*.'[9] I will say no more, though if I were to follow my inclination, I'd begin all over again!

Let me see and hear that you are all so bound and fastened into Christ sweet Jesus that no devil or creature can ever prise you away from so sweet and delightful a bond. Love, love, love one another. Abide in the sweet and holy love of God. Sweet Jesus. Jesus, Love.

---

[1]   Cf. Gardner, pp. 171–8.

[2]   Cf. I Peter 4:8.

[3]   lit. 'It is a weapon'.

[4]   I Peter 5:8.

[5]   Cf. Romans 7:21–23.

[6]   The details of what was for Catherine an accepted fact (cf. letters 38 & 60) remain obscure, but see Papàsogli, p. 133, text and footnote.

[7]   Raimondo would seem to have attributed his ability to perform some act of virtue to Catherine's possession of it – an idea she characteristically rejects.

[8]   Philippians 4:13.

[9]   'Lord, now lettest thou thy servant depart in peace, according to thy word.' Luke 2:29.

# GROUP II

## *Letters written in Avignon and on the return journey*

LETTER 23    (Dupré LXXI; Tommaseo 255; Gigli 13).

*To:    Pope Gregory XI, in Avignon.*[1]
*Date:*  June or July 1376.

Sweetest and most Holy Father,
Catherine, your unworthy daughter in sweet Jesus,
recommends herself to you in his precious blood. I desire
to see you a real man, fearless and making no concessions
to self-love, whether for yourself or for any of your blood
relations, for I believe and see in the sight of God that this
more than anything else is keeping you back from your
good and holy desire[2] and thwarting the honour of God
and the exaltation and reform of holy Church. For this
reason, my soul's one desire is for God, in his infinite
mercy, to take all disordered affection and lukewarmness
out of your heart and make a new man of you, that is,
remake you with glowing and ardent desire, for in no
other way can you hope to implement what God wills and
his servants long for.

Alas, alas, sweetest father, forgive my presumption in
what I have said, indeed am forced to say, by the sweet
First Truth. His will, father, is this; this he requires of
you: he requires you to take action against the abundant
wickedness being committed by those who are feeding
and grazing in the garden of holy Church, for he says it is
not right to give man's food to beasts.[3] He has committed
the authority to you, and you have accepted it, so you *must*
exercise the power vested in you; if you will not use it, it

would be better to resign – more to God's honour and your own salvation.

The other thing he requires of you is this: to make peace with all Tuscany with which you are now at war. Make what terms you can with all your wicked children who have rebelled against you – as far as possible without war, but not without punishing them, as every father must punish the son who offends him. The sweet goodness of God also requires you to give full authorization to those who are asking to be allowed to undertake the crusade, for what seems impossible to you is possible to his sweet loving Goodness, who has ordained and wills that it should be so.

See to it, as you value your life, that you are not negligent in this, nor mock at the workings of the Holy Spirit which *you* are being asked to implement, for you can do it if you will. Justice you can mete out; peace you can have, if you disentangle it from perverse pomp and worldly luxury and retain only God's honour and what is due to holy Church. The authority to delegate authority to those who ask for it: that, too, is yours. Since, then, you are not poor but rich – for you hold in your hands the keys of heaven and to whomsoever you open it, open it is, and against whomsoever you shut it, shut it remains[4] – if you fail to do this, you will be severely reprimanded by God. If I were you, I would be very fearful of the divine judgement. And so, with all my heart I beg you, in the name of Christ crucified, to be obedient to God's will – which I know is what you really want to be – lest you have to hear that dread rebuke: 'Cursed be you, for time and power were given to you and you did not use them.' I believe, father, that by God's grace and relying also on your own holiness, you will so act that none of this will come upon you.

I will say no more. Forgive, please forgive me; my great desire for your salvation, and great sorrow when I see it in danger, makes me speak. I would gladly have said all this to you personally so as to unburden my conscience completely. When it shall please your Holiness to receive me, I shall come willingly.[5] See to it that I am not forced to complain about you to Christ crucified. I can complain to no one else, as there is none higher than yourself on earth!

Abide in the sweet and holy love of God.

I humbly ask your blessing. Sweet Jesus. Jesus, Love.

---

[1]   See note 5.
[2]   to return to Rome.
[3]   Cf. Matthew 15:26.
[4]   Matthew 16:19.
[5]   Some of the Pope's entourage, fearing Catherine's influence with Gregory, had prevailed on the timid Pope to see her less frequently.

# LETTER 24   (Dupré LXXII; Tommaseo 230; Gigli 197).

*To:*   *The* Otto di Guerra *in Florence.*[1]

*Date:*   (in ms.) 28 June 1376.

Dear fathers and sons in Christ sweet Jesus,

I, Catherine, servant and slave of the servants of Jesus Christ, write to you in his precious blood, desiring to see you such true, humble and obedient sons towards our father[2] that you will never look back[3] but be truly sorry and really regret having offended him, for unless one who commits an offence turns away from it with deep contrition he deserves no mercy. So I invite you to true humility of heart, a humility that does not look back but presses forward in pursuance of your newly-formed holy resolution, growing more steadfast in it from day to day. If you want to be taken into your father's arms, be like dead children begging for life, and I hope by God's goodness you shall have it, provided you are in earnest in humbling yourselves and acknowledging your faults.

But I have a serious complaint against you if what is being said here is true, namely that you have levied a tax on the clergy. If this is true, it is a grave evil for two reasons. Firstly because you are offending God, for you cannot levy such a tax with a good conscience.[4] You seem to me to be losing every other good thing along with your conscience; to care only about sensual transitory things which come and go like the wind, while we fail to see that we are mortal and must die, we know not when! So it is very foolish to deprive our own selves of the life of grace and encompass our own death. I don't want you to persist in doing this, for it amounts to looking back, and you know that it is not the beginner but the man who perseveres to the end[5] who earns the crown of glory. So I warn you that you cannot hope to achieve peace unless you persevere in your humility and give up offending and insulting the priests and ministers of God's Church.

And this is the other thing that I was saying was bad and harmful for yourselves, besides the harm that comes from offending God, as I have said: you are jeopardizing the prospect of peace because, if the holy Father should hear of it, he would be more angry with you than ever. Some of the cardinals, who themselves eagerly desire and are working for peace, have said just this. Their reaction on hearing this news was: 'The reports about their wanting peace do not seem to be true; if they were, surely they would avoid even the slightest action against the will of the holy Father and the practice of holy Church.' I believe that sweet Christ-on-earth may well say the same, and will have right and reason on his side if he does.

Dearest fathers, I tell you, indeed I urge you, not to impede the grace which, through no merit of your own, the Holy Spirit in his mercy is prepared to grant you. And you would be exposing me to shame and abuse, for nothing but shame and ridicule can result if I say one thing and you do another. I beg you to desist, and to make every effort, in word and deed, to show that you desire peace and not war.

I have spoken with the holy Father: by the goodness of God and his own, he heard me graciously and made it clear how eagerly he longs for peace in that, like a good father, he is less interested in the offence his son has committed against him than in whether he is genuinely sorry, so that he can be completely merciful towards him. Such was his great joy that my tongue cannot describe it.[6] At the end of my fairly long interview with him, he said that if things with you were as I had reported them, he was prepared to receive you as sons and to deal with you as I had suggested. No more about this here.

The holy Father felt quite unable to give any other answer until your ambassadors arrive. I am astonished that they have not yet come. I shall be with them as soon as they get here, and then go to the holy Father.[7] Then I will write and tell you how things are. But you yourselves with your new taxes are spoiling what is being sown here. Do, please, desist, for the love of Christ crucified – and in your own interest! I will say no more.

Abide in the sweet and holy love of God. Sweet Jesus. Jesus, Love. Given at Avignon on the twenty-eighth day of June 1376.

---

[1]   A group of 8 magistrates elected by the people of Florence to conduct the war against the Church.

[2]   the Pope.

[3]   Cf. Luke 9:62.

[4]   Lay taxation of the clergy was forbidden by a decree of the fourth Lateran Council (*Decretals* X 3.49.7) and by Pope Boniface VIII's Bull *Clericis Laicos* (*Sext* 3.23.3).

[5]   Cf. Matthew 10:22.

[6]   The 'refrain' from I Corinthians 2:9 again.

[7]   But the composition of the *Otto di Guerra* changed every two months; the ambassadors who eventually came to Avignon represented men who had no use for Catherine and spurned her attempts at mediation.

LETTER 25   (Dupré LXXXIII; Tommaseo 240;
Gigli 169).

*To:*   *Monna Lapa (Benincasa), Catherine's mother.*

*Date:*   October/November 1376, from Genoa, where
Catherine and her party were delayed by sickness
on the way home from Avignon.

Dearest mother in Christ sweet Jesus,
Your unworthy daughter Catherine writes to comfort
you in the precious blood of God's Son. With desire I
have desired to see you really mother of my soul as well as
of my body, for it seems to me that when you come to love
the soul more than the body all undue tenderness will die
in you and my physical absence will not cause you so
much pain. Rather, it will be a consolation to you, and you
will desire to bear every burden for God's honour when
you realize that I am being used for this and that it cannot
be accomplished without an increase of grace and virtue
in my soul. So it is indeed true, sweetest mother, that if
you love my soul more than my body, you will be consoled
and not disconsolate.

I urge you to learn from our sweet mother Mary who,
for God's honour and our salvation, gave us her Son, who
died on the wood of the most holy cross. When she was
left alone after Christ ascended into heaven, Mary stayed
with the disciples. This greatly consoled them all, and to
separate made them disconsolate, yet for the glory and
honour of her Son and for the good of the whole world,
Mary agreed, indeed chose, to let them go. She chose the
pain of parting from them rather than the consolation of
keeping them with her, solely through her love for God's
honour and our salvation. I beg you to learn from her,
dearest mother. You know I have to follow God's will and
I know you want me to follow it. It was his will that I
should go, and go for a reason,[1] nor has my journey been
fruitless; far from it. It has been his will, too, not that of
any man, that I should stay away – if anyone says other-

wise, he is wrong. And so I must continue to act, following in his footsteps however and whenever it shall please his inestimable Goodness.

Like a good sweet mother, you must rest content and not be disconsolate, bearing the burden for God's honour, and for your own salvation and mine. I remember that you did this for temporal goods, when your sons were leaving you to acquire temporal riches.[2] Yet now, when the stake is eternal life, you find it so burdensome that you say you will fade away if I don't answer quickly! And all because you are loving the part of me that came from you (that is, your flesh that you clothed me with) more than the part I received from God. Lift then, lift your heart a little to that sweet and holy cross where all affliction is alleviated. Will to bear a little finite pain and so escape the infinite pain we deserve for our sins.

Be comforted for the love of Christ crucified instead of thinking you have been abandoned either by God or by me. You shall have your consolation, and to the full. However great the pain may have been, the delight will be even greater. By God's grace we shall soon be home; we would not now be still on the way were it not for the delay caused by Neri's serious illness. Maestro Giovanni[3] and Fra Bartolomeo[4] were ill, too, etc. [lacuna in ms.][5] No more now. Greetings, etc. [further lacuna].[5] Abide in the sweet and holy love of God. Sweet Jesus. Jesus, Love.

---

[1]    Italian: *mesterio*, a 14th century form of the modern Italian word *mestiere* meaning 'trade, occupation,' and hence, here, 'need' or 'necessity'; cf. Dante, *Purgatorio* I, 92 *'Non c'è mestier lusinghe'* (There is no need for flattery).

[2]    A reference to her 3 brothers leaving home to start a dyeworks in Florence; cf. letter 4.

[3]    for *Neri* (Pagliaresi); see letter 3, note 5b; for *Maestro Giovanni* (Tantucci), see letter 21, note 1a.

[4]    *Fra Bartolomeo* (Dominici) OP, see letters 2 & 7.

[5]    Cf. letter 4, note 3 and letter 6, note 9.

LETTER 26  (Dupré LXXXV; Tommaseo 246; Gigli 51).

*To:*   *Prior of Benedictine Monastery of* S. Girolamo della Cervaia, *near Genoa.*

*Date:*  Probably October/November 1376, from Genoa.

Beloved and most dear father (out of reverence for the most sweet Sacrament) and son (I call you this on account of my true and holy desire which gives birth to your soul by fervent prayer in the sight of God, as a mother gives birth to a child).

I, Catherine, poor wretched servant and slave of the servants of Jesus Christ, spur you on and recommend myself to you in the precious blood of the Son of God, desiring to see your heart and soul utterly consumed in the consummate burning love that engulfed, consumed and destroyed all our iniquities on the wood of the most holy and venerable cross. Yet this sweet Fire did not burn itself out – and never will, for if his love in us were to cease, we would cease to be, since that which gave us being would have ceased: the fire of his love that alone moved him to draw us out of himself. Moreover, God in his inestimable charity seems to have anticipated the fragility and wretchedness of man, always only too ready to offend his Creator, by providing him with a medicine against his infirmities.

The medicine is that fire of love which you can never put out and which the soul receives as medicine when it sees the standard of the most holy cross set up within it, for we ourselves were the rock in which that cross was embedded; neither nail nor wood could have held the sweet and spotless Lamb had not love held him to it. Seeing such sweet costly medicine within itself[1] must not make the soul careless. Rather let it raise itself up with love and desire, stretching out its hands with hatred and distaste of self, like a sick man who hates his illness but welcomes the medicine the doctor gives him.

Dear son and father in Christ Jesus, let us raise ourselves up with the fire of burning love, with [self]-hatred and profound humility, recognizing that of ourselves we are nothing and submitting our infirmities to Christ Jesus, our doctor. Let us stretch out our hand to take the bitter medicines we are given, namely the bitterness a man often encounters: darkness, temptation, confusion of mind, or other trials that come from without, which seem very bitter to us at the time. But they will become exceedingly sweet to us if, like wise invalids, we look at the love of the sweet Jesus who gives them to us, and see that he does it, not out of hatred, but out of his very great love for us, for he cannot want anything other than our sanctification.[2] Once we have seen his goodness, we have seen our own great need also. Great indeed is our need of these [medicines]; without them we would fall into ruin, for they make us know ourselves, rouse us out of our sleep of negligence and rid us of our ignorance by making us vomit up our pride! The result is the birth in us of justice, combined with a sweet and holy patience, making us ready to endure every pain and torment, and consider ourselves unworthy of peace and tranquillity of mind. A soul in love with God and possessing perfect hatred of self does just this. The eye of its understanding is open and it sees within itself the inestimable goodness and charity of God. It finds suffering so sweet and wholesome that it feels unable to delight in anything else; its one thought is to discover how it can suffer out of love for its God. My soul longs and yearns to see you making your way towards this goal, so that if God leads us, and graciously allows us, to toil and even perhaps give our lives for him, the ship of our soul will be well stocked with the blood and fire of divine Charity that we shall thus have sought and procured. I will say no more.

Keep a careful eye on the members of your community; shut it to nothing.

Abide in the sweet and holy love of God. Sweet Jesus. Jesus, Jesus.

LETTER 27   (Dupré LXXXVI; Tommaseo 247; Gigli 355).

*To:*   *Monna Giovanna, wife of Corrado Maconi, of Siena.*¹
*Date:*   End of November 1376, from Pisa.

Dearest sister and daughter in Christ Jesus,
I, Catherine, servant and slave of the servants of Jesus Christ, write to you in his precious blood, desiring to see you clothed with the wedding garment² seeing that, without it, a soul can neither please its Creator nor come to the wedding feast of eternal life. So I want you to be clothed; and that you may don it more easily, I want you to strip off all earthly love you may have for yourself, your children, or any created thing outside God. You must not love yourself or anything else except in God, for a man cannot serve two masters; if he serves one, he will despise the other.³ No one can serve both God and the world as they are incompatible. The world seeks honour, status, wealth, good positions for their children,⁴ noble birth, sensual pleasure and delight – all of which are rooted and grounded in perverse pride. God, however, seeks and wants quite the opposite. He wants voluntary poverty, humility of heart, contempt of self and of all worldly pleasure and delight. He does not want [a man to be] seeking his own honour. He must seek God's honour and his neighbour's salvation, and be concerned only about how to become clothed with the blazing fire of charity and adorned with sweet and solid virtue, and with true

and holy patience, so that he will not want to avenge any injury he may suffer at the hands of his neighbour. Enduring all things patiently, he seeks only to take vengeance on himself for his own offences against the sweet First Truth. Whatever he loves, he loves in God and nothing at all apart from him.

You might ask: 'How am I to love?' My answer is that you must love your children and everything else for the love of him who created them and not either for your own sake or theirs; and you must never offend God on account of them or of anything else. In other words, you must not love them because of any useful purpose they may serve, or as if they belonged to you, but only as something on loan – for everything we have been given in this life has been given to us on loan for our use, and is left with us only for as long as it shall please the divine Goodness who gave it to us. So you must use all things as though dispensing them on behalf of Christ crucified: whether it be material wealth – insofar as you have a say in its distribution to the poor who stand in the place of God[5] – or the care of your own children, whom you must always feed and bring up on the fear of God, preferring that they should die rather than offend their Creator. Please, oh please, offer both yourself and them in sacrifice to God. And if you see that God is calling them, do not pull against his sweet will. Rather, if they are holding out one hand, do you, like a true good mother who loves their salvation, stretch out both. Don't be wanting to choose their state in life according to your own ideas – this would be a sign that you were loving them outside God – but whatever state God may call them to, with that be content. Often a mother who loves her children in a perverse worldly way will say: 'I want my children to serve God, but they can do that as well in the world as in any other way.' But such simple-minded mothers, who *will* submerge their children in the world in this way, often find that they finish up not having them at all either in God or in the world! And it is only right that women who thus show themselves so full of pride and ignorance, and want to dictate how the Holy Spirit is to call their children, should be deprived of them both physically and spiritually. Such mothers love neither in God nor for God but outside God, in a selfish, all-too-human way, being more concerned about their children's bodies than their souls.

Dearest sister and daughter in Christ Jesus, Christ crucified can never be put on without first stripping off this kind of love. I hope that, in God's goodness, this will not be true of you but that you, like a true good mother, will devote yourself and them to the honour and glory of God's name, and so be clothed in the wedding garment. And that you may don it more easily, I want you to turn your desires and affections away from the world and all it stands for and to open the eye of your understanding to know God's love for you; for in his love he has given you the Word, his only-begotten Son, and the Son has given you his life with such burning love, opening his veins in order to bathe us in his Blood. What wretched fools we are, for we fail to recognize or to love such bounty, and all because our eye is tight shut; if it were open and fixed on Christ crucified, it could not ignore or be ungrateful for so much grace. I urge you, then, to keep this eye always open; fix it unswervingly on the Lamb slain in sacrifice so that such ignorance may never affect you.

Up, then, dearest daughter, let us delay no longer but make up for lost time with true and perfect love so that, having been clothed, in this life, in the grace of this garment, we may all – you, your husband and children – rejoice and exult at the wedding feast of eternal life. Draw all your strength and sweetness from Christ sweet Jesus. Be patient, and don't be concerned because I have kept Stefano too long. I assure you I have taken good care of him, for I am now one with you in love and affection and so I have taken your things as if they were mine! I think you will not have minded too much? I want to do everything I possibly can for you and for him until death.

You, his mother, gave birth to him once, and now I want to give birth to you, to him, and to all your family in sweat and tears, by means of continuous prayers and desire for your salvation. I'll say no more.

Please convey my greetings to Corrado and bless the rest of the family for me, especially my new seedling who has just been planted out again in the garden of holy Church.[6] Take it that he is entrusted to your special care, and that you are to feed him on virtue so that he may give off a sweet scent among the other flowers. May God fill you with his most sweet grace.

Abide in the sweet and holy love of God. Sweet Jesus. Jesus.

---

[1]   The Maconi family belonged to the lesser Sienese nobility. They made Catherine's acquaintance when the pious Giovanna prompted her son Stefano to seek her aid in settling a feud with rival families on a point of honour. Stefano soon became a devoted and ardent disciple (and secretary) for whom Catherine seems always to have had a special affection. He went with her to Avignon (see Gardner pp. 168 et seq. and letters 28, 49 & 50).

[2]   of charity; cf. Matthew 22:1–14, and parallels.

[3]   Matthew 6:24.

[4]   Catherine well knew Giovanna's worldly ambitions for Stefano, and already sensed his incipient vocation for the religious life.

[5]   Cf. Matthew 25:31–46.

[6]   This is almost certainly a reference to Stefano's conversion. Yielding reluctantly to his mother's insistence, he had returned to Siena ahead of the rest of the party, perhaps bearing this letter with him.

LETTER 28   (Dupré LXXXVII; Tommaseo 195; Gigli 253).

*To:*    *Stefano Maconi, a young Sienese nobleman.*[1]

*Date:*   November/December 1376, from Pisa.

Dearest son in Christ sweet Jesus,

I, Catherine, servant and slave of the servants of Jesus Christ, write to you in his precious blood, desiring to see you strong and persevering in the battle, so that you may receive the crown of glory for, as you well know, only to those who persevere is the crown and fruit of their toil awarded.[2] 'But', you will object, 'how can I have this strength, since I am so weak and fragile that the least little thing floors me?' I'll tell you. I know you are weak and fragile in your sensual nature, but not in your reason and strength of spirit, for in the blood of Christ we are made strong; the only weakness is in our sensuality. This being so, we can see, and I now tell you, how to acquire the glorious virtue of fortitude and great perseverance: since our reason is made strong in the blood of Christ, we must drown ourselves in this sweet and glorious Ransom, seeing it, with the eye of understanding and the light of holy faith, in the vessel of our soul; knowing that our being is from God, as is the new being we received from him by grace in the blood of his only-begotten Son, which took our weakness from us. So gaze, and rejoice, dearest son, for you are yourself a vessel containing the blood of Christ crucified, if only you will savour it in love.

O pity-full Blood, channel of pity-full mercy! You are that glorious Blood wherein ignorant man can know and see the truth of the eternal Father, for in this truth and in ineffable love we were created to the image and likeness of God. His truth was this: that we should share in the joy of the supreme goodness he savours in himself. In your blood, you have revealed this truth to us; for this one end you created man. O Blood, scattering the darkness and giving man light that he might know the eternal Father's truth and holy will, you have filled the soul with grace, giving it life and preserving it from eternal death. You make it grow fat on the food of God's honour and the salvation of souls; you sate it with the insults and abuse the soul itself longs for and endures for the love of Christ crucified. You burn and consume it in the fire of divine charity, burning out anything in it that is alien to God's will, yet you do not torment or parch it, as mortal sin does.[3] O tender Blood, you strip off the self-love which weakens any soul that wears it; then you clothe it in the fire of divine charity, for a soul cannot savour you, O Blood, unless you clothe it with fire when you draw near to the soul, for by the fire of love were you yourself shed. And since there is no love without strength and no strength without perseverance, you strengthen and reassure the soul in every adversity.

So you see, beloved son, that the way to become absolutely strong is to put the whole of yourself into the fire of divine charity which you will find in the Blood, and in the Blood to drown and destroy every trace of your own will. Then you will have supreme Strength himself at your side, and so be strong and persevering, dealing death to the weakness of your own sensuality while yet savouring sweetness in the midst of bitterness and peace in the midst of war.

Be comforted, my son. Do not give way under the discipline God has imposed on you until your hour comes. Reflect that digging the foundations is always the most laborious part of the work. Once they have been completed, the building itself is easily done. You, now, are laying your foundation; once you have done that, the rest will be easy. I don't want you to find it arduous; but that the difficulties melt away when you think of the Blood. Bear up, bear up, become a bearer! But I will say this . . . [lacuna in ms.].[4] As to this, however, do whatever the Holy Spirit prompts you to do. I can hardly keep myself from saying to you those words of Christ . . . (further lacuna).[5] When the time and place are right, I hope it will come about. Meanwhile, get on with provisioning the little ship of your soul and filling the vessel of your heart with Blood. No more now.

Abide in the sweet and holy love of God. Sweet Jesus. Jesus, Love.

¹   See letter 27 note 1. Note: This is probably Catherine's first letter to Stefano.
²   Matthew 10:22.
³   Conjectural translation
⁴   Yet another tantalizing series of omissions by the early editors, who included Stefano himself, to whom we owe an invaluable collection of 205 of Catherine's letters.
⁵   Only on her deathbed did Catherine make it clear to Stefano that she thought it was God's will for him to join the Carthusians, which he did early in 1381.

LETTER 29   (Dupré LXXXVIII; Tommaseo 252; Gigli 11).

*To:*   *Gregory XI, during the halt he made at Corneto in the Papal States, on his way to Rome.*

*Date:*   December 1376/January 1377, from Siena.

Most reverend and holy father in Christ sweet Jesus,
Your wretched and unworthy daughter Catherine recommends herself to you in his precious blood, desiring to see your heart made firm and strong in true and holy patience, for I consider that a weak, volatile and impatient heart cannot achieve great things for God. Every rational creature that desires to serve God and be clothed with virtue must have this constancy, fortitude and patience, otherwise it could never have God in its soul.

[Catherine develops the idea that as vice drives out virtue, so virtue drives out vice – humility pride, patience impatience, etc. – for 'we can neither acquire nor become perfect in virtue without its opposite' (cf. letter 22).]

Most holy father, *dolcissimo babbo mio*,[1] open the eye of your understanding and let your intelligence see that if virtue is so very necessary to all men so that each may save his soul, how much more does one in your position, whose responsibility it is to feed and care for the mystical body of holy Church, your bride, stand in need of such constancy, fortitude and patience? You know that when you were but a seedling in the garden of holy Church, you had to equip yourself with virtue in order to resist the devil, the flesh and the world, the three chief enemies ranged against us night and day, for they never sleep. I trust in the divine Goodness, which has already enabled you to resist these enemies to some extent, and will help you to do so entirely, so that he may accomplish in you the end for which he created you, namely that you should give glory and praise to his name and rejoice in his goodness when you attain to his eternal vision wherein lies his bliss.

And now you are Christ's vicar and must toil and struggle for the honour of God, the salvation of souls and the reform of holy Church; all these things mean pain and suffering for you in addition to those every soul endeavouring to please God has to endure, as we said. Since, then, yours is the heavier burden, you must be all the more daring and courageous of heart, and not fearful of anything that may happen. Well you know, holy Father, that when you took holy Church as your bride, you took on the task of toiling and striving on her account and of facing up to the many cross-winds of much pain and suffering which were already bearing down on you to contend with you for her. With true manliness, then, go out and meet these dangerous winds with fortitude, patience and long-suffering. Let neither pain, dismay nor servile fear make you look back, but rather persevere, rejoicing in the midst of the storm and the battle.

Let your heart rejoice indeed, for in the many adverse situations that have, and will, come about, God's work is being well done, nor was it ever done in any other way! And so we see that the purpose of this persecution of the Church, and of all tribulations, when endured by a virtuous soul, is the peace that is attained through true patience and perseverance; it comes out of it all crowned with glory. This, then, is our remedy. This is why I said, most holy father, that I longed to see your heart firm, immovable, and fortified in true and holy patience.

I want you to be a tree of love grafted into Love the Word, Christ crucified; a tree that, for God's honour and the salvation of your flock, is well-rooted in deepest humility. If you are such a tree, sweetly rooted in this way, you will find in yourself – at the tree's top – the fruit of patience and fortitude, and at its centre, perseverance already crowned. In the midst of your sufferings you will find peace, serenity and consolation when you see that by suffering you are being conformed to Christ crucified. By thus enduring with him, you will come joyfully from great war to great peace.

Peace, peace, most holy father! May it please your Holiness to receive your sons who have offended you, their father.[2] Let your graciousness overcome their wrong-headedness and pride. It will not be undignified for you to stoop down to pacify your wayward child; indeed, it will be greatly to your honour, and to your advantage, before God and worldly-minded men. Alas, my father, no more war! In some way or other – but without going against your conscience – there can be peace. Let the war be dispatched against the infidels, where it ought to go, [while you] imitate the meekness and patience of the spotless Lamb, Christ sweet Jesus, whose vicar you are. I am confident *in Domino nostro Jesu Christo*[3] that in this and in the other things he will be so much at work within you that he will fulfil your own desire and mine, for my one desire in this life is to see God honoured, your peace restored, holy Church reformed and the life of grace in every rational creature.

Be consoled about the situation here;[4] as far as I can gather, they want you as father nonetheless, especially this poor foolish city[5] which has always been daughter to your Holiness but was forced by circumstances to act against your wishes. They feel they had no alternative. Excuse them yourself to your Holiness and thus catch them with the hook of love.

I beseech you, for the love of Christ crucified, to move on as fast as you can to where you [and] the glorious apostles Peter and Paul belong. For your part, try to go in safety and for his part God will provide whatever may be needful for you and the good of your bride. I will say no more. Please forgive my presumption.

Be comforted and trust in God's true servants, that is in their prayers, for they are earnestly praying and beseeching God for you. I and your other children humbly ask your blessing. Abide in the sweet and holy love of God. Sweet Jesus. Jesus, Love.

---

[1]   See letter 15, note 2.

[2]   This almost certainly refers to an embassy from Siena seeking, perhaps unofficially, to pave the way for a reconciliation with the Pope.

[3]   'in our Lord Jesus Christ'. Catherine would have been very familiar with this phrase which occurs frequently in the liturgy.

[4]   Either Tuscany or the 'poor foolish city'; see note 5.

[5]   This could be Pisa (where Catherine is known to have remained until 8 December 1376) but is more likely to be Siena. Two manuscripts record the name of the bearer: Tommaso Guelfaccio – who may well have been a member of the delegation to which Catherine refers (see note 2).

# GROUP III

## Letters written between January 1377 and December 1378

LETTER 30   (Tommaseo 45, Gigli 266).

*To:     Francesco Malavolti, a Sienese nobleman.*[1]
*Date:*  ? Early 1377.[2]

Dearest and more than dearest son in Christ sweet Jesus,

I, Catherine, servant and slave of the servants of Jesus Christ, write to you in his precious blood, desiring to get you back into the fold with your companions, for the devil seems to me to have you so well hidden that he will not let you be found. I, your wretched mother, go round searching for you and sending for you because I long to lift you onto the shoulder of the bitterness and compassion I feel for your soul.[3] So open the eye of your mind, dearest son, and rid it of darkness. Acknowledge your sin – not with confusion of mind, but with knowledge of yourself and hope in the goodness of God. You see you have squandered the substance of grace your heavenly Father gave you, so do what the prodigal son did who had spent all his substance in loose living.[4] When he began to be in want, he acknowledged his fault and ran to his father for mercy. Let you, now, do the same, for you are impoverished and in want and your soul is dying of hunger. So run to your Father for mercy; he will help you. Far from spurning your desire, if it springs from remorse for your sin, he will graciously fulfil it.

Alas, alas, where are those sweet desires of yours? I, poor forlorn creature, find that the devil has stolen both your soul and your holy desire. The world and its minions have ensnared you with their unlawful pleasures and delights. Do get up and take the remedy. Sleep no longer. Bring consolation to my soul, and don't be so cruel to your own as to make yourself scarce. Don't let the devil fool you by either fear or shame. Sever the knot. Come, do come, dearest son. Well can I call you 'dear' since you are costing me so much in tears and sweat and great anguish! Please come back to your fold. Before God I ask pardon that I can do no more. In begging you to come back and stay back I only ask you to do God's will.

Abide in the sweet and holy will of God. Sweet Jesus. Jesus, Love.

---

¹    This devoted though somewhat unsteady disciple became an Olivetan friar some time after Catherine's death.
²    Gardner (p.208) suggests that Francesco had slipped back into his old ways during Catherine's absence in Avignon.
³    Cf. Luke 15:5.
⁴    Luke 15: 11-32.

## LETTER 31   (Tommaseo 34; Gigli 73).

*To:*    *Frate Girolino, Prior of an Olivetan Monastery just outside Siena.*

*Date:*    Unknown, but presumably before the start of the schism, which is not mentioned.

Beloved father (out of reverence for the most holy Sacrament) and dearest brother in Christ sweet Jesus,

I, Catherine, servant and slave of the servants of Jesus Christ, write to you in his precious blood, desiring to see you a good and manly shepherd, diligently feeding and watching over the sheep entrusted to you,¹ as did the sweet Master of Truth, who laid down his life for us, his sheep, when we had strayed from the way of grace. It is true, dearest brother in Christ sweet Jesus, that you cannot do this without God, and that we cannot have God on earth. But I see a lovely solution. Since your heart is small and low, I want you to do what Zacchaeus did.[2] Being small of stature, he climbed up into a tree in order to see God. His eagerness won him the reward of hearing those gracious words: 'Go home, Zacchaeus, for I must eat with you today'. We must do the same. We, too, are small of stature; our hearts are narrow and we are low in charity. Let us, then, climb the tree of the most holy cross, for then we shall see and touch God and find the fire of his inestimable charity with the love that made him run to meet the shame of the cross and raised him on high, hungering and thirsting for the Father's honour and our salvation.[3]

Behold our sweet good Shepherd, who gave his life with such famished desire and burning love that, disregarding his own suffering, our ignorance and ingratitude for such a gift, and the insults of the Jews, like a man in love he submits to his Father in perfect obedience. So, if we are willing (and our negligence does not keep us back), our climbing the tree can bring about in us that word spoken by the sweet mouth of Truth: 'If I shall be raised on high, I will draw everything to myself'.[4] Truly, a soul that has climbed up there sees the Father's goodness poured out, and the power that empowers the blood of the Son to wash away our sins. There we see the obedience of Christ crucified who dies obeying, and obeys with such longing that the anguish of his desire far exceeded his bodily suffering. We see, too, the abounding clemency of the Holy Spirit, the ineffable Love that held him fast to the wood of the cross, for neither nail nor rope could have bound him there without the bond of love. Only hearts as hard as diamonds could fail to be softened by such measureless love. And truly, a heart once pierced by this arrow rises up with all its strength (though it is not the whole man that is made clean but his soul, for which

God made everything).[5]

And if you say: 'I can't climb this tree; it's too high,' I answer that he has hollowed out steps for you in his body. First raise yourself, heart and soul, to the feet of God's Son; then climb up to the heart, which is open and utterly spent for us, and so arrive at the peace of his mouth[6] where you will learn to savour souls and make them your food,[3] and in this way become a true shepherd ready to lay down your life for your sheep. Keep your eye on them all the time, so that vice may be rooted out and virtue planted in its place.

I am sending you two more little sheep; give them time in their cell and to study. Feeding them both will be no trouble and you will derive great joy and consolation from them. No more now.

Strengthen and encourage one another, binding yourselves together in the bond of love and climbing up that most holy tree bearing the fruits of virtue that have ripened on the body of God's Son. Keep running.

Abide in the sweet and holy love of God. Sweet Jesus. Jesus, Love.

---

[1]  Cf. John 22:15 et seq.
[2]  Luke 19:1–9.
[3]  See letter 11, note 3.
[4]  John 12:32.
[5]  The text is unsatisfactory and the translation conjectural, but cf. letter 34, p.155.
[6]  Cf. the fuller expression of this idea in letter 18. Both letters foreshadow one of the key images used by Catherine in the *Dialogue*.

LETTER 32   (Tommaseo 242; Gigli 37).

*To:*   *Messer Angelo Ricasoli, Bishop of Florence.*[1]

*Date:*   ? Spring of 1377 (but see note 5).

Most dear and reverend father in Christ sweet Jesus,

I, Catherine, servant and slave of the servants of Jesus Christ, write to you in his precious blood, desiring to see you stout-hearted and free from fear so that you can valiantly serve Christ's sweet Bride,[2] working by every spiritual means for God's honour according to her needs today. I am sure that if you lift up the eye of your mind to see this need you will act promptly and without fear or negligence. A soul that gives way to servile fear does nothing perfectly. Whatever position such a man may hold, be he dealing with trivial matters or important affairs, he will prove inadequate and fall short of perfection in anything he undertakes. How dangerous this fear is! It severs the arms of holy desire and so blinds a man that he can neither see nor know the truth, for his fear is itself the product of blind self-love. As soon as the rational creature loves itself in a sensual way, it becomes fearful, because its love and reliance rest on a poor weak thing that possesses neither solidity nor stability but is come and gone like the wind.

O perverse love, ruin of all in authority, temporal or spiritual, and of their subjects! A prelate who loves like this will never utter a rebuke for fear of losing his position and displeasing his subjects. It is the ruin, too, of those under authority, for there is no humility but only deep-seated pride in one who loves himself in this way, and a proud man never obeys. If he is a temporal lord, he will not uphold justice but pronounce only corrupt false judgements by consulting only his own convenience or that of others. And by this failure to correct faults and uphold justice those under authority are made worse because they are left to feed on their own vices and wickedness.[3]

Since self-love and this disordered fear are so dangerous, we must fly from them, opening instead the eye of
our intelligence and fixing it on our rule and doctrine,
the spotless Lamb. He is the One we must follow, for he is
love itself, and truth, who seeks only his Father's honour
and our salvation. He did not fear the Jews and their
persecution, or the devil's wiles, or ignominy, mockery
and treachery; nor did he fear, at the end, the shameful
death of the cross. And we, now, are pupils attending his
sweet and gentle school. So, my very dear father, I want
you, with great eagerness and prudence, to fix the eye of
your mind on this Book of life that contains such sweet
winning teaching. Give your whole attention to God's
honour, the salvation of souls and the service of Christ's
sweet Bride. By this light you will strip off your own
self-love and be clothed in divine love. You will seek God
for his infinite goodness alone, for he is worthy to be
sought after and loved by us. You will love yourself and
virtue, but hate vice, for God; and with this love you will
love your neighbour too.

You see clearly that the divine Goodness has placed
you in the mystical body of holy Church[4] and let you feed
at her breast solely in order that you may eat the food of
God's honour and the salvation of souls at the table of the
most holy cross. He does not want it eaten anywhere but
on the cross, by bearing both bodily fatigue and countless
anguished desires as the Son of God himself simulta-
neously endured physical torment and the agony of desire,
but his cross of desire cost him [more than] the actual
cross. The desire was his hunger for our redemption in
obedience to his Father's will, and it ached within him
until the moment of fulfilment. Moreover, being the
wisdom of the eternal Father, he saw who were sharing in
his blood and who, because of sin, were not. His blood
was given for all, and so he grieved over the ingratitude
of those who did not wish for it. This crucified desire was
with him from start to finish, and even when he had given
his life, the desire remained, though the torment of the

cross did not.

This, then, is what you and every rational creature must do. Give [to God] your bodily fatigue and the fatigue of your desire as you grieve over God being offended and so many souls being damned and perishing. It seems to me, dearest father, that the time has come for us to give the honour to God and our toil in his service to our neighbour. This is no time to be indulging in sensual love of self, or servile fear. Rather, let true love and a holy fear of God govern our actions. And if we have to give our lives for God's honour, then we must give them, let alone mere temporal goods! I trust, in the infinite goodness of God, that being stout-hearted you will do this and persevere, as you have begun, as a faithful son of holy Church, attaining to great perfection by the practice of virtue. I am overjoyed at the perseverance and constancy you have displayed up to now.[5] I beg you not to look back until death but to continue being the virtuous man and fragrant flower that you ought to be in the garden of holy Church, for it seems to me that those who are not manly in virtue are not constant either.

[Catherine again urges the Bishop to be stout-hearted and free from fear. She ends with a reference to the spotless Lamb 'our King, who came so meekly and humbly to meet us on the way' (Zech. 9:9). The use of this text perhaps suggests that the letter was written on or near Palm Sunday, but see note 5 below.]

---

[1]   See letter 11.
[2]   the Church.
[3]   Cf. Dante, *Purgatorio*, VI, 76 ff.
[4]   Catherine makes a distinction between the 'mystical' body of the Church (bishops and priests, and in some cases specifically the cardinals) and the 'general' body (the faithful in general). Cf. Dialogue, p.285 and note 24.
[5]   The mss. record that, to avoid being compelled by the War Party to violate the interdict, the bishop had fled from

Florence and suffered the confiscation of his property there
as a result; cf. Fawtier, p.173. However, for reasons largely
connected with the parallel letter Catherine sent to the
Florentine cardinal, Pietro Corsini (Tommaseo 11), Fawtier
dates both letters several years earlier.

LETTER 33   (Tommaseo 49; Gigli 177).

*To:*     *Monna Alessa dei Saraceni.*[1]

*Date:*   Late summer/early autumn of 1377, while
          Catherine was on a mission of reconciliation to the
          Salimbeni and other prominent Sienese families in
          the wild and inhospitable Val d'Orcia, near Siena.[2]

Beloved daughter in Christ sweet Jesus,
   I, Catherine, servant and slave of the servants of Jesus
Christ and your poor unworthy mother, long for you to
attain that perfection to which God has called you. It
seems to me one should pursue this aim with moderation,
not without it. [Yet] all our actions should be both with
and without moderation! No moderation in our love for
God – no, no limit, nor measure nor rule, simply measureless love.[3] But in order to reach such perfection of
love, rules are necessary. Let the first rule be to shun
mere conversation with others, except when charity
requires it. Love a great many but hold converse with few.
And learn how to use moderation even when conversing
with those you love in a spiritual way. Otherwise, without
realizing it, you would be imposing a limit on the measureless love you owe to God by bringing a finite creature
into it and giving the measureless love to the creature
instead of to God, thereby impeding your own perfection. So, though your love of creatures be spiritual, there
must be due moderation in it.
   Be a drinking-cup that you fill, and drink, in the fount.
Granted that you may have drawn your love from God,

who is the fount of living water,[4] yet unless you continued to drink in him your cup would soon be empty. And the sign that you are not drinking fully in God will be when you find yourself pained by the thing you love, either because of a conversation you have had, or because you have been deprived of some consolation you had grown accustomed to, or because of some other thing that has happened. To be pained by this, or by anything else other than an offence against God, is a clear sign that your love is still imperfect and that you have withdrawn your cup from the Fount.

Is there a method,[5] then, for making the imperfect perfect? This is it: correct and chastise the movements of your heart with true self-knowledge and with hatred and regret for your imperfection; for having been so churlish as to give a creature the love due entirely to God, dispensing with all moderation in loving the creature while moderating our love for God. It is our love for God that must be measureless while our love for others must be measured against our love for God and not by the yardstick of our own consolations, whether spiritual or temporal. So try to love everything in God and to correct every disorderly affection.

Make two dwelling-places for yourself, my daughter. One will be your actual cell, to keep you from wandering about from place to place except out of necessity, to obey your prioress,[6] or for the sake of charity. Make the second dwelling-place a spiritual one that you take everywhere with you, namely the cell of true self-knowledge, wherein you will find knowledge of God's goodness [at work] in you. This second cell is really two cells in one and when you are in one, you need to be in the other too, as otherwise your soul would fall into either confusion or presumption. Self-knowledge alone would result in confusion of mind, whereas to abide solely in knowledge of God would lead you to presumption. Each needs to be seasoned with the other and made into one and the same thing; if you do this, you will come to perfection.

Self-knowledge will teach you to despise your own sensual nature and so turn you into a judge seated on the bench of your conscience, pronouncing sentence and not letting the fault escape your judgement. From this knowledge springs the vein of humility: always unaffected, never shocked, patiently and joyfully enduring every injury, every loss of consolation, every suffering, whatever their origin. Humiliations then look like glory, great persecutions like refreshment. In all this [the soul] rejoices to see itself punished for the perverse law of its own self-will, and also being conformed to Jesus Christ crucified, who is the way and the doctrine of truth.

In knowledge of God you will find the fire of divine charity. And your delight? On the cross with the spotless Lamb, by seeking his honour and the salvation of souls in humble and unceasing prayer. Herein lies all our perfection. Many other things, too, but this is the main one from which we receive so much light that we cannot go wrong in all the lesser operations that flow from it.

Delight, my daughter, in conforming yourself to the ignominy of Christ. And keep guard over the movements of your tongue, lest it sometimes utter those of the heart. Swallow down what is in your heart with hatred and distaste for self. Make yourself the least of the least, subject, in your humility and patience, to every creature for God's sake; not excusing yourself but saying 'it was my fault'. In this way the vices in your own heart and in that of the person you would have spoken to are overcome by the virtue of humility.

Plan out your time: keeping vigil at night, after you have given your body its due in sleep, and sweet prayer in church in the morning. And don't spend the time not allocated to prayer chattering! Let nothing draw you away from prayer – or anything else – except necessity, obedience or charity, as I have said. After the main meal, withdraw for a while and be recollected, then work with your hands, according to your need. At vespers time, go and do something: whatever the Holy Spirit prompts you to do, that do [and no more]. Then return home and take every care of your old mother, providing for all her needs; let this burden be yours. The rest after my return. Try to go about things so as to fulfil my desire for you. No more now.

Abide in the sweet and holy love of God. Sweet Jesus. Jesus, Love.

---

¹   See letter 1, note 2.
²   See Introduction, p.26 and Papàsogli, pp.248–252.
³   Cf. St. Bernard, *Liber de diligendo Deo*, I, 1 & VI, 16.
⁴   Cf. John 4:10 and 7:37.
⁵   Italian: *modo*, meaning both 'method' and 'moderation' gives Catherine scope for an elaborate word-play that is not fully reflected in our translation.
⁶   of the Sisters of Penance, or *Mantellate* (see letter 1, note 2) to which both Catherine and Alessa belonged.

LETTER 34   (Tommaseo 253; Gigli 194).

*To:*   *Messer Trincio dei Trinci, ruler of Foligno, and his brother Corrado, petty tyrants of a type common in Catherine's day.*¹

*Date:*   14 September 1377.²

Dearest brothers in Christ sweet Jesus,

I, Catherine, servant and slave of the servants of Jesus Christ, write to you in his precious blood, desiring to see you true servants of Christ crucified, bound together in the sweet bond of charity that bound God into man and man into God so perfectly that neither death nor anything else could ever separate them.³

O true sweet Bond, so strong that you kept the God-Man nailed fast to the wood of the most holy cross! – for nails and iron could not have held him had he not been held there by his love for his Father's honour and our salvation. So strong was this love, dearest brothers, so tenacious, that no devil and no creature could make it release its hold. In spite of the injuries they heaped on him then and we heap on him now, creatures could not and cannot slacken it; neither could their ingratitude then nor ours now; nor can the devils prevent him from loving us, however much they molest us. Nor did he himself abandon his obedience to his Father, but persevered to the death of the cross. With great patience and perseverance, this sweet and loving Word, God's only-begotten Son, shows us the will and sweet Truth of his eternal Father. His will is our sanctification,[4] and his truth, too. For this end God created us, that we might be sanctified in him to the praise and glory of his name, and relish the joy of his eternal vision.

Dearest, sweetest brothers, I urge you to gaze into the abundance and abyss of his Charity. Seeing that man had been blinded and kept in ignorance through his own sin and was unaware of God's sweet truth and will, God chose to abase himself to man. O wretched pride! Well may a soul be ashamed of being proud when God is humbled and has given us his Word, veiled and clothed in our humanity. Who could add anything to the mere thought of the Most High having descended so low, and bound himself into man and man into God. Open, then, the eye of your understanding and see the great outpouring of the blood of God's Son, for the opening up of his body has shown us how immeasurably God loves us and wants only our good; had he wanted anything else he would not have given us such a Ransomer. O inestimable, O sweetest Charity! The cavern of your body is open through the heat of the fire of your love for our salvation. You, eternal God, have made yourself visible, and have given us a visible Ransom, so that our low understanding can have no excuse for not raising itself up – since you have abased yourself and so brought our lowness up to your own Highness! Let the impetus of love, then, raise up man's understanding and affections, knowing the abasement of your humility and then the highness and excellence of your charity, O eternal Godhead. You yourself said this, sweet and loving Word: 'If I am lifted up from the earth, I will draw all things to myself';[5] as though the sweet eternal Truth were saying: 'If I am abased to the humiliation of the shameful death of the cross, I will draw your hearts to the height of the Divinity and uncreated Charity'; for once a man's heart has been drawn, all his affections and powers, with all his activity whether spiritual or temporal, can be said to be drawn too. Indeed, since every created thing has been made subject to man, once man has been drawn, all things have been drawn, and that is why he said: 'If I am lifted up from the earth, I will draw all things to myself.'

It is well, then, to open the eye of the mind and gaze into the Creator's love. So I urge you to reflect, dearest brothers, that when the eye of the mind is clouded with sensual self-love, it cannot know this truth. For, as a sore eye that is full of grit and the flesh round it swollen cannot see the sun, so the soul's eye cannot see if it is covered with the grit of disordered love and attachment to the world, that is, to these fleeting things that come and go like the wind; or if it is obscured by fleshly passion, by unclean living, the wretched involvement in the mud of the flesh that turns a man into a brute beast and deprives him of light and knowledge. Such men, I say, cannot know this truth; indeed, they have become lie-lovers, following in the footsteps of their father, the devil, the father of lies.[6]

I want you, then, to turn the eye of your mind away from these transitory things and from all carnal vice, and to cleanse your souls in holy confession. I am not saying that you should give up your position, except in so far as the Holy Spirit may inspire you to do so, but I do want you to hold it with holy fear of God, standing upright like virtuous men – rather than idiots or animals – and ruling your subjects with justice and kindliness. Hold, too, to the

state of matrimony and don't be wanting to contaminate
it, that is to break it up by any unruly appetite. Rather,
check your feelings with the memory of Christ's blood
and of the union of the divine and human natures. With
this holy thought in mind, your wretched flesh will be
ashamed of stooping to such wretchedness, will sense the
odour of purity and so abide in holy matrimony with awe
and fear of God. And hold in respect the days commanded by holy Church.[7] You will thus be fruitful trees,
bearing good fruit to the praise and glory of God's name,
and grafted into Christ sweet Jesus, the tree of life, who
will bind you with that strong bond of love that kept him
nailed fast to the cross. Once bound to God and your
neighbour with this sweet bond, you, too, will share in this
strength so that no devil or creature can tear you away or
stop you being strong and persevering until death. No
ingratitude shown by those you serve in failing to
appreciate you,[8] nothing the devil may put into your
heart in the way of hatred or annoyance with your neighbour, will slacken this love or rob you of its strength when
you are made one, and bound in the bond of charity, as I
said. Rather, in your own sphere you will be true servants
of Christ crucified. Otherwise you cannot share in the life
of grace, and that is why I said that I longed to see you
true servants of Christ crucified, bound in the sweet bond
of charity.

[The letter ends with a series of brief reflections on
God's appreciation for any service rendered to him in
the Church, Catherine, too, graciously thanking the
two brothers for what they themselves have done.]

---

[1]    The two brothers had sided with the papal forces in·the war
against Florence, a fact which partly accounted for Trincio's
assassination on 28 September, 1377. Corrado's absence from
Foligno at the time saved him from a similar fate. He made a
violent come-back in the following December.

² So Gardner, p.222; but cf. Fawtier's comment, p.240. Both scholars suggest that Catherine may have written the letter ('in a trance' according to the mss.) at the request of the two men's sister, Bianchina Salimbeni, whose guest Catherine was about this time; cf. letter 36, note 4c.

³ Cf. Romans 8:38–39.

⁴ I Thess. 4:3.

⁵ John 12:32.

⁶ John 8:44.

⁷ Here, as elsewhere, Catherine recommends the accepted medieval practice of observing continence on great feastdays.

⁸ This may be a reference to Gregory XI's tendency to take his few loyal supporters rather too much for granted.

LETTER 35    (Tommaseo 250; Gigli 65).

*To:*    *Giovanni di Gano, Abbot of the Williamite Abbey of Sant'Antimo.*¹

*Date:*    Probably late summer/early autumn of 1377, from one of the Salimbeni strongholds in the Val d'Orcia.²

Dearest father in Christ sweet Jesus,

I, Catherine, servant and slave of the servants of Jesus Christ, write to you in his precious blood, desiring to see you possessing the true and most sweet light the soul needs; that is, opening the eye of your understanding to see, consider and discern God's supreme eternal will in you. This sweet awareness makes a man prudent and enlightened; cautious, too, and not given to judging men's intentions lightly, as God's servants frequently do, under the guise of virtue and loving but misplaced zeal.³ It brings courage and drives out fear. It gives a man due reverence in discerning what is God's will for him; whatever God permits, be it persecution or consolation, whether from men or from the devil, he sees all as done for our sanctification.[4] He delights in God's measureless charity, and trusts in his providence that provides for all our needs, giving all things in due measure – and the greater the trial meted out to us, the greater the power we are given to bear it.[5]

All this the soul sees and knows, once the eye of the understanding has been enlightened and it has known God's will and so come to love it. Being thus enlightened, it forms no judgement about the intentions of God's servants, or of any other creature – other than to hold, and in due reverence, that they are guided by the Holy Spirit – and so does not venture to criticize them but leaves judgement to God.[6] One might perhaps ask: 'Is any servant of God so enlightened that no other can ever see more than he does?' No, indeed; which is why, in order that God's magnificence may be manifested and the order of charity respected, all God's servants must together use and share all the light, graces and gifts they receive from God, and this in order both that the light and magnificence of sweet Truth itself be shown to be – as it is – not finite, but infinite, and also so that we may humble ourselves to recognize God's light and grace in his servants. He sets them here and there like springs, one yielding one kind of water and another another,[7] their purpose in this life being both to pour life into themselves and to console and refresh others who thirst for these waters, that is, for the many gifts and graces God pours into his servants. It is thus that God supplies our needs.

Truly, then, no one is so enlightened as not often to need light from others: even so, one who has been given light concerning God's sweet will [in any matter] will himself impart it under the light of faith, neither judging adversely, nor taking scandal concerning the one he wishes to advise, but in such a way as always to remain untroubled. Hence, if the other abides by his counsel, he is pleased, but if not, he sweetly concludes that, under God's will and providence, this was to serve some purpose,[8] some design. And so he remains untroubled and suffers no hurt, for he is clothed with that will. Rather than waste his breath informing others of his own views, he endeavours to drown and mortify them in God's view of things by entrusting to him any doubts or fears he may entertain on the matter, and freely offering to God both himself and his doubts about his neighbour. In this sweet prudence do those who are enlightened with this true light live and move, and so have a foretaste of eternal life even in this.

The reverse is true of those who, though they serve God, are nonetheless ignorant, for they still cling to their own views and opinions, under colour of virtue and misplaced zeal. This is why we frequently fall into serious defects and into all sorts of scandal and backbiting. So a true, penetrating light is needed. But I hardly think we can hope for this without first dispelling the cloud and darkness of self, and so making our own point of view give way.

Oh glorious Light! O soul so drowned as to be lost to view in this light, for you no longer see yourself as such but only the light within you, and in that light alone you see and judge your neighbour,[9] seeing, loving and revering him in that light and not in your own opinion or false judgement disguised as loving zeal! So let us open wide, and use, the eye of our understanding and keep [self-] will lost and drowned. Guided thus by true love[10] and true respect for God's will and that of his servants, we shall have light and attain such true and perfect purity that we shall not be scandalized by anything God's servants do. Not being their judges, we shall be at peace concerning them, ready to rejoice over whether they go or stay and over everything they do, through having seen and recognized God's will in them.

Up, then, dearest father and son, let us nestle at the breast of divine Charity and there savour this sweet wholesome milk which will bring us to the perfection of the saints and make us follow the footsteps, and the rule,

of the Lamb. Losing our fear, we shall face thorns and
tribulations and shirk no toil, while yet grieving over the
offence that murmurers commit and the scandal they
give, bringing them before God with great compassion.
Moreover, we shall go on doing the holy deeds we began
for the honour of God and the salvation of souls, and
finish them according to his sweet will. I will say no more
about this, except that we should drown ourselves in the
blood of Christ crucified; fearlessly, I say, knowing that if
God is for us no one can be against us.[11]

I don't know when I shall be able to come.[12] I cannot
know how long I shall remain [here]. I will get away as
quickly as I can, but always fulfilling God's sweet will in
myself – in going and in staying – not that of men. I want
you to know – you and the others who let so many hurts
and fancies into your hearts – that I neither stay, nor go
on wearisome journeys, with all my infirmities, out of
pleasure, but only when compelled by God, for his honour and the salvation of souls. Nor can I do otherwise,
even if sick hearts choose to draw evil out of good. What I
must never do, though, is to turn back and abandon the
ground that has already been ploughed[13] as this would
make us seem to have ploughed at the behest of men, and
so cause cockle to grow and choke the wheat.[14] I will say
no more.

Abide in the sweet and holy love of God. Sweet Jesus.
Jesus, Love.

---

[1]   Catherine held this holy man in high esteem, valuing his
judgement in all matters connected with the religious life affecting herself or others; cf. Raymond, p.216, text and footnote.

[2]   See Fawtier, p.189, and letter 36, notes 4 & 5.

[3]   Ital. *zelo d'amore*. Our translation tries to convey Catherine's
antithesis between (misplaced) 'zeal of love' and 'true love'. Cf.
Cavallini, Letter X, notes 3 & 25.

[4]   I Thess. 4:3.

[5]   Cf. I Cor. 10:13.

[6]   Translation conjectural.

⁷ In the days before piped water and in an area rich in thermal springs the relative merits of particular springs would have counted for much. (The water from the *Fonte Branda* near Catherine's home remained clear and drinkable until a few years ago).

⁸ See letter 25, note 1, for this use of the word *misterio*.

⁹ Cf. Psalm 36:9.

¹⁰ See note 3 above.

¹¹ Romans 8:31.

¹² to visit the monastery; cf. letter 37, note 6.

¹³ Cf. Luke 9:62.

¹⁴ Cf. Matthew 13:24–30.

## LETTER 36   (Tommaseo 118; Gigli 175).

*To:*   *Monna Caterina dello Spedaluccio and Giovanna di Capo, in Siena.*¹

*Date:*   Autumn 1377, while Catherine was staying at *Rocca d'Orcia*, a Salimbeni stronghold some distance from Siena.

Beloved daughters in Christ sweet Jesus,

I, Catherine, servant and slave of the servants of Jesus Christ, write to you in his precious blood, desiring to see you obedient daughters, united in true and perfect charity. Obedience and love will help you to digest all suffering and darkness: obedience, by removing the cause of distress, perverse self-will, which is drowned and killed by real holy obedience; [the love of] charity, by melting away your darkness, for God *is* Charity and he is the supreme eternal Light. No one guided by this true light can go astray. And since it is so very necessary, I want you, dearest daughters, to strive to lose your own wills and to acquire that light.

This is the teaching I remember that you have always been given, though you have not grasped much of it. I beg you, dearest daughters, to do now what has hitherto been left undone, for if you don't, you will be in continual distress and keep me in it too; though I, poor wretch, deserve it.

We must do, for God's honour, what the holy apostles did – once they had received the Holy Spirit, they separated from one another and from that sweet mother, Mary. It would have given them great joy to stay together, but they sacrificed their own pleasure and sought instead the honour of God and the salvation of souls. And though Mary sends them away, they do not conclude from this either that there is any lessening of love, or that they are deprived of her affection. We too should live by this rule. I know my presence is a great consolation to you. Nevertheless, to be truly obedient, for God's honour and the salvation of souls you must not seek your own consolation, or allow the devil to suggest to you that you are being deprived of the love and affection I have for you, body and soul. Otherwise [love] would not be rooted in you. Of this I do assure you, that I myself do not love you, except for God! Why be so inordinately distressed at what has to be? How shall we accomplish great deeds when we fall so far short in little ones? Whether we are to be together or separated must be determined by the need of the moment, and just now our sweet Saviour wills and permits us to be separated, for his honour.

You two are in Siena; Cecca and Grandma are at Montepulciano[2] where Fra Bartolomeo and Fra Matteo have already been and will be again.[3] Alessa and Monna Bruna are with the Countess and Madonna Isa at Monte Giovi, eighteen miles from Montepulciano.[4] Fra Raimondo and Fra Tommaso, Monna Tomma, Lisa and I are among rascals here at the Rocca,[5] where we are eating so many incarnate devils that Fra Tommaso says his stomach aches.[6] Even so, he cannot have his fill. Indeed, they are asking for more, and finding work here for a good wage.[7] Ask the divine Goodness to give them big bitter-sweet mouthfuls. Think what a joy it is to see so clearly God being honoured and souls being saved! You must neither wish nor long for anything else. By doing this, you can do nothing more pleasing to the supreme eternal will of God, and to mine. Bestir yourselves, then, my daughters, and begin sacrificing your will to God. Stop wanting to be kept on milk;[8] we need to get the teeth of our desire ready to chew hard mouldy bread if necessary!

I will say no more. Bind yourselves in the sweet bond of charity; in this you will show yourselves to be daughters, not in anything else. Draw your strength from Christ sweet Jesus and then strengthen all the others (lacuna in mss.) We shall return as soon as we can, as it pleases the divine Goodness. Abide in the sweet and holy love of God. Sweet Jesus. Jesus, Love.

---

[1]   Two more of Catherine's many devoted female disciples who were also members of the Order of Penance.

[2a]   *Cecca* – Francesca Gori, see letter 2, note 8.

[2b]   Ital. *la nonna* – Catherine's mother (see letter 25), who was known as 'Gradma' because Catherine herself was *mamma* to her disciples (see letter 20, note 8).

[2c]   *Montepulciano*, a monastery of Dominican nuns not far from Siena; see letter 1, note 8; letter 9, note 1 and letter 55, introductory note.

[3a]   *Fra Bartolomeo* Dominici OP, see letters 2 and 7.

[3b]   *Fra Matteo* Tolomei OP, whose family was at loggerheads with the Salimbeni. His mother tried in vain to force Catherine to send her son back to Siena (see Tommaseo 120).

[4a]   *Alessa* Saraceni, see letters 1, 2, 7 & 33.

[4b]   *Monna Bruna*, probably a *Mantellata*.

[4c]   *Countess* – probably Contessa Bianchina, widow of Giovanni Salimbeni and mistress of *Monte Giovi*.

[4d]   *Isa*, her daughter.

[4d]   *Monte Giovi*, a castle on Monte Amiata, about 30 miles from Siena, owned by the Salimbeni family. (Note: the phrase '18 miles from Montepulciano' may have been interpolated by one of the early editors).

[5a]   *Fra Raimondo* of Capua OP; see letter 9, note 1, and passim.

[5b]   *Fra Tommaso* della Fonte OP; see letter 1.

[5c] *Monna Tomma*, probably another *Mantellata*, not elsewhere mentioned.

[5d] *Lisa*, Catherine's sister-in-law; see letter 2, note 8 and letter 55, note 1.

[6a] One of Catherine's favourite metaphors for saving souls (see letter 11, note 3) is here made playfully explicit.

[6b] The phrase 'incarnate devils' reflects Catherine's first-hand experience of the evil ways of many of the inhabitants of the Val d'Orcia and is endorsed by the evidence given by Fra Tommaso Caffarini OP at her Canonization Process. Speaking of this apostolic expedition, he said: 'I was aware of the many sinners she brought to repentance, including some who had not been to confession for forty years.' (Translated from text as given in Papàsogli, p. 250, note 4).

[7]  Luke 10:7.

[8]  Cf. I Cor. 3:2 and Hebrews 5:13.

## LETTER 37  (Tommaseo 121; Gigli 201).

*To:*   *The lord Defenders and 'Captain of the People' of the Republic of Siena.*

*Date:*  August/October 1377.[1]

Dear Lords in Christ sweet Jesus,

I, Catherine, servant and slave of the servants of Jesus Christ, write to you in his precious blood, desiring to see you true lords with manly hearts – that is, lording it over your own sensual nature with true solid virtue by following our Creator. Otherwise you could not justly hold the temporal lordship God has graciously entrusted to you. It is fitting that a man who is to be lord and governor over others should first be so over himself. Could a blind man see to lead others?[2] Can one dead man bury another?[3] One invalid care for another? Or one pauper finance another? No indeed.

Truly, my dear lords, if a man is blind and has clouded the eye of his understanding with mortal sin, he knows neither himself nor God, so he will hardly be able to see or correct faults in his subjects. And even if he does correct them, he will do so with the darkness and imperfection that are in himself. Many times I have seen, and still see, a lack of knowledge lead to non-existent faults being punished, while evil and wicked deeds deserving of a thousand deaths go unpunished. Lack of light obscures the truth and conjures up calumny where there is none; it makes men suspicious of the very people they can most rely on and trust (God's servants, that is, who are all the time giving birth to them with tears and sweat, and with holy and unceasing prayers, exposing themselves to danger, pain and torment of all kinds for God's honour and for their own and the whole world's salvation), yet ready to trust men whose root is self-love and who sway with every wind. And all through lack of light and the darkness of sin. So light is needed.

I say [too] that one dead man cannot bury another;[4] that is, that a man who is dead to grace has neither the urge nor the strength to bury the corpse that is his neighbour's defect, for he feels he is himself as dead as the other, and so neither desires nor knows how to correct him. Since he is unconcerned about his own illness, he remains unconcerned when he sees one of his subjects ill. Yet the illness of mortal sin is so serious as to be incurable unless a man sets about curing himself. [Moreover], falling into mortal sin at once makes a man a pauper for, by not following in the footsteps of Christ crucified, he loses the riches of true solid virtue and so is unable to help when another pauper is deprived, as I said, of the riches of divine grace. Because of the darkness he has lost the light, and so does not see where the fault is. Hence injustice is done, not justice. His illness robs a man of the vigour of true and holy desire for God's honour and his neighbour's salvation – and he gets steadily worse unless he has recourse to the doctor, Christ crucified, and spews the filthy poison out of his mouth in a good confession.[5] If he does this, he receives both life and health, but if not

it is death for him – and one dead man cannot bury
another, as I said. And can there be any greater poverty
than to be deprived of the light of health and faith? I
know of nothing worse. Hence such men are quite
unsuited to govern others, for they do not govern themselves.

So you do require these things, and that is why I said
that I longed to see you truly lords. But thinking as I do
that there is no true lordship where a man is not first lord
of himself by making his reason lord over his sensual
nature, therefore I am pointing out to you all the difficulties encountered by those who let their own wretchedness
lord it over them, instead of the other way round; lest you
fall into this trap. Open, do open the eye of your understanding! Don't be so blinded by such misplaced fear. Put
your faith and trust in the servants of God and not in the
devil's wicked minions who, to cover up their own iniquity, make you see things that are not there.

Avoid setting the servants of God against you, for it
would seem that God will suffer everything else more
readily that the exposing of his servants to injury, scandal
and defamation. What you do to them you do to Christ:
let that be your warning! Never allow either yourselves or
others to defame Christ's servants, my very dear brothers
and lords, but cut out the tongue of the defamer by a
reprimand and by paying no heed to the talebearer. By so
doing you will practise virtue and eliminate many scan-
dals, though seemingly our sins make us as yet undeserv-
ing of so much. Indeed, the opposite seems to be happening: evil men are given a hearing and good men despised.
For I have heard that suspicion has been sown in your
minds, either by the archpriest of Montalcino or by
someone else, to cover up his own malice towards the
abbot of Sant'Antimo,[6] who is the greatest and most perfect servant of God these parts have known for a very
long time. If you had even a glimmer of light, not only
would you not be suspecting him, but you would hold
him in due reverence. I beg you therefore, for the sake of

Christ crucified, not to stand in his way but to assist him by giving him the help he needs. Day in day out you complain that priests and other clerics go uncorrected, yet now when you find some willing to correct them, you stand in their way and complain about *them*!

I have been told – though I don't know how true this is – that you have also been hearing complaints and made suspicious about my coming here with my family.[7] Certainly, if you had as much value in your own eyes as you have in mine and theirs, you and all the other citizens would not yield so easily to such thoughts and feelings, but would stop your ears against them. I and the others have unceasingly sought, and seek, your salvation in soul and body, shirking no toil, offering sweet and loving desires to God, with copious tears and sighs, in order to shield you all from the divine judgement we all deserve for our sins. I myself am not so virtuous as to be able to do anything except imperfectly, but the others can, for they are perfect and are concerned only for God's honour and the salvation of souls. And no ingratitude or stupidity on the part of my fellow citizens will keep us from striving until death for your salvation. We will learn how from that sweet Paul who said: 'The world reviles us and we bless; it persecutes and casts us out, but we endure patiently'.[8] We shall do this too, making his rule ours. By the truth we shall be set free.[9] I love you more than you love yourselves, and am as concerned for your peace and protection as you are. So do not believe that I or any member of my family[7] is doing anything else. We have been set to sow the word of God and to reap the fruit of souls. Each one must practise his own trade, and God has put us at this one, so we must practise it and not bury our talent[10] – for which we would deserve a severe rebuke – but work away always, everywhere, and in everyone. God is no acceptor of places or of creatures,[11] but of true and holy desires. With this, then, we must work.

I see the devil grieving over the loss that, through God's goodness, he has suffered and will suffer through

our coming here. I came only to eat and relish souls, and
to snatch them from the hands of demons. I long to give
my life for this, or a thousand if I had them. And to this
end I shall move on or stay put as the Holy Spirit makes
me. Pietro[12] will inform you by word of mouth of the
main reason why I came and why I am still here. I will say
no more.

Bathe yourselves in the blood of Christ crucified, if you
wish for life. Otherwise we shall fall into everlasting
death. Do not be annoyed at having to read and listen, but
bear it all patiently, for my sorrow and my love produce a
torrent of words: love for your salvation, that is, and
sorrow at our waywardness. May God in his divine
judgement not deprive us of the light to know the truth. I
really will say no more!

Abide in the sweet and holy love of God. Sweet Jesus.
Jesus, Love.

---

[1]   See Fawtier, pp. 188 & 248, and also note 6 below.

[2]   Luke 6:39.

[3]   Cf. Matthew 8:22.

[4]   Catherine ingeniously adapts the Mt. 8:22 text to make a
rather different point.

[5]   Cf. Revelation 3:16.

[6]   According to the mss., Catherine wrote this letter from the
Williamite Abbey of Sant'Antimo – in the Val d'Orcia – where
her great frind and counsellor Giovanni di Gano of Orvieto (see
letter 35) was abbot. Little more is known of the background to
the incident she refers to, though Gardner (p.213) states that
the archpriest was claiming jurisdiction over the abbot and so,
presumably, attempting to thwart the latter's efforts at reform.

[7]   See letter 20, note 8.

[8]   I Cor. 4:12–13.

[9]   John 8:32.

[10]   Mt. 25:25.

[11]   Cf. Acts 10:34, A.V. & Douai.

[12]   *Pietro* Ventura, another of Catherine's 'inner circle' of early
and devoted disciples; see Gardner p.114 and letters 12 (note 5)
and 49.

LETTER 38 (Tommaseo 226; Gigli 89).

*To:* *Fra Raimondo of Capua, OP, in Rome.*[1]
Date: 14 April, 1378, from Florence.[1]

To you, beloved father and son in Christ Jesus, given to me by that sweet mother Mary,[2] I, Catherine, servant and slave of the servants of Jesus Christ, write to you in his precious blood, desiring to see you[3] true sons and proclaimers of the incarnate Word, God's Son, not only in word but also in deed, learning how from the Master of Truth who first practised virtue and then preached it. In this way you will bear fruit and be the conduit God uses to channel his grace into the hearts of your hearers.

I tell you, my children, we cannot lead good lives and hunger for God's honour and the salvation of souls, or even learn how, unless we attend the school of the Word, of the Lamb who was slain and abandoned on the cross, for only there is the true doctrine to be found, as he said: 'I am the Way, the Truth and the Life' – and no one can go to the Father except through him.[4]

So open your eye of knowledge and let it see; unstop your ears and hear his teaching. See yourselves, for in him you find yourselves and in yourselves you find him. That is, in him you find yourselves in that, by grace and not as your due,[5] he creates you in his image and likeness; and in yourselves you find the measureless goodness of God, who became like us when he united the divine nature with ours. Oh, let our hearts burst and split open to see such flaming, burning love: God grafted into man and man into God! O inestimable Love! However highly man prized it, he could never do so enough.[6] So make for this sweet school, children, for this great love will lead you and be your life.

I say, then: Open your ears to hear his doctrine, the doctrine of voluntary poverty, patience in the face of insult, returning good to those who do us evil; being little, humble, trodden underfoot and abandoned by the world; enduring mockery, torments, insults, treachery, detraction, back-biting, tribulation and persecution from the world, from devils visible and invisible, and from one's own stinking flesh, that rebel ever seeking to rebel against its Creator and war against the spirit.[7]

Such is his doctrine: to endure with patience and to fight back with the weapon of hatred and love. O sweet and wholesome doctrine, the treasure he chose for himself and left to his disciples as the greatest riches he could leave them. For if divine Goodness had seen that dainties and delights, pleasures and self-love, vanity and fickleness of heart, were good things, he would have chosen them for himself. But because the Wisdom of the Word incarnate saw and knew this other to be the better part,[8] he immediately loved it and, in his love, clothed himself with it, as his servants and children do when they follow in their Father's footsteps.

I want no such ignorance to befall you, nor any drawing back from this sweet and delightful way, this wholesome school. Rather, like true children, [I want you] to wrap yourselves so tightly in this garment as to make it a second skin that can never be stripped from you until you are stripped of life itself, when we shall lay aside our garment of suffering and remain clothed in the garment of delight,[9] eating the fruit of our toil at the table of the Lamb.

The sweet herald Paul did just this, for he put on Christ crucified and was stripped of his joy in the divine Essence.[10] He puts on Christ the man, that is, the sufferings and opprobrium of Christ crucified; indeed he seeks to glory in nothing else, saying: 'Far be it from me to glory in anything but the cross of Christ crucified'.[11] And in this the apostle found such joy that, as he himself once told his servant[12] 'Dearest child, I fastened that joy so tightly with the thong of love and desire that I was never stripped of it nor was it even loosened until life itself was taken from me.' Sweet Paul certainly seemed to have studied this doctrine. He was so thoroughly versed in it that he took to eating and relishing souls. Like a sponge that absorbs water, so he, as he travels the way of opprobrium, absorbs the inestimable charity and goodness whereby God so supremely loves his creatures. He sees that [Christ's] will is this: to will our sanctification;[13] that is, to will the eternal Father's honour and our salvation; and so he gave himself up to death in order to accomplish this sanctification in you. Paul grasps and understands this doctrine. Having understood it, he devotes himself at once to honouring God and toiling for his neighbour. He proclaims the truth manfully, not held back by negligence, but eagerly, for he has become a vessel of love,[14] filled with fire, to carry and to preach the word of God.

And this my soul desires, for with intense and ardent desire I have desired to keep [this] Pasch with you;[15] that is, to see my desire fulfilled and consummated. What bliss for my soul when I see you[16] above all others set and firmly established in your Object, Christ crucified [and] being fed and nourished by the food of the soul. For when a soul sees not self for self's sake, but self for God and God for God, inasmuch as he is supreme eternal Goodness, all-worthy of our love – contemplating in him the effect of his fiery and consummate love – it finds in him the image of his creature, and in itself, that image, it finds him. That is, the love a man sees that God has for him, he, in turn, extends to all creatures, and so at once feels compelled to love his neighbour as himself, for he sees how supremely he himself is loved by God when he beholds himself in the wellspring of the sea of the divine Essence. He is then moved to love self in God and God in self, like a man who, on looking into the water, sees his image there and seeing himself, loves and delights in himself. If he is wise, he will be moved to love the water rather than himself, for had he not first seen himself, he could not have loved or been delighted by himself; nor removed the smudge on his face revealed to him in the well.

Think of it like this, my dearest sons: we see neither our dignity nor the defects that mar the beauty of our soul unless we go and look at ourselves in the still sea of the divine Essence wherein we are portrayed; for from it we came when God's Wisdom created us to his image and likeness. Therein we find the grafting of the Word into our humanity. We find and see and savour the furnace of his Charity,[17] which was the instrument that gave us to ourselves[18] and then 'oned' the Word into us and us into the Word when he assumed our human nature. This was the powerful bond that kept [him] nailed and fastened to the cross, and we shall see all this when we see ourselves in God's goodness. In no other way shall we savour him in the life that never ends, nor shall we see him face to face, unless we first savour him by burning love and desire in this life, in the way I have said.

However, we cannot show our love for him directly by being of any use to him, for he does not need our good deeds; but we can and ought to show it through our brothers, by seeking in them the glory and praise of God's name. No more negligence, then, no more torpid ignorance! Rather, with your hearts full of fiery courage, urge on your sweet and loving desires to set about giving honour to God and tireless service to men, never taking your eyes off our one Object, Christ crucified.[19] Only think! He is the wall you must lean on in order to see your reflection in the water! Run, run up to it and lock yourselves into the wounds of Christ crucified. Rejoice, rejoice and exult for spring will soon be bringing her fragrant flowers. And don't be surprised if you see the opposite coming about; rather, be all the surer on that account.

Alas, alas, my wretched soul! Would that I might never rest until I see a knife coming to pierce my throat for the honour of God, to pour out my blood into the mystical body of holy Church! Alas, alas, I am dying and cannot die. I will say no more. Forgive my ignorance, father.[20] And may your own heart burst and melt in the heat of such Love.

I say nothing of the things God has done and is doing, as no tongue or pen would be equal to it.[21] You wrote urging me to rejoice and exult, and sent me news to that end that filled me with great delight; but already, the day after I was separated from you, the sweet First Truth, the eternal Bridegroom, desiring to treat me as a father his daughter or a bridegroom his bride, when he cannot bear her to be in distress but finds new ways of giving her joy, so did the Word, supreme eternal high Deity, treat me – think of it, father! – giving me so much joy that the very limbs of my body seemed as wax melting in the fire. My soul found itself abiding in three places at once. In one I was with devils, through knowledge of myself, and through the many battles, torments and threats they inflicted on me, for they never ceased knocking at the door of my conscience. Then I arose with hatred, which I took with me to hell,[22] desiring to make my confession to you. But divine Goodness gave me more that I asked, for when I begged for you, he gave me himself and himself gave me absolution and the remission of my own sins and yours, going once again over lessons he had given me in the past, and overshadowing me with an immense fire of love and so great a sense of security and purity of mind that the tongue is quite unable to describe it. And to complete my consolation he gave me Christ's dwellings on earth[23] for I seemed to be journeying along a road, as it seemed, a road from the most high eternal Trinity, where one was bathed in indescribable light and knowledge in the goodness of God. And [while he] revealed things to come in the future, we were moving among and conversing [both] with the truly blessed and with Christ's little family on earth. I saw new tidings of great joy and peace approaching and heard the voice of the sweet First Truth saying: 'My daughter, I do not despise true and holy desires; indeed, I fulfil them. Be consoled, then, and be a good instrument, manfully proclaiming the truth, for I shall always be with you.' I seemed to sense the exaltation of our archbishop, so that when I heard your description of what had happened, joy upon joy swept over me.[24]

My dear sweet son, I make my obstinate and hardened heart known to you so that you may press for vengeance and justice on me that I do not burst and split asunder in the heat that comes from such burning Love. Ah! And in some wonderful way those three places enhanced rather than interfered with one another. As salt seasons oil and gives the finishing touch to a dish, so the chatter of the demons, producing humility and [self]-hatred, and the hunger and converse of holy Church, producing love and desire, together caused me to enter into and to taste, along with the truly blessed, the life that never ends. I will say no more. I tell you, I am bursting and yet cannot burst.

I have news for you of my father, Fra Tommaso, who by God's grace has conquered the devil with virtue.[25] He is a completely changed man, his heart now resting in great affection and love. I beg you to write to him sometimes and to open your heart to him. Celebrate the fact that my lost children have been found and restored to the flock, and have left the darkness. No one can now urge me to do anything that I don't already want to do.

I, Catherine, your unworthy daughter, ask for your blessing. I recommend all my sons and daughters to you that you may take good care of them, lest the infernal wolf snatch any of them from me. I think Neri[26] will be joining you, as I feel it is advisable to send him to Court. Tell him what steps need to be taken to secure peace with these putrid members who have rebelled against holy Church, for I see no sweeter means of securing peace in body and soul. [I know] you will act promptly in this as in whatever else is needed, aiming always at God's honour and that alone. Having said this, though, do whatever God prompts you to do and what seems best to you, whether to send him or not.

Abide in the sweet and holy love of God. Sweet Jesus. Jesus, Love.

¹ The accuracy of these details depends on correctly identifying the circumstances in which the letter was written. Cf. Fawtier, pp.195–197, and notes 15, 24 and 26 below.

² See letter 22, note 6.

³ The use of the plural form of address in the first half of the letter suggests that Catherine had others in mind besides Fra Raimondo – perhaps some or all of the community at the Minerva in Rome of which he was prior.

⁴ John 14:16.

⁵ Romans 4:4–5.

⁶ *or* If man had prized it, it would have been enough.

⁷ Cf. Romans 7:21–23.

⁸ Cf. Luke 10:42.

⁹ Cf. II Cor. 5:4.

¹⁰ The reference is to Paul's description of 'being carried up to the third heaven' (cf. II Cor. 12:1–10), from which it is clear that despite his joy in that vision, Paul was happy to do without its continuance; like Christ, to endure suffering, weakness and humiliation, and so to be 'stripped of joy in the divine Essence'.

¹¹ Galatians 6:14.

¹² Catherine herself, in a vision.

¹³ I Thessalonians 4:3.

¹⁴ Cf. letter 2, note 4.

¹⁵ Ital. *fare pasqua*, which in Catherine's day had the meaning of celebrating any feast, not necessarily Easter. However, the gospel read at Mass on the Wednesday in Holy Week included the Luke 22:15 text: 'With desire I have desired to eat this Pasch with you before I suffer', etc., which Catherine uses so often and here, clearly, with full emphasis (cf. Fawtier, p. 198).

¹⁶ The pronoun here is still plural (*voi*) but the paragraph is addressed to Raimondo alone; it is the *voi* of respect. In the next two paragraphs, Catherine again addresses her 'sons', after which her words are again for Raimondo alone.

¹⁷ Charity is here personified as the Holy Spirit.

¹⁸ i.e. gave us free-will; cf. letter 6, p.65.

¹⁹ Cf. Hebrews 12:2; Galatians 3:1.

²⁰ The remainder of the letter is addressed to Raimondo alone.

²¹ Cf. I Cor. 2:9.

²² i.e. I reflected on the pains of hell which such sins would incur were I to commit them (Papàsogli, p.280).

²³ Catherine seems to mean the Church in general, and perhaps also the hearts of faithful Christians.

²⁴   It is not easy to identify this 'archbishop'. One possibility is the theory outlined by Fawtier, p.197 (following a hint given by Gigli, II, pp 570–71, note H), namely that the reference could be to Bartolomeo Prignano, Archbishop of Bari. If so, 'what had happened' was that he was elected Pope on 8 April 1378 and crowned in St Peter's on Easter Sunday, 10 days later. News of the election reached Florence on 12 April. (Cf. also suggested date for this letter, and notes 1 and 15).

²⁵   *Fra Tommaso* della Fonte OP; see letters 1, 36 and 50. The reference is obscure and may be at least half teasing.

²⁶   *Neri* Pagliaresi, see letter 3, note 5b. According to Fawtier's hypothesis, Catherine wanted to send her trusted messenger to the papal court in order to assess prospects for peace with Florence under the new pontificate.

LETTER 39   (Tommaseo 292; Gigli 129).

*To:*   *Bro. William of Flete,*¹ *Messer Matteo di Cenni, Fra Santi, and other disciples, in Siena.*²

*Date:*   ? April/May 1378, from Florence.

Beloved sons in Christ sweet Jesus,

I, Catherine, servant and slave of the servants of Jesus Christ, write to you in his precious blood, desiring to see you bound in the bond of charity, for it is clear to me that without this bond we cannot please God, since it is the sweet sign by which to recognize the servants and children of Christ.³

But remember, my sons, that this bond needs to be pure and unstained by self-love. So, if you love your Creator, love him and serve him because he is supreme and eternal Goodness and worthy of being loved, and not out of self-interest, for that would be a mercenary love, like a miser who loves money because of his avarice. So let your love of others be pure. Love, oh love one another, for each is neighbour to the other. But beware! If your love were based only on the self-interest and pleasure of each, it would not last but fade away, leaving your soul empty. A love that is rooted in God must be such that the other is loved in view of virtue[4] and because he is a creature made in God's image; then, even if the pleasure or advantage I was deriving from the one I love comes to an end, the love, if rooted in God, does not, because one is loving the other for virtue's sake and God's honour, and not out of self-interest. I tell you, when the love is God-centred, even if the other's virtue fails, the love does not. Love for the non-existent virtue is missing, but not love for the person as God's creature, and his member, bound into the mystical body of holy Church. Indeed, one who loves thus will develop a great and true compassion, and give birth to the other by desire, in God's sweet presence, with sighs, tears and unceasing prayer.

This was the love Christ left to his disciples: a love that never fails or fades; that endures injury with patience; that does not grumble or take offence, for the other is loved, not for his own sake, but for God's.[5] This love neither judges nor wishes to judge the will of men, but the will of the Creator who seeks and desires only our sanctification,[6] and so it delights at whatever God may allow, in whatever way, for it seeks only the Creator's honour and the neighbour's salvation. We can truly say that such people are bound in the bond of charity by the very bond that nailed the God-Man fast to the wood of the sweet and most holy cross.

But remember, children: you will never attain this perfect union unless you make Christ crucified your goal and follow in his footsteps. You will find this love in him, for he loved you as a free gift and not as your due.[7] And because he loved you freely, he never let his love go slack on account of our ingratitude, our ignorance, our vanity or our pride but persisted in it even to the shameful death on the cross that destroyed our death and gave us life. Let you, now, do the same. Learn, oh learn from him. Love, love one another with a pure and holy love in Christ sweet Jesus. I say no more, because soon I hope, when it pleases the divine Goodness, to see you again.

Abide in the sweet and holy love of God. Sweet Jesus. Jesus, Love.

---

[1]   See letter 10.

[2]   a. *Matteo* di Cenni, having been converted from a dissolute youth by the influence of William of Flete, devoted himself to a life of practical charity. As rector of the *Misericordia* Hospital, he had every opportunity to know and admire Catherine's own devotion to the sick and suffering, especially when the plague raged in Siena in 1374.

b. *Fra Santi* had already been a hermit for many years when he became Catherine's disciple. Saying that he found more quiet and peace of mind and made more progress in virtue from being in her company and listening to her than ever he had in the solitude of his cell, he gave up his habitual way of life to be with her wherever she went. (Raymond pp. 310–311).

[3]   Cf. John 13:35.

[4]   Cf. St Thomas, *Summa theol*. 2a 2ae 23,1; *Commentary on Nic. Ethics of Aristotle*, VIII, lect. 1–3.

[5]   Cf. I Corinthians 13:4–7.

[6]   I Thess. 4:3.

[7]   Romans 4:4–5.

## LETTER 40   (Tommaseo 293; Gigli 26).

*To:    Cardinal Pedro de Luna of Aragon.*[1]

*Date:*   Latter half of May 1378, while Catherine was in Florence and the Cardinal in Rome. (Note: The early mss. record that Catherine dictated the letter in a trance).

My very dear father in Christ sweet Jesus,

I, Catherine, servant and slave of the servants of Jesus Christ, write to you in his precious blood, desiring to see you set as a solid pillar in the garden of holy Church and stripped of the self-love that weakens every rational creature; to see nothing living in you but true love, embedded in the living Rock, Christ sweet Jesus, and always following his footsteps. Such a love makes the soul strong by consuming the one thing that weakens it, so that not only is the soul itself made strong but it frequently passes this strength on to others. You yourself, and those in a similar position, strengthen others in a special way when you set before your own subjects and other layfolk the example of holy and upright lives combined with doctrine embedded in truth. For sound teaching and good living make it clear that one has been stripped of one's weakness and made strong against man's three principal enemies: against the devil and his malice; against the world, by not following after its vanities but rather rejecting the status and delights it offers; and against his own frail flesh. Such a man has indeed trodden down his flesh with the feet of desire and the light of reason – not indulging it with bodily pleasure and choice food but rather steeping it[2] in penances, fasting, vigils, and humble and unceasing prayer. In this way that servant girl, frail flesh, is not given the upper hand but rather reason; to which we must give it if the soul is to be the mistress, as it should be, and sensuality the servant. Great is that man's shame and discomfiture who, from being his own master, free with so great a freedom that no one can rob him of the city of his soul, becomes the wretched servant and slave of these three enemies. They turn him back into nothing, depriving him of the being that is grace. Hence, whoever has been made strong is free, for he is out of his enemies' grip, and has furnished the city of his soul with a company of true solid virtues. How easily such men, with their hunger and zeal for God's honour and the salvation of souls, impart strength to others, inspiring them, by their own good lives, to practise virtue and so to free themselves of self-love, which is what makes a man weak, as I said. And that is why I said that one who has himself been made strong has often strengthened his neighbour too.

So I want you, my very dear father, to be a pillar, firm, solid and never changing whatever the world may choose to do to us, or even if persecution should come from among your own clerical body, the mystical body of holy Church.[3] Unless you were first stripped of self-love, you would undoubtedly weaken and in your weakness collapse;[4] which is why my soul longs to see you so strongly set up that not only will you not collapse yourself, whatever happens, but rather brace yourself to help and support others who are weak. Give, oh give, Christ's blood to your soul, so that, on fire with love, it will rush into battle and fight like a man. Let your memory be filled with this precious Blood; let your understanding see and comprehend the wisdom of the Word, God's only-begotten Son, and with what wisdom he overcame, by his blood, our own malice and the malice of the age-old demon whom he caught with the hook of our humanity. And let your will, as if inebriated with the blood of Christ wherein it has found the abyss of his charity, make all haste to love, loving him with heart, soul, and strength until death, with no thought for self but only for Christ crucified; [run, too,] to climb up to the table of the cross, and there partake of the food of souls for the honour of God by enduring with true patience until death, bringing our neighbour's faults before God with great compassion and accepting patiently any injury done to ourselves. Let us do this, dearest father, for now is the time.

I seem to have heard of the beginning of discord there between Christ-on-earth and his disciples.[5] This grieves me unbearably through the dread I have of heresy,[6] which I greatly fear may come about on account of my sins. And so I beg you, by that glorious and precious Blood that was shed with such burning love, never to turn away either from virtue or your Head; and I plead with you to plead persistently with Christ-on-earth to conclude this peace quickly[7] (to have to fight inside as well as outside would be too much) so that he can concentrate on barring any way in which this evil might arise. Tell him to provide himself with good pillars, now that he will be creating new cardinals;[8] let them be manly men, men who do not fear death but are equipping themselves with virtue in order to stand firm till death for the love of truth and the reform of holy Church; and to give their lives, if necessary, for the honour of God. Alas, alas, waste no time; don't put off applying the remedy until the rock falls on our heads. Alas for my soul's misfortune! Any other evil, whether war, dishonour or other tribulation, would seem to us less than straw or a shadow compared with this. Believe me, I tremble at the mere thought of it, especially after hearing from a certain person[9] who was shown in her reason how grave and dangerous [the situation] was, so much so that the war itself – think of it – seemed to her as nothing in comparison. I tell you, her heart and her life seemed to have parted from her body through grief, whereupon she called out and pleaded with Mercy to remedy so great an evil, and longed for her body to spurt blood under the impetus of her holy and burning desire, for she felt that satisfaction could not be made by sweating mere water, and that is why she wanted to sweat blood. Willingly would she have willed her body to be drained of blood.

Dearest father, I think it better for me to be silent than to talk about these things, but I beseech you in every way I know and can to beseech Christ-on-earth and the others to conclude this peace quickly and to employ whatever ways and means are appropriate to God's honour and the reform of holy Church, and to the elimination of this scandal. And if it should come nonetheless, may you be strengthened in virtue so that with the help of others of like virtue the darkness may be resisted and driven out, and light may prevail. I have no doubt at all that God will accomplish this in his infinite mercy, and will sweep the darkness and stench away from his Bride so that, in due time, whenever it shall please the measureless and infinite goodness and charity of God, only the perfume and light remain. In this thought I take comfort and my soul is uplifted; otherwise I believe I would die in anguish. So be a man for me, and a pillar that never gives way, while I pray and get others to pray to God to make you just that. I will say no more.

Abide in the sweet and holy love of God. Forgive my presumption, father, in presuming to say so much, but let love and sorrow excuse me before you. Sweet Jesus. Jesus, Love.

---

[1]   This lone Spanish cardinal had been a key figure in the election of Urban VI, as he was, later, in the events leading up to the election of the first anti-pope and the start of the Great Schism.

[2]   Ital. *macerare*, to macerate, which has as its primary meaning 'to soften hemp or other fibres by steeping', a connotation which would have been very familiar to a dyer's daughter and one which Catherine, with her delight in word play, would hardly have been able to resist.

[3]   Cf. Dialogue, p.285 for Catherine's distinction between the 'mystical' and 'general' body of the Church.

[4]   This intuition was borne out by events. The Cardinal's extreme scrupulosity and hesitancy in making decisions coupled with his somewhat legalistic mentality – he had been a professor of canon law before becoming a cardinal – would seem to have contributed to his desertion of Urban. See G.G. Meersseman, 'Spirituali romani, amici di Caterina da Siena', in *Ordo Fraternitatis. Confraternite e pietà dei laici nel medioevo*, Rome, 1977, pp. 535–573; and note 5 below.

[5]   Urban VI and his cardinals. The newly-elected Pope's 'sincere and uncompromising hatred of the corruption of the Curia' (Gardner) and determination to reform it, together with his extremely tactless vehemence of expression and demeanour quickly alienated even the most loyal of the cardinals who, by early May, were already quietly withdrawing from Rome and soon afterwards began plotting Urban's overthrow. Pedro de Luna did not join them until the end of June, apparently in the hope of winning them over to Urban; instead he was himself so completely won over to the anti-Urbanist cause as eventually to accept election as the anti-pope Benedict XIII. See Gardner, pp. 272–74, and Meersseman, op. cit. pp. 564–5, who highlights the fact that Fra Raimondo and others of Catherine's friends and disciples were on intimate terms with the Cardinal, on

whom they pinned most of their hopes.
6   the impending schism.
7   with Florence and her allies.
8   It was customary for a recently-elected pope to create a
number of new cardinals.
9   Herself.


## LETTER 41   (Tommaseo 302; Gigli 16).

*To:*   **Urban VI**

*Date:*   Late June/early July 1378, from Florence.[1]

Most holy and sweetest father in Christ sweet
Jesus,
I, Catherine, servant and slave of the servants of Jesus
Christ, write to you in his precious blood, desiring to see
you really shepherd and ruler of your sheep, whom it is
your task to nourish with the blood of Christ crucified. So
your Holiness must take great care to see to whom it is
entrusted and through whose agency. I mean, most holy
Father, that when shepherds are being appointed to the
garden of holy Church, let them be men who seek God
and not high office; equally, let whoever presents a candidate for office do so straightforwardly, not in an
underhand way.
O most holy Father, please be patient when these
things are said to you. They are only said for the sake of
God's honour and your own salvation, as any son should
do who loves and cares for his father and cannot bear
anything to happen that would bring shame or injury
upon him. In his concern, he is always on the alert,
realizing that though his father bears responsibility for
the whole family, he has only one pair of eyes, so that,
unless his legitimate children keep an eye on their
father's honour and interests, he would often be
deceived.

And so it is, most holy Father. Your Holiness is lord and father of the whole body of Christians and we are all under your wings.[2] As to authority, you can do all things, but as to seeing, you are only one. Hence your children must do the seeing, and endeavour in simplicity of heart and free from servile fear to secure whatever is to God's honour, and to the salvation and honour of yourself and of the sheep under your crook. I know your Holiness greatly desires to have helpers to help you, but you must be patient and listen!

I am sure that two things are giving you pain and affecting your state of mind, and I don't wonder at it. The first is that when you hear of sins being committed, you are grieved that God is offended, for this offence – and the sins – upset you and you feel stung at heart. There is no question of being patiently patient in this, or of not grieving that God is offended. That would make us seem to approve these very vices. The other thing that might pain you would be when one of your sons comes to you to tell you something that he feels is an offence against God, harmful to souls and showing little respect for your Holiness, but does so in a foolish way, refusing on grounds of conscience, in your very presence, to tell you the truth pure and simple, as it is; whereas nothing should be kept secret or hidden from you.

I beg you, holy Father, not to be upset by the pain you feel when your foolish son offends in this way. Simply reprimand him for his foolishness. I say this because, according to what I have been told by *Maestro* Giovanni,[3] Fra Bartolommeo[4] grieved you by his over-scrupulosity and made you angry. Both he and I are much distressed on this account, for he feels he has offended your Holiness. I beg you, for the love of Christ crucified, to inflict on me every pain he has caused you. I am prepared for whatever discipline or correction your Holiness pleases. I believe my own sins were the cause of his foolish behaviour, so I must accept the penalty. He himself is most anxious to acknowledge his fault to you, wherever it

may please your Holiness for him to come to you. Please
bear patiently with his faults, and with mine. Bathe yourself in the blood of Christ crucified and draw strength
from the sweet fire of his charity. Pardon my presumption.

I humbly ask your blessing. I thank the divine Goodness and your Holiness for the great grace you accorded
to me on St John's Day.[5]

Abide in the sweet and holy love of God. Sweet Jesus.
Jesus, Love.

---

[1]   See Fawtier, pp. 151–2.
[2]   Cf. Matthew 23:37, Psalm 91:4 and parallels.
[3]   *'Master' Giovanni* Tantucci; see letter 21, note 1a.
[4]   *Fra Bartolomeo* Dominici OP; see letter 2.
[5]   24 June, Feast of St John the Baptist, principal patron of
Florence. The 'grace' may have been an indulgence, which
would have been especially important to Catherine in a city still
bound by the papal interdict, where she was unable to receive
the sacraments.

LETTER 42   (Tommaseo 193; Gigli 224).

*To:*   *Messer Lorenzo del Pino, a learned and influential
lawyer in Bologna.*

*Date:*  Not known.[1]

Dearest brother and son in Christ sweet Jesus,
I, Catherine, servant and slave of the servants of Jesus
Christ, write to you in his precious blood, desiring to see
you loving and following truth and despising falsehood.
But one can neither have nor love this truth without first
knowing it. Who is Truth?[2] God is supreme and eternal
truth. In whom shall we know it? In Christ sweet Jesus
who by his blood reveals to us the eternal Father's truth as

regards ourselves; namely that he created us in his image and likeness in order to give us eternal life and enable us to share in and enjoy his own Goodness. But as man's sin kept this truth from being fulfilled, God gave us the Word, his Son, imposing on him, under obedience, the task of restoring man to grace through much suffering; he was to purge man's sin in his own person and show the truth of God in his blood. Thus man, through the ineffable love that he finds God showing him in and by Christ's blood, perceives that God seeks and wills only our sanctification.[3] For this end we were created, and whatever God gives or allows to happen to us in this life is so that we may be sanctified in him. One who knows this truth never forgets it but ever loves and follows it, treading in the steps of Christ crucified. And since it was for our instruction and example that this sweet and loving Word despised the world and all its delights and chose to endure hunger and thirst, shame and reproach even to the shameful death on the cross, for the Father's honour and our salvation; so whoever loves the truth that he has known by the light of holy faith will also follow these ways, these footsteps. Without this light, one could not know that truth, but having it, one knows it, and knowing it one loves it, and so comes to love what God loves and hate what he hates.

Here lies the difference between a man who loves the truth and one who hates it: one who hates the truth is lying in the darkness of mortal sin, hating what God loves and loving what God hates. God hates sin and inordinate indulgence in the pleasures of this world, whereas such a man loves it, feeding on the world's wretchedness and corrupting himself, whatever his position. Thus, if his position requires him to minister in some way to his neighbour, he does so only in so far as he thinks this will serve his own interests, and no further; he loves only himself. The blessed Christ gave his life for us, but this man will not part with a single word to help his neighbour that has not first been paid and more than paid for.[4] And if his neighbour is a poor man without means, he keeps him on tenterhooks before giving him the facts, and may even not do so but simply make fun of him. Where he ought to be merciful and a father to the poor, his wronging the poor makes him cruel to his own soul. The wretched man does not see that the supreme Judge will render to him only what he has received from him, for every sin is justly punished and every good deed rewarded. Christ embraced voluntary poverty and was a lover of continence, whereas the wretch who has taken to following and loving falsehood does the opposite. Instead of being content with what he has, or giving it up for love of virtue, he steals what others have. Instead of being content with the state of matrimony (in which, if he respects it as he should, he can remain with a good conscience) he plunges into every wretchedness like a wild beast on the loose, and wallows in unchastity like a pig in the mire.

But we would say: 'What will become of me who am rich and married, if these things are damning my soul?' Dearest brother, a man can save his soul and retain the life of grace in himself whatever his state [in life], but not while he is in mortal sin. Every state is pleasing to God, who is the acceptor not of particular states but of holy desires.[5] So, we may keep these things provided our will is rightly ordered concerning them, for all that God has made is good and perfect except sin, which was not made by him and so is not deserving of love. A man may keep riches and worldly position, if he wishes, without offending God or harming his soul, though to give them up would be more perfect, as to renounce rather than retain [them] is the greater perfection. And even if he chooses not to renounce them in fact, he must do so by holy desire, centring his affections not on them but on God alone, while continuing to use them for his own needs and those of his family, but as things lent him, not as his own property. By so doing he need never suffer pain on account of any created thing, for what is lightly loved is lightly lost. We see, then, that by their love of falsehood the servants of this world endure much pain and excruciating torment to the very end of their lives. And why? On account of the disordered love they show for themselves and created things by loving them apart from God – for divine Goodness has ordained that all such inordinate affection be insufferable even to itself.

Such a man always puts his faith in falsehood because there is no knowledge of truth in him. He fancies he can hold onto the world, live in luxury, be god of his own body and make a god of anything else he loves in a disordered way,[6] whereas he must let them all go. For we see him let them go at death – or else God allows them to be taken from him even sooner! We see it happening every day: one moment a man is rich, the next he is poor; today he goes up in the world, tomorrow he comes down; now he is well, now ill. We can rely on nothing, for all things are either whisked away from us just when we thought we had grasped them, or we are whisked away from them by death.

You see, then, that all things pass. This being so, we must be moderate and enlightened in our possession of them, and love them only as we ought. Thus to possess things is to possess them not sinfully but according to grace; large-heartedly, not avariciously; with compassion, not cruelty, towards the poor; humbly, not proudly; gratefully, not ungratefully, acknowledging that all things come from the Creator and not from self. Such a man will love his children, his friends, his relatives, and all rational creatures with the same well-ordered love. His use of matrimony, too, will be rightly ordered, as the sacrament it is, and he will respect the days commanded by holy Church.[7] He will be, and behave, like a man, not an animal; without observing absolute continence, he will yet be continent and self-controlled. Such a man will be a fruitful tree bearing the fruits of virtue; a fragrant tree, too, giving off a sweet perfume though it stands in the mire. And the seed it bears will be good and fertile.

So you see you can have God whatever your state in life. It is not our state in life that robs us of him, but our lack of good will. When the will is set on loving falsehood, it is disordered and poisons all we do. But if a man loves Truth, he follows in his footsteps, hating what Truth hates and loving what Truth loves, so that all he does is good and perfect. Otherwise he could have no share in the life of grace and nothing he did would bear the fruit of life.

Since, then, I know of no other way, I said I longed to see you loving and following truth and despising falsehood. That is, [to see you] hating the devil, the father of lies,[8] and your own sensuality that goes after such a father, but loving Christ crucified, who is the way, the truth and the life.[9] Whoever takes him as his way attains the light and is clothed in the gleaming garment of charity, the ground of all the virtues. When this charity and ineffable love are in a man's soul, the state common to most men[10] no longer satisfies him, but he wants to go further. He yearns to pass from mental to actual poverty, from mental to actual continence, in order to observe Christ's counsels as well as his precepts, for he begins to weary of the filth surrounding him. And sensing how very difficult it is to stand in the mire without getting soiled, he longs with intense desire and burning charity to disentangle himself from the world altogether, in so far as he can. And where he cannot do so in fact, he endeavours to be perfect in the state that is his: at least the desire[11] is not lacking.

So then, dearest brother, let us sleep no longer but rouse ourselves from our slumber. Open the eye of your mind with the light of faith to know, love, and follow this truth, which you will know in the blood of the humble loving Word. The Blood, in turn, you will know in knowing yourself, for the soul's face is washed in it, and the Blood is ours and no one can take it from us unless we choose. No negligence, than; rather, like a vessel, be plunged into and brimming over with the blood of Christ crucified. I will say no more.

Abide in the sweet and holy love of God. Sweet Jesus.
Jesus, Love.

---

¹   The early mss. record only that the letter was written 'in a
trance'.
²   John 18:38, but Catherine writes *Who* and not *What*.
³   I Thessalonians 4:3.
⁴   In the form of often exorbitant legal fees even for relatively
trivial services and advice.
⁵   Cf. Acts 10:34.
⁶   or 'make a god of his own body, etc.;' cf. Phil.3:19.
⁷   See letter 34, note 7.
⁸   John 8:44.
⁹   John 14:6.
¹⁰   lit. 'the common state' – as distinct from the religious life
calling for the express practice of the counsels. For this distinction between precepts and counsels, cf. *Summa Theol.* 2a 2ae,
184, 1–3.
¹¹   to disentangle himself.


LETTER 43   (Tommaseo 266; Gigli 229).

*To:     Ristoro Canigiani, of Florence.*¹
*Date:*   ? July/August 1378.²

[Writing to her 'beloved son in Christ sweet Jesus',
Catherine states her desire to see quite spent in him the
self-love that deprives the soul of light by clouding the
eye of the intellect, thus plunging it into a dark ignorance of the things it most needs to know.]

. . . What do we need to know? God's great goodness
and ineffable charity towards us; and then the perverse
law in us that is always at war with the spirit,³ and our own
wretchedness. Possessed of this knowledge, the soul

begins to repay its debt of praise and glory to God by loving him above all things and its neighbour as itself. In its hungry desire for virtue, it has only hatred and loathing for itself, hating its own vices and the sensual nature that gives rise to them. Through this self-knowledge, if one remains in its light, one attains to every virtue and grace. Where else but in the house of self-knowledge can the soul find the riches of sorrow for its sins and the abundance of God's mercy?

Now let's see if we too can find these things. Let's talk a bit about this because you say in your letter that you want to have contrition for your sins and have been refraining from holy communion because you find contrition impossible. We will consider whether this is a reason for refraining.

You know that God is supremely good; that he loved us before ever we existed; that he is eternal Wisdom and that his power and goodness are immeasurable. Therefore, we can be certain that he has the power, the knowledge and the will to give us whatever we need. We see the proof of this in the fact that he gives us more than we know how to ask for and what we have not asked for.

[Catherine instances the fact that we are rational creatures made in the image of God and not just animals; also our redemption, and the gift of the Eucharist.]

Since he gives us so much without our asking for it, how much the more will he fulfil our desires when what we desire is just? Indeed, who but God moves us to desire and ask for this? If he moves us to ask, this is a sign that he wants to fulfil our desire by granting our request.

'I grant you all that,' you will say, 'but how is it that I so often ask for contrition and other things and do not seem to be given them?' Here is my answer. Either this is because a person makes the request without due prudence, asking for the thing in words but not in real earnest. Of such people, our Saviour said that they call him 'Lord, Lord,' but he will not know them[4] – not that he

really does not know them, but on account of their sins
they will not be known to his mercy.⁵ Or else, a person is
asking for something that, were he given it, would hinder
his salvation. Hence, in not getting what he asks for, he
does in fact get it; he asked for it thinking it to be good for
him, whereas precisely his not having it is good for him;
so that in not granting his request God has in fact fulfilled
the desire that prompted it . . . Sometimes, too, God does
not grant what we ask for as soon as we would wish in
order to make us yearn and hunger for it all the more, for
he delights to see his creatures hungering [for his gifts].

Sometimes he will give us the grace in fact but without
our feeling that we have it. This is his providence at work,
for he knows that if such and such a man felt he had
received the grace, he would either let the cord of his
desire go slack⁶ or become presumptuous; so God with-
holds the awareness of it, but not the grace itself. Others
will both receive and be aware of the grace, as it pleases
the sweet goodness of our Physician to deal with us, his
patients, treating each of us in the way most appropriate
for our malady. So you see, whatever happens, the creature's underlying desire in making his request is always
fulfilled.

And now let us see what we are to ask for and with what
degree of prudence.

It seems to me that the sweet First Truth teaches us
what we are to ask for when, after reproving man for
excessive solicitude in procuring and holding onto
worldly wealth and status, he said in the holy gospel: 'Do
not be anxious about tomorrow. Let the day's trouble
be sufficient for the day.'⁷ Here he reminds us to be
prudently aware of the shortness of life; then he adds:
'Ask first for the kingdom of heaven, for your heavenly
Father knows you need these other little things.' What is
this kingdom? And how do we ask for it? It is the kingdom of eternal life, and also the kingdom of our soul,
which never enters the kingdom of God except as
governed by reason.⁸ And how do we ask for this? Not

with words only (as was said above, those who ask only with their lips are not known by God) but with desire for true solid virtue. It is virtue that pleads for and wins possession of this kingdom of heaven; the virtue that makes a man prudent, so that he can work prudently and maturely for God's honour, and his own and his neighbour's salvation, prudently accepting and tolerating his defects and prudently ordering his charity aright by loving God above all things and his neighbour as himself. The order of things prudent charity calls for is to be ready to part with one's bodily life for the salvation of souls, and with temporal goods for one's neighbour's bodily needs. Lack of prudence would reverse this order, as many do who practise a mad and foolish kind of charity. Very often, in order to rescue their neighbour (and not even his soul, but only his body), they will part with their own soul by spreading lies and giving false witness, thus losing their own charity through not seasoning it with prudence.

So we have seen that we should ask for the kingdom of heaven with prudence. Now I will give you my answer about our attitude to holy communion and how we are to receive it.

In this matter, we must not practise a stupid humility, as worldly-minded people do. I tell you we *must* receive this sweet Sacrament; it is the food of our soul and without it we cannot live in grace. The strongest of ties can, indeed must, be severed so that we can approach this sweet Sacrament. For his part, a man should do all he can, and that is enough.

And how are we to receive it? With the light of most holy faith and the mouth of holy desire. First you will gaze upon God and Man whole and entire present in the Host by the light of faith; and then the heart, which follows the understanding, will receive it with deep love and an awed awareness of its own faults and sins, leading to contrition as you ponder the depths of God's inestimable charity in giving himself so lovingly to us as our food.

And not seeming to have the kind of perfect contrition and dispositions he would like must not make a person hold back; one's good will and efforts to have the right dispositions are quite enough.

[Catherine applies to the Eucharist the symbolism of the various rituals for eating the paschal lamb prescribed in Exodus 12, then continues:]

I said that we ought not, nor do I wish you, to behave like many imprudent worldlings who go beyond what the Church commands in saying: 'I am not worthy', and so live for long periods in mortal sin without the food of their souls. O senseless humility! Who does not see that you are not worthy? When do you think you *will* be worthy? Don't wait, for you will be as unworthy in the end as you were to begin with. However upright we may be, we never will be worthy. God is the One who is worthy, and he makes us worthy with his own worthiness, which will never diminish. So what must we do? Make our preparation, and carry out this sweet commandment. If we don't do this, but refrain from communion in the belief that we are avoiding sin, we only fall right into it.

To conclude, therefore, I urge you not to entertain any such foolish notion but to prepare yourself to receive holy communion like a faithful Christian in the way suggested. The more you abide in true self-knowledge, the more perfect will this preparation be; otherwise not, for in this knowledge you will see everything clearly. Don't slacken your holy desire, whatever pain, injury, insult or ingratitude you may experience from those you have served, for then, with true and long-suffering perseverance, you really will persevere until death. I beg you to do this for the love of Christ crucified. I say no more.

Abide in the sweet and holy love of God. Sweet Jesus, Jesus, Love.

---

[1]    This man of strong character and personality shared with his

father, Piero, and younger brother, Barduccio, a deep devotion to Catherine. By profession a lawyer, he was prominent in the counsels of the Guelf (pro-papal) party, though he advised against accepting some of the more preposterous terms offered by the Pope and his advisers during the war with Florence and her allies. His house was burnt down during a violent uprising in June 1378 – when Catherine herself narrowly escaped death – and he fled to Pistoia; see Gardner, pp.172, 223 & 239.

²    One of a series of five letters which began when Ristoro wrote to tell Catherine of his desire to turn over a new leaf. They could be connected with the change in his fortunes and flight to Pistoia.

³    Cf. Romans 7:21–23.

⁴    Matthew 7:21–23.

⁵    Cf. Dialogue, pp.291–2.

⁶    Cf. Hosea 11:4.

⁷    Matthew 6:31–34.

⁸    See letter 40. Characteristically Catherine sees the way of salvation as normally through the achievement of virtue.


## LETTER 44    (Tommaseo 279; Gigli 230).

*To:*     *Ristoro Canigiani of Florence.*¹

*Date:*    ? July/August 1378.


Beloved son in Christ sweet Jesus,

I, Catherine, servant and slave of the servants of Jesus Christ, write to you in his precious blood, desiring to see you grounded in true and perfect charity, for it is the mother and wet-nurse of all the virtues and makes a man so constant and steadfast in them that neither devil nor creature can part him from them without his consent. This charity is utterly sweet, with no trace of any bitterness that afflicts the soul; yet it brings a sweet bitterness,² filling out the soul with true self-knowledge whereby it knows the faults, past and present, it has committed against its Creator. It is a knowledge accompanied by the bitterness of regret for having offended such supreme eternal Goodness and soiled the face and beauty that had been washed in the blood of the humble, spotless Lamb. In this blood the soul knows the fire and abyss of [God's] Charity, so that now, and only now, can it begin to love; for the creature loves its Creator in the degree that it sees itself loved by him. Hence, our coldness of heart is entirely due to our not perceiving how much we are loved by God. And why do we not perceive it? Because the cloud of self-love has darkened the eye of the mind wherein is its pupil, the light of most holy faith.

This light leads us to perfect love for God, and also for our neighbour. A soul in love with its Creator wants to love what he loves. Seeing that he greatly loves his creature, it is constrained by the fire of charity to love the creature too, and to serve him with all diligence and care. And that usefulness which it cannot offer to God, who has no need of us, it desires to offer to its fellow-creatures, by sharing with them all the spiritual and temporal graces and gifts it has itself received from God. And all for a spiritual motive, for a frank and open-hearted charity seeks nothing for self,[3] seeing that it loves neither self, nor Creator, nor creatures, for its own sake, but loves all things for God alone.

Charity is not feigned or two-faced, seeming to be one thing outside but inwardly being quite another. It is humble and not proud – indeed, humility feeds charity in the soul. Not faithless but faithful, faithfully serving God and neighbour, trusting in God and not in self. Not imprudent, and so using all things with great prudence. It is just and gives to each his due:[4] to God giving glory, and the praise of his name, by the practice of holy virtue; to others, kindness; and to oneself hatred of the faults one has committed and displeasure at one's own weakness. Charity is strong, and cannot be weakened either by impatience in adversity or undue elation in times of prosperity. It makes peace between disputants, keeps anger in check, and stamps out sloth and envy, by welcoming and delighting in the neighbour's good as if it were its own. Charity clothes the soul in the garment of grace, making it so strong that no dart can strike home but rebounds at whoever threw it. Thus we see that if someone injures us and we bear it patiently, the poisoned impact of the offence rebounds at whoever threw it; and if we are displeased when the world strikes at us through pleasure, luxury and status, the blow recoils on it with hatred; and if the devil strikes at us with all kinds of temptations, then we strike back at him with all the might of our will by remaining firm, unswerving and persevering until death, and not yielding to his crafty malicious promptings.

While we hold this citadel, no blow can harm us, for our will alone commits the fault or practises the virtue, as it chooses. If impurity tries to assail us, we just strike back with the odour of purity which, with continence, makes a soul angelic, purity being charity's own daughter.

[Developing this theme, Catherine invites Ristoro and his wife to aim at the ideal of complete continence while they are still young for 'God would not be very pleased if you wait to give him something you can't keep anyway!']

It is because I long to see you attain this perfect and excellent state, and consider you cannot do so except through charity, that I said, and repeat, that I long to see you grounded in that true and most perfect charity which embraces all good and recoils and flies from all deliberate evil. And since this charity is so sweet and delightful, we mustn't be negligent or waste time but get up eagerly by the light of holy faith. This will show us that we are loved; perceiving this we shall know his goodness; knowing it, we shall love it, and with this love drive out the self-love that deprives us of the life of grace.

Fill your memory with the blood of Christ crucified. No more now.

Abide in the sweet and holy love of God. Sweet Jesus. Jesus, Love.

¹   See letter 43, notes 1 and 2.
²   See letter 26 note 1.
³   For this and what follows, cf. I Cor. 13 passim.
⁴   Cf. Romans 13:7.

## LETTER 45   (Gardner IV).

*To:*   *The Priors of the Arts Guilds and the* Gonfaloniere di Giustizia¹ *in Florence.*

*Date:*   Early August 1378, immediately after Catherine's departure from Florence.²

My lords and beloved brethren in Christ sweet Jesus . . .

[Stating her desire to see the city's rulers bound together in the bond of charity, Catherine lists the various ways in which the strength and endurance of this bond make it possible to withstand all attempts by the world, the devil and our own sensual nature to break or sever it (cf. letters 40, 49 and others). She dwells in particular on the virtue and practice of justice (cf. letter 59), then continues:]

You are anxious to reform your city, but I tell you that you will never succeed unless you endeavour to throw down hatred and rancour of heart, and your own self-love; that is, unless you are concerned not only for yourselves but for the general good of the whole city. I beg you, therefore, for the love of Christ crucified, and also in your own real interest, not to be trying to have one rather than another appointed to rule the city, but to select men of virtue, wise and discreet, who by the light of reason will bring about the order needed to secure within and maintain without the peace that God in his infinite

mercy has granted to us: that of seeing the sons reconciled to their father, and ourselves, his sheep, restored to
the fold of holy Church. So make sure you are not
ungrateful for the great gift God has bestowed on you
through the tears and ceaseless prayers of his servants –
not by any virtue of our own, though, but solely by virtue
of the burning love of God,[3] who does not spurn the
prayers and desires of his servants. I tell you, if you are
not truly grateful to your Creator for all this, the spring
of his compassion[4] will run dry for us.

I urge you, therefore, to do all in your power to show
your gratitude by arranging as soon as possible for the
prescribed Masses and Absolution (so that the Office can
once again be said in praise to God)[5] and for a procession,
held with due devotion, so that the devils who have
occupied the city because of our sins, depriving men of
light and knowledge, will be driven out, tied together
with this sweet bond of charity in such a way that they can
no longer harm us, but rather we them. In this way you
will fulfill your own desire, and mine, of putting your city
back in order and keeping it in true and perfect peace.[6]
But if each of you is wanting things done his way for no
good reason, you will never succeed, for where there is no
unity, a man cannot govern his own household, let alone
a city like this. Mature and skilful men are needed, not
children, so I beg you to be just this. Find ways of keeping
people inside the city, not out abroad; exiling people was
never in a city's best interests, and this one I consider
mine. My sorrow at seeing it in such travail must speak for
me.

I did not expect to have to write to you, for I thought I
would be saying these things to you in person, for the
honour of God and your own benefit. I had intended to
call on you in order to celebrate with you the holy peace
for which I have toiled for so long in every way I could, to
the measure of my possibilities and little virtue. If I had
had more virtue, I would have achieved more.[3] Only
after rejoicing with you, and thanking the divine Good-

ness and yourselves, did I intend to leave and go back to
Siena. Now it seems that the devil has unjustly set people's
hearts very much against me, and I did not want one
offence to be added to another (the more they heap up,
the greater the harm done), so I have gone, with the grace
of God, and I pray the supreme eternal Goodness to
bring peace to your hearts, making them one and binding
them in such charity that no devil or creature will ever be
able to part you. Whatever I myself can do to further
your salvation I shall gladly do until I die, despite the
visible and invisible demons who are out to frustrate
every holy desire.

I leave with the consolation of seeing accomplished
what I had set my heart on when I entered your city,
namely never to leave it again, even if it meant dying
here, until I had seen all you children reconciled to your
father, for I saw such danger and damage to body and
soul. Sadly and sorrowfully I go, to leave the city in such
bitterness. But the ever-living God who consoled me in
the first thing will console me in this second one of seeing
and hearing you bring about a good stable and perfect
state of peace, so that you may be free to devote yourselves to the glory and honour of [God's] name and not
have to endure being under arms. I hope that the
Loving-Kindness of God will turn again the eye of his
mercy and grant the desire of his servants. I will say no
more.

Abide in the sweet and holy love of God. Sweet Jesus.
Jesus, Love.

---

[1]    Supreme Magistrate of the Florentine Republic.

[2]    Catherine probably left the city almost as soon as news of the
signing of the longed-for peace treaty between the city and the
Pope reached Florence on 1 August. See Gardner pp.249–50
and Fawtier p.245.

[3]    Catherine plays on the word *virtú* which means both 'virtue'
and 'valour, merit'.

[4]    Ital. *fonte della pietà*; cf. letter 47, note 5.

[5] Catherine must have left the city even before the first informal absolution from the papal interdict was proclaimed there on 10 August.

[6] Cf. Isaiah 26:3.

## LETTER 46    (Tommaseo 316; Gigli 165).

*To:*    *Suor Daniela of Orvieto.*[1]

*Date:*    Late October/early November 1378.[2]

Beloved daughter in Christ sweet Jesus,

I, Catherine, servant and slave of the servants of Jesus Christ, write to you in his precious blood, desiring to see you with true and perfect light, so that you may know the fullness of truth. How very necessary this light is, dearest daughter. Without it we cannot go by the bright life-giving way of Christ crucified, but must go in the dark, beset by fierce storms and bitterness.

But if I'm not mistaken we need to have this light in two ways. First, there is a general light that every rational creature must have in order to see and know what to love and whom he should obey – seeing, by the eye of the understanding with its pupil of most holy faith, that he is bound to love and serve his Creator (loving him *directly* and with the whole heart and soul) and to obey the commandments of the law, namely to love God above all things and one's neighbour as oneself. On these principles all the rest depends. This general light obliges us all; it would be death for us without it; deprived of the life of grace we would follow the devil's dark way.

But there is another light, not separate but united with the first: indeed, the first leads to the second [in that] those who keep God's commandments grow in another, most perfect light. With great and holy desire they rise from imperfection and come to perfection by observing both commandments and counsels in thought and deed. One should bring this light into play with hungry desire for the honour of God and the salvation of souls, gazing with this light into the light of the sweet and loving Word, where the soul tastes the ineffable love for his creature shown to us through the Word who, for his Father's honour and our salvation, ran as one enamoured to the shameful death of the cross.

Once a soul has known this truth in the perfect light, it rises above self and all sense-feelings. In an agony of sweet and loving desires, it runs in the footsteps of Christ crucified [along the way] of suffering, shame, mockery and insult, with much persecution from the world and frequently also, under colour of virtue, from the servants of God. Hungrily it seeks God's honour and the salvation of souls, and is so delighted with this glorious food that it despises self and all else; seeking this alone, it goes out of self. Those glorious virgins and other saints, whose one joy was to partake of this food with their Bridegroom at the table of the cross, were in this perfect light. To us, too, dearest daughter and sweet sister in Christ sweet Jesus, he has granted the great grace and mercy of being numbered among those who have passed from the general to the particular light (that is, he has made us choose the perfect state of the counsels[3]). By this true light, then, we are to follow this sweet straight way perfectly and not look back on any account, or go our own way, but God's, enduring suffering sinlessly until death, thus snatching souls from the hands of demons. For this is the way and the rule the eternal Truth gave you, writing it in his body with such large letters that no one has so little understanding as to be excused [from reading it]. Look at the great initial capitals, each one illuminating the eternal Father's truth: the ineffable love by which we were created – indeed yes! – simply so that we might share in his supreme eternal Goodness. This our Master was raised up on the Chair of the cross so that we could study him better and not fool ourselves by saying: 'But he taught me down on the ground, not raised aloft.' That is not so. He climbed onto the cross seeking, with his suffering, to give full honour to the Father and to restore beauty to the soul. Let us then choose the heart-felt love, founded on truth, shown us in this book of Life.

Lose self in all things; the more you lose, the more you will find, and God will not spurn your desire, but will himself direct you and show you what you are to do; and give light to whoever is over you, provided you are acting on his advice. It is because a soul given to prayer must have a holy jealousy, and delight always to be guided in all it does by both prayer and counsel that you wrote to me, and from my understanding of the letter it seems you are under stress. And no small stress at that; in fact, greater than any other, for on the one hand you feel yourself being called in your mind in new ways by God; but his servants are opposed to it, saying it is not a good thing. I deeply sympathize with you, for I know of nothing so wearisome as distress of this kind, because of the soul's jealous concern for itself. [While] it cannot resist God, it would yet fulfil the will of his servants, trusting their light and knowledge more than its own; but does not seem able to. Here now is my answer, according to the little I see at my low level. Don't insist on getting your own way, but as you feel yourself called, not on your own initiative, so respond. Hence, if you see souls in danger and can help them, don't close your eyes, but earnestly set about helping them, even to death. Don't let your own resolutions, or silence, or anything else, stand in the way, lest afterwards the words 'Cursed be you that said nothing', be addressed to you. Our one principle and foundation is the love of God and our neighbour; all other exercises are but instruments and buildings erected on this base. You must not take such pleasure in the instrument or in the building as to neglect the principal foundation of God's honour and love of neighbour. Work away, then, dear child, in the field to which you feel God is calling you; and don't be pained or grieved in mind because of what I have said; just bear up manfully. Fear and serve God selflessly and don't let what creatures say bother you, except to be sorry for them.

As for your desire to leave home and be in Rome, entrust it to the will of your Bridegroom. If it be to his honour and your own salvation, he will send you the way and the means when you least expect, and in a way you would never have thought of. Leave it to him, while you lose yourself – only mind you don't lose yourself anywhere but on the cross, where you will find yourself most perfectly. But this you cannot do without the perfect light, which is why I said I longed to see you with this special perfect light, as well as the general one I spoke of.

No more sleep! Let us wake from our negligence, roaring[4] with humble and continous prayer over the mystical body of holy Church and over Christ's vicar. Pray unceasingly that he may be given light and strength to withstand the blows of incarnate self-loving devils who are wanting to contaminate our faith. It is a time for weeping[5].

As for my coming to you, ask the supreme eternal Goodness to bring about whatever is to his honour and the salvation of souls, especially now that I am about to go to Rome to do the will of Christ crucified and of his vicar. I don't know which route I shall take.[6] Ask Christ sweet Jesus to send us by whichever one will most serve his honour and the peace and quiet of our souls. I say no more.

Abide in the sweet and holy love of God. Sweet Jesus, Jesus, Love.

---

[1]   Little more is known about this person than that she was a Dominican tertiary and that Catherine seems to have had a special affection for her.

[2]   See Fawtier, pp.220–1.

[3]   Cf. letter 42, note 10.

[4]   Medieval bestiaries seemed to suggest that lion cubs are born dead but brought to life after three days when the male lion

'roars' over them. (Dupré, p.255, note 15).

5  Ecclesiastes 3:4.

6  One of the two routes open to Catherine would have taken her through Orvieto; see Fawtier, p.221.

## Letters written from Rome (December 1378 — shortly before Catherine's death on 29 April 1380).

**LETTER 47**   (Tommaseo 310; Gigli 31).

*To:*   *Cardinals Iacopo Orsini of Rome,*[1] *Pietro Corsini, a Florentine, and Simone da Borzano, Archbishop of Milan, some time after they had been present (without voting) at the election of Clement VII, the first anti-pope of the Great Schism, which took place at Fondi, near Rome, on 20 September 1378.*

*Date:*   *? December 1378/January 1379, from Rome.*[2]

Dearest brothers and fathers in Christ sweet Jesus, I, Catherine, servant and slave of the servants of Jesus Christ, write to you in his precious blood, desiring to see you return to the true light from the darkness and blindness into which you have fallen. Then you will be fathers to me; otherwise not. Thus, I address you now as 'fathers' only in so far as you turn away from death and return to life (at the moment, you have turned away from the life of grace and are as limbs severed from the head that gave you life) by being united in faith and perfect obedience to Pope Urban VI, for in this obedience stand all who possess the light whereby they know and therefore love the truth. One cannot know what one cannot see; whoever does not know cannot love; and he who neither loves nor fears his Creator is bestowing a carnal love on himself and on anything else he may set his heart on, whether pleasures, or honours, or worldly position. Man was created through love, and so cannot live without it. Hence either he loves God, or he loves himself and the world with the love that brings death, fixing the eye of his mind, dimmed by self-love, on these transitory things that come and go like the wind, wherein he can know neither truth nor goodness but only falsehood, for he is without light. For truly, if he had light, he would know that such love as this contains and causes nothing but pain and everlasting death, with a foretaste of hell even in this life, for a man who loves himself and the things of this world in a disordered way becomes unbearable even to himself.

O human blindness! Do you not see, luckless man, that you think you are loving something solid and stable, something delightful, good and beautiful, whereas in fact these are transient, utterly wretched, ugly, devoid of all goodness? Not in *themselves* – for all are created by God who is supremely good – but because of man's inordinate attachment to them.[3] How transient are wealth and worldly renown for the man who would have them without God, that is, without fearing him! Rich and great today, poor tomorrow. How repulsive is our bodily life, with the stench we give out from every part of our bodies! Simply a sack of excrement, food for worms, food for death! Our life and the beauty of youth pass away like the beauty of a flower once it is plucked. No one can restore this beauty, or retain it, when it shall please the supreme Judge to pluck this flower of life by death, and none knows when!

Wretched man! The darkness of self-love keeps you from knowing this truth. Did you but know it, you would choose any suffering rather than live as you do. You would set about loving and longing for the One who IS; you would steadfastly savour his truth and not flutter like a leaf in the breeze; and you would serve your Creator, loving all things in him and nothing apart from him. Oh, how this blindness will be rebuked and reproved on the last day in every rational creature, and much the more in those whom God has drawn out of the mire of the world

and endowed with the greatest possible dignity, making
them ministers of the blood of the humble and spotless
Lamb! Alas, alas, what have you come to by not matching
your dignity with virtue? You were put to feed at the
breast of holy Church. You were the flowers put in to fill
the garden with the scent of virtue. You were set up like
pillars to give strength to this ship and guard Christ's
vicar on earth.[4] You were set as lamps on a lampstand to
give light to all faithful Christians and to spread the faith.
You yourselves well know if you have fulfilled the purpose for which you were created [cardinals]. Certainly
you have not, for self-love has kept you from knowing
that only in order to give strength and light, and the
example of a good and holy life, were you placed in this
garden. Had you known this sweet truth, you would have
loved it and clothed yourselves with it. And where is the
gratitude you owe to the Bride who fed you at her breast?
I see only ingratitude, which makes the spring of piety
run dry.[5]

What convinces me that you are ungrateful, cowardly
and mercenary? The way in which you, with the others,
have persecuted and continue even now to persecute this
Bride, when you should be shields warding off from her
the blows of [the] heresy[6] [you persist in] though you well
know the truth: that Pope Urban VI is truly Pope, the
Supreme Pontiff, elected by regular election and not out
of fear – indeed, more by divine inspiration than by your
human efforts. And you announced it so to us, the truth
as it was. Now you have turned your backs, like mean
paltry knights afraid of your own shadows. You have
departed from the truth, which gives courage, and clung
to falsehood, which weakens you in body and soul, depriving you of all grace, spiritual and temporal.

What made you do it? The poison of self-love, which
has infected the world. It has turned you from pillars to
worse than straw; from sweet-scented to stinking flowers
that make the whole world reek; from being lamps set on
a lampstand to spread the faith to having your light

hidden under a bushel of pride,[7] not spreaders of the faith but its contaminators, shrouding yourselves and others in darkness. Rather than the angels on earth you ought to be, set to snatch us from the path of hell's demon, and undertake the angelic office of leading the sheep back into the fold of obedience to holy Church, you have assumed the task of devils, wishing to infect us, also, with the evil you have in yourselves, by drawing us, too, away from our obedience to Christ-on-earth and into obedience to antichrist, that limb of the devil – which is what you are too, for as long as you persist in this heresy.

This is no blindness due to ignorance – ignorance due to men having reported one thing to you when in fact the reality is different. No, for you know what the truth is and it was you who announced it to us, not we to you. What madness to give us the truth while yourselves choosing to relish the lie! And now you wish to corrupt this truth and convince us of the opposite by claiming that you elected Pope Urban out of fear. This is not so, and whoever says it is (and I address you now without reverence, for you have forfeited your right to it!) is lying in his teeth. Anyone who chose could see that the one you claim to have elected out of fear was *Messer di S. Pietro*.[8] You could say to me: 'Why do you not believe us? We who elected him know the truth better than you do.' To which I reply that you yourselves have shown me that you are departing from the truth in many ways and that I must not believe [your story] that Pope Urban VI is not the true pope. If I look back at your lives in the past, I do not know you to have been so good and holy that you would have scrupled about telling lies! And what shows me that your lives are disordered? The poison of heresy.

Going back to the regular election: you yourselves told us that you elected him canonically and not out of fear. We've already said that the one you presented out of fear was *Messer di S. Pietro*. But what shows me that your election of Messer Bartolommeo, Archbishop of Bari, now Pope Urban VI, was canonical? The truth of this is shown in the ceremony of his coronation. And that this ceremony did take place is shown by the homage you paid him and the favours you sought from him, and have made use of in every sphere. Only by lying can you deny this truth.

Fools, worthy of a thousand deaths! Like blind men, you do not see what straits you are in; you have fallen into such confusion that you are making liars and idolators of yourselves. For, even if it were true (which it is not; indeed I confess and do not deny[9] that Pope Urban VI is the true pope), but if what you are now saying were true, wouldn't you have been lying to us in saying that he was the supreme pontiff, which he is? And wouldn't you have been paying homage to him under false pretences by revering in him Christ on earth? And wouldn't you have been guilty of simony in seeking for favours and making illicit use of them? Indeed you would. And now they have made an antipope, and you along with them, to judge by your behaviour and demeanour in consenting to be there on the spot, when those devils incarnate elected their devil.[10]

You could say to me: 'No, we didn't elect him.' I don't know that I believe that for [if you did not], I hardly think you would have borne being there even at the risk of your lives; the mere fact of your having suppressed the truth and not burst out with the fact that this[11] was not in your power makes me inclined to believe that you did. For, even conceding that your intention was less evil than that of the others in what you did, nevertheless you went through with the evil together with them, so what can I say? I can say that he that is not for the truth is against it;[12] that he that was not then for Christ-on-earth, Pope Urban VI, was against him. And so, I tell you that you, with him,[10] did evil. I can say, too, that you have elected a limb of the devil, for if he were a member of Christ he would have chosen death rather than consent to so great an evil, since he, too, knows the truth and cannot make ignorance his excuse. And now there are all the faults you have committed and are still committing with regard to this devil by acknowledging him to be pope, which he certainly is not, and by paying homage to a man when you shouldn't. You have turned away from the light and gone off into the darkness, from the truth to join up with lies. I see nothing but lies all around me. You well merit retribution and in truth I tell you (and so ease my conscience) that unless you make due submission in true humility, that retribution will come.

O misery upon misery, blindness upon blindness! preventing a man from seeing his own evil and the harm threatening soul and body. Had you seen this you would not, in your servile fear, have deserted the truth so easily. But, driven by your passions and your pride, and being accustomed to pick and choose among the pleasures and delights of the world, not only could you not endure corrective measures, but even a harsh word of reproof made you lift your heads in rebellion. And this is why you left. Herein we see the truth of the matter, for until Christ-on-earth began to bite, you acknowledged him and revered him as the vicar of Christ, which he is. But this last deadly fruit that has come from you shows what kind of trees you are, set in the soil of pride born of that love of self which has robbed you of the light of reason.

Alas, no more of this, for the love of God. Take refuge in humbling yourselves under the mighty hand of God[13] and in obedience to his vicar, while you yet have time, for once time has gone, all is lost. Acknowledge your faults so that you can humble yourselves and know God's infinite goodness in not commanding the ground to swallow you up[14] or animals to devour you,[15] but instead giving you time to put your souls in order. If you will not acknowledge what has been given to you by grace, it will stand in judgement against you; but if you choose to return to the fold and to feed in all truth at the breast of Christ's Bride, you will be received with mercy by Christ in heaven and by Christ-on-earth, in spite of the great wrong you have done. I beg you to delay no longer and not to ignore the goad of conscience that I know is continually stabbing at you. And do not become so distressed in mind at the evil you have done as to think, in your helplessness and hopelessness, that it cannot be put right, and so despair of your own salvation. This you must not do. Rather, with living faith, place all your hope in your Creator and humbly come back to your yoke; for the last offence of obduracy and despair would be worse, and more displeasing to God and the world. Up with you, then, in the light, for without it you would walk in darkness, as you have done up to now.

Knowing in my soul that without this light we can neither know nor love the truth, I said, and now repeat, that I desire with great desire[16] to see you rise up from darkness and become one with the light. My desire extends to all rational creatures, but most of all to you three, on whose account I have suffered more and whose fault has caused me greater dismay than any of the others who committed it; for, though all were abandoning their father, you ought to have been the ones to support him by proclaiming the truth. Even though he did nothing but reprimand you, still you ought not to have turned Judas[17] by denying his Holiness in every way. Even naturally speaking (though as far as virtue goes we are all to be equal), but from a human point of view, since Christ-on-earth is an Italian and you are Italians, could you not have been moved by love of your country, as the Ultramontanes[18] were? Your self-love seems to me to be the only explanation. Throw it down, once and for all, without waiting for time which will not wait for you, and trample on it with the feet of hatred of vice and love of virtue. Come back, I beg you to come back, without waiting for the rod of justice, for we cannot escape God's hands. In his hands we are, for justice or for mercy. Better, then, to acknowledge our sins and so remain in the hands of his mercy than to persist in sin in the hands of his justice,[19] for our sins do not go unpunished, especially not those against holy Church.

But I am willing to bind myself to bring you before God with tears and unceasing prayer, and to do penance together with you, provided only that you will return to your Father[20] who, like a true father, is waiting for you with the wings of his mercy held wide. Alas, alas, do not flee or despise this mercy, but accept it humbly, paying no heed to evil counsellors who have encompassed your death. Alas, sweet brothers! Yes, sweet brothers, and fathers too, if only you will draw near to the Truth. Yield at last to the tears and sweat streaming from God's servants in such abundance that you could wash from head to foot in them! If you spurn these, not to mention the anguished, sweet and doleful desires they are offering for you, so much the harsher will your sentence be. Fear God and his true judgement. I hope in his infinite goodness that he will accomplish in you the desires of his servants.

Do not take offence at my goading you with words; my love for your salvation has made me write. I would prefer to do so by word of mouth, did God but allow it – his will be done – though in fact you deserve deeds rather than words! I will end here, and say no more; yet if I were to follow my inclination, I would not have done even now, so overwhelmed is my soul with pain and sorrow at seeing so much blindness in the very men who were set up to give light but who, instead of lambs feeding on God's honour, the salvation of souls and the reform of holy Church, are more like thieves snatching at the honour they owe to God and keeping it for themselves; or like wolves devouring the sheep. Hence my great distress. I beg you for the love of that precious Blood which was poured out for you with such burning love to ease the anguish of my soul that seeks your salvation. I will say no more.

Abide in the sweet and holy love of God. Bathe yourselves in the blood of the spotless Lamb wherein you will lose all servile fear and remain with the light in holy fear. Sweet Jesus. Jesus, Love.

¹ See letter 5.
² See Gardner, Ch. XII, pp.252 et seq. for an account of the circumstances attending the election of Urban, his abandonment by the Cardinals and the start of the Schism. (Note: Fawtier, p.169, dates this letter several months earlier, i.e., almost immediately after the election of the anti-pope.)
³ Cf. letter 42 and Dante, *Convivio*, IV, XI, 4–5.
⁴ Catherine here runs together the two images of 'pillars' and 'ship' of the Church.
⁵ On piety as a virtue, cf. St Thomas, *Summa theol*. 2a 2ae, 101, and Dante, *Convivio*, II, x, 5–6.
⁶ the Schism.
⁷ Cf. Matthew 5:15.
⁸ The aged Cardinal Tebaldeschi, archpriest of St Peter's and a Roman by birth, whom the terrified Cardinals presented as pope to the mob that erupted into the conclave demanding the election of a Roman. The fiction was maintained for about 24 hours; see Gardner, p.265.
⁹ Cf. John 1:20.
¹⁰ the anti-pope, Clement VII.
¹¹ to proceed to a second election.
¹² Matthew 12:30.
¹³ I Peter 5:6.
¹⁴ Cf. Numbers 16:31.
¹⁵ Cf. II Kings 2:24.
¹⁶ The Luke 22:15 text is again explicit.
¹⁷ We accept the reading *'Giuda'* from the Harleian ms. – cf. Gardner, p.305, note 1.
¹⁸ the French cardinals.
¹⁹ Cf. Dialogue pp.291–2.
²⁰ The word 'father' here is ambiguous. It could refer either to God the Father (as the translation suggests) or to the holy Father.

# LETTER 48   (Tommaseo 83; Gigli 237).

*To:*   *Conte di Conte, of Florence.*¹
*Date:*   Late 1378 or early 1379.²

[Stating her desire to see in Conte the light of faith which will show him the way of truth, Catherine stresses that faith and love go together. We love and so are faithful; by our fidelity in the face of trials and temptations we learn to love God and do his will].

But why does [God] allow us to endure all this toil and rebelliousness? To test our virtue, and also so that by the light [of faith] we may recognize our own imperfection and how God helps the toiling, beleaguered soul; that we may recognize, too, his glowing love in the good will which he has preserved in the soul during the darkness, temptation and trials.[3]

Thanks to this knowledge gained in its time of trial, the soul frees itself from imperfect faith, coming to perfect faith through all this experience, which it has had and taken to heart while still imperfect. The light of faith does away with all confusion of mind and that not only in times of battle, but even if a man has actually fallen into mortal sin; whatever the sin, faith lifts him up again. For by this light he gazes into the loving-kindness, the fire and abyss of God's love; stretching out the arms of hope, he receives into them, and presses to himself, the fruit of the Blood wherein he has found this sweet and loving Fire. With perfect contrition he humbles himself before God and, for God's sake, before his neighbour, considering himself the least and vilest of creatures. He thus extinguishes the fault in his soul by contrition and by the hope he derives from the Blood, instilled into him by the light of faith. And so he comes to such perfect and intense love of the divine loving Fire that he can say with blessed Gregory: 'O happy blessed fault, meriting such a redeemer!'[4]

Was Adam's fault happy? Not the fault, but the fruit we received from it, namely God's clothing of his Son with our humanity and his imposing on him the great act of obedience which restores mankind to grace, whereupon the Son, like a man in love, ran to pay the price [for us], his own blood. And so it is with the soul. Its fault is not happy, but the fruit of charity is – the fruit it receives from the great and perfect amendment it has made by the light of faith, as I said, and from its growth in knowledge and humility. Joyfully, it sets about obeying God's commandments, shouldering this yoke with hatred and love,[5] and hastens like a lover to give its life, if necessary, for the salvation of souls, for it has seen, by the light of faith, that it cannot return to God the love and graces it has found in him. Or rather, it can return the love, but not its debt of service for the graces received from him, since God has no need of us. However, by being of service to its neighbour, it can make through him the return it cannot make directly to God. This is the true state of things. If we care lovingly for our neighbour we demonstrate, in him, our love for the supreme eternal Truth, for such charity is the test as to whether or not virtue is present in the soul. Obediently, then, the soul runs, having bound its own will to do God's will in its neighbour, without faltering on account of suffering, or anything else, until death.

This light gives us a foretaste of eternal life as we feed lovingly at the breast of Christ crucified, where we delight in the chance to 'steal' the virtues, the way of life, and the maturity of those who certainly enjoyed that foretaste – seeing that they are now citizens of the blessed life – while they were yet pilgrims and wanderers in this. With this faith we carry the key of the Blood that opens the way to eternal life. Faith relies not on itself but on its Creator; there is no wind in it of proud self-importance. This, together with pride, impurity and every other fault and wretchedness are the fruits of our lack of faith in God and our self-reliant presumption, which is a worm hidden under the root of the tree of our soul.[6] A man must kill it with his dagger of hatred or it will gnaw away at the tree, making it grow twisted or bringing it down altogether unless the soul acts with great diligence and humility. Often a man's self-love makes him so dense that he fails to notice the worm in its hiding place. And that is

why God permits so many trials and persecutions, letting
the tree become twisted or even fall. He does not permit
the will to evil, but he does give man time in which to be
guided by his own free will, and this simply in order that
he may come to his senses – that, now humbled, he may
use the light [of faith] to seek out that worm and kill it.
Has not such a soul cause to rejoice and to acknowledge
the grace from God which made him see and find within
himself what he did not know was there? It certainly has.
In every way, then, dearest son, and whatever state a man
may be in, whether he is in sin or not, whether he is
upright or a sinner, or has fallen and picked himself up
again, he needs this light.

How many difficulties come from not having it! I won't
start enumerating them, or say more than this, as it would
take too long. Let what I have said suffice. I don't know
how to tell you in words or in writing how useful and
delightful it is to have this light, but may God in his
infinite mercy grant you to experience it. My wish is that
it may be so. And that is why I said I longed to see in you
the light of faith.

[Commenting on Conte's letter to Barduccio,[7]
Catherine urges him not to think of leaving the con-
fraternity he belongs to unless he desires to be a religious, and warns him against yielding to confusion of
mind. Let both himself and herself make a fresh start,
using the antidotes outlined in the letter.]

---

[1]   This disciple may have belonged to one of the many religious
confraternities whose members devoted themselves to good
works, as he is known to have been in charge of the famous
Florentine prison 'Le Stinche' in later life. The letter suggests
that he was somewhat unsettled. According to one of the early
mss., he had recently fallen into sin.

[2]   See Fawtier, p.263.

[3]   Cf. letters 22 & 55.

[4]   As in letter 21, Catherine uses an idea from the *Exsultet*, an

Easter vigil chant attributed in her day to Pope St Gregory the Great.

5 hatred of self (or sin) and love of God (or virtue).

6 Cf. Jonah 4:7.

7 *Barduccio* Canigiani, the pious and delicate younger brother of Ristoro (see letters 43 and 44), became an ardent (and favourite) disciple of Catherine's during her prolonged stay in Florence. He went with her to Rome and has left an invaluable and moving account of her last illness and death. He himself died of consumption just over two years later. (Raymond, p.312).

## LETTER 49   (Tommaseo 332; Gigli 264).

*To:     Pietro Ventura and Stefano Maconi, in Siena.*[1]

*Date:   (in ms.) 1 January 1378.*[2]

Beloved sons in Christ sweet Jesus,

I, Catherine, servant and slave of the servants of Jesus Christ, write to you in his precious blood, desiring to see you such brave knights that you will prevail over your three main enemies. These three, sweetest sons, are the devil, the world and the flesh.

We can easily prevail over the first two, because the devil's power over us was taken from him by the blood of God's Son, and so he now has no hold over us – as to sin – except what we choose to give him. He can certainly torment us with all kinds of thoughts, but he cannot force us into the slightest fault, for the blood of the spotless Lamb has made us strong and released us from bondage to him. As for the world, what can it do to us? Nothing. True, it can strike at the outer shell, our bodies, with countless vexations, torments, jeers, slanders, and insults – but how much of all this does a servant of God feel in the kernel of his soul? Not a thing. While the world spends itself in afflicting him, he rejoices, for his heart is centred on God, the source of all joy. He has chosen to suffer for

Christ crucified; so the more he sees himself suffering, without sin, the happier he is, as he is thus more closely conformed to Christ. So, these two enemies can indeed be easily overcome.

But the third enemy, the flesh, that is our sensuality, is a perverse law always at war with the spirit.[3] It is nearly always trying somehow to kick against God's will, making us turn our backs on all the good inspirations God's mercy puts into our hearts, and so act on none of them so long as we defer to it. By contrast, all the wicked thoughts the devil gives us – is allowed by God to give us, but only so that we may increase in perfection and grace, *not* so that we let ourselves be overcome by them! – yes, our perverse sensual nature makes us act on all these. In short, it is this that deprives us of God and keeps us in a constant state of bitterness in this life. So we must certainly arm ourselves against this enemy.

Therefore, I want each of you to divide himself into two parts, sensuality and reason, and let these be locked in deadly combat, reason's weapon being the sword of hatred and love. And let there be no half-measures; it must be war to the death – death of the enemy who deprives us of the life of grace by making us rebel against God. Sometimes this cursed law will play a clever trick designed to make us fall all the more heavily. It will go to sleep and seem to be dead within us, for we cease to experience any conflict; at such times, all our actions and thoughts are directed with great fervour towards God, with a sweetness that seems a foretaste of eternal life. But if we do not press home the war, if we lay the sword aside and fail to keep ourselves fighting fit, [our enemy] will wake up stronger than ever and perhaps bring us down miserably.

Hence my desire for you both to undertake this war with the intention of never making peace but of waging it ever more fiercely, always dealing out to the fellow the things he doesn't like and never conceding to him anything he does. Let the watchdog of conscience bark to warn reason, who must not admit a single thought to the heart without first inspecting it; or allow a single wicked thought to go unrebuked. Let this wretched sensuality be the servant-girl, and reason the mistress, as is only fitting.[4] If you let yourselves grow negligent or lukewarm, you will never defeat either this third enemy or the other two. And that is why I said I longed to see you brave knights, so that you may be victorious. Up with you, then, my children! Take a grip on this sword and never let it be out of the hand of free will until death for, by God's permission and for our own good – so that our virtues, with the help of grace, may be acquired by sweat and toil – this enemy of yours will last out until then.

Now I will answer the letters you sent me, Pietro. I shall indeed see whether you want to leave home and come here! If this *is* what you want, you will lose no time in disentangling yourself and winding up those outstanding affairs of yours so that, once free, you can follow Christ crucified completely. But you are a negligent fellow. You have not taken hold of the sword I spoke of, and are not acting on the holy desire God has given you. I am sure you don't think I want to abandon you. May death find you and the others such as I give birth to you anew every day, in the sight of God, by unceasing prayer; and more where more is needed! Hurry then and make a new man of yourself. And the same goes for you, Stefano. Do your best to get away from the world and run to God who awaits us with open arms. Come quickly.

By God's mercy, holy Church and Pope Urban VI have recently received the weightiest piece of news to come for some time.[5] I am sending with this a letter intended for the Bachelor;[6] you will see from it how God is beginning to pour out his graces on his sweet Bride. And I hope that in his mercy he will continue to do so more and more from day to day. I know his truth cannot lie, and he has promised to reform her through much endurance on the part of his servants and by means of humble and unceasing prayer, with sweat and tears.[7]

And so I invite you once again to knock persistently on the door of his Mercy, for I promise you that if we persist in knocking, it will be opened to us.[8] Say this to all the other sons there, and bless them all for us.

Grandma, Lisa and the rest of our poor little family comfort you in Christ[9] . . . [lacuna in original]. Abide in the sweet and holy love of God. When you do come, Stefano . . . [further lacuna]. Sweet Jesus. Jesus, Love. Given at Rome on the first of January 1378.[10]

---

[1]   for *Pietro*, see letters 12 (note 5) and 37; for *Stefano*, see letters 27 & 28. The two young men were close friends.

[2]   1379 according to our calendar. The Sienese year began on 25 March.

[3]   Cf. Romans 7:23.

[4]   For parallel development of this theme, cf. letter 40.

[5]   This may refer to the report of England's official support for Urban's cause (Fawtier p.273).

[6]   William of Flete; see letter 10.

[7]   Cf. Dialogue, p.289.

[8]   Luke 11:10.

[9]   Catherine's mother and sister-in-law; see letters 2, 25 & 36.

[10]   See note 2.

## LETTER 50   (Tommaseo 329; Gigli 262).

*To:*   *Stefano Maconi, in Siena.*[1]

*Date:*   Late January/early February 1379.[2]

Dearest son in Christ sweet Jesus,

I, Catherine, servant and slave of the servants of Jesus Christ, write to you in his precious blood, desiring to see you cutting the knots, not stopping to untie them; for that takes time and you are not sure of having it, it goes so quickly. Better, then, to make one clean cut, with true and holy resoluteness. What joy when my soul shall see that you have indeed cut yourself away from the world – in fact as well as in spirit – and from your sensual nature, and have been joined to eternal Life, a join so delightful, so sweet and appealing, that it destroys all bitterness and lightens every load.

Who, then, would hesitate to draw his sword of hatred and love and slash self away with the hand of free will? So powerful is this sword that once a man has made the cut, it makes the join! But you will say to me, dearest son: 'Where can I find such a sword, and where is it forged?' So I reply: 'You will find it in the cell of self-knowledge, where you conceive hatred for vice and for your own frailty, and love for your Creator and your neighbour, with true solid virtue. As for the forging, that is done in the fire of divine charity, on the anvil of the body of the sweet and loving Word, God's Son.' Fool indeed, and deserving of severe rebuke, is the man who has within him the weapon he needs to defend himself, yet tosses it from him!

I don't want you to be numbered among such fools. No, I want you, in true manly fashion, to make haste and respond to Mary's loving summons. The blood of these glorious martyrs[3] who gave their blood and their lives in their love for Life is boiling hot, calling on you and the others to come and endure, here, for the glory and honour of God's name and of holy Church, and for the testing of your virtue. For to this holy land where God manifested his dignity, calling it his garden, was he summoning his servants when he said: 'Now is the time for them to come and test the gold of virtue.'[4] So let's not pretend to be deaf. If our ears are blocked because of the cold, let us take the hot Blood – hot because mingled with Fire! – and wash them out with it; all trace of deafness will then disappear. Hide yourself in the wounds of Christ crucified; flee from the world; leave your family home; take refuge in the cavern, the side of Christ crucified, and so come into the promised land.[5] The same goes for

Pietro.[6] Sit down, both of you, at the table of the cross and there, drunk with Blood, devour the food of souls: enduring suffering, disgrace, mockery, treachery, hunger, thirst and nakedness, and glorying – with Paul, that sweet vessel of election[7a] – in the shame of Christ crucified.[7b] If you make the cut, as I said, to suffer will be your glory; otherwise not, but rather your bane, and your own shadow enough to scare you.

When my soul reflects on all this in its hunger for your salvation, I yearn to see you make the cut without waiting to do the untying, so that you can run all the more quickly. Clothe yourself in the blood of Christ crucified. No more now. Abide in the sweet and holy love of God.

I received your letters and was greatly consoled to hear of Battista's recovery,[8] both because I hope he will yet be a good plant and because of my compassion for Monna Giovanna.[9a] But I was far more delighted at the news that God has sent you a means by which you can get away from the world, and also at how well disposed you tell me the Lords and other citizens are towards our sweet *babbo*,[10] Pope Urban VI – may God in his infinite mercy keep things so, and grant an ever greater increase in reverence and obedience to him. As long as you and the others are there, be sure to sow the truth and confound the lie[11] in every way you can.

My very special greetings to Monna Giovanna and to Corrado.[9b] Comfort Battista, too, and the rest of the family. Comfort all my children there; ask each one to forgive me if I don't write, but I am finding it very difficult. Comfort Messer Matteo.[12a] Ask him to let us know what it is he wants as it has slipped my memory and Fra Raimondo[12b] left so soon that we did not have a chance to ask him. Then I'll do what I can at once. And tell Fra Tommaso[12c] that I have not written to him as I don't know if he is there; if he is, comfort him for me, and ask him to give me his blessing. Greetings from our Lisa[12d] and all the family. Neri[12e] hasn't written to you as he has been at death's door, but now he's on the mend.

May God give you his everlasting blessing. Tell Pietro[12]f
to come if he can as we need him to do something for us.
Sweet Jesus. Jesus, Love.

Deliver all these letters, or arrange to have them delivered, and pray to God for us. Give the second bundle of
letters as it is to Monna Caterina;[12]g she will distribute
them.

---

1   See letters 27, 28 and 49.
2   See Fawtier, pp. 272–3.
3   The words 'whose bodies are buried here in Rome' seem to
have been interpolated here by one of the early editors; cf.
Dupré Theseider, E., 'Il problema critico delle lettere di S.
Caterina', in *Bullettino dell'Istituto Storico Italiano e Archivio
Muratoriano*, no. 49 (1933), p.206.
4   perhaps a reference to a vision, but cf. Psalm 12:6.
5   Cf. Exodus 12:1 et seq.
6   *Pietro* Ventura; see letter 49.
7a  Acts 9:15.
7b  Cf. Gal. 6:14.
8   Stefano's younger brother, who had been ill.
9a  Stefano's mother
9b  and father; see letter 27.
10  See letter 15, note 2.
11  that Urban was not the lawful pope.
12  Close friends and disciples in Siena:
    a. *Messer Matteo*, Rector of the Misericordia Hospital, see
    letter 39, note 2a.
    b. *Fra Raimondo* of Capua OP, who left Rome early in
    December bearing letters from Urban to the King of
    France, the University of Paris, the Duke of Anjou and
    others; see Gardner, pp.291–293 and letter 57, note 1.
    c. *Fra Tommaso* della Fonte OP, early confessor and close
    friend; see letters 1, 36 & 38.
    d. Catherine's sister-in-law, see letter 2, note 9.
    e. *Neri* Pagliaresi, beloved disciple and secretary; see letters
    3 (note 5b) and 53.
    f. *Pietro* Ventura, see letters 37 and 49.
    g. *Caterina* di Ghetto, a disciple and *Mantellata*; see letter 1,
    note 2.

LETTER 51 (Tommaseo 328; Gigli 130; Cavallini XXXII. Note: Our translation is based on the text as given by Cavallini).

*To:*    *Fra Antonio of Nice.*[1]
*Date:*  Before Easter (10 April), 1379.[2]

Beloved son in Christ sweet Jesus,
I, Catherine, servant and slave of the servants of Jesus Christ, write to you in his precious blood, desiring to see your foundation laid on the living Rock, Christ sweet Jesus, so that the building you erect on it will never be brought down by any wind that may beat against you but may endure, solid, firm and stable until death, in the way of truth.[3]

How badly we need this true solid foundation, and I, ignoramus, don't know it, for if I did I would not be laying the foundation on myself, who am worse than sand, but on that living Rock I spoke of. Following Christ by the way of insults, mockery and treachery, I would deprive myself of every consolation, whether from within or without, in order to conform myself to him. I would not be seeking myself for my own sake, but have my whole attention fixed on God's honour, the salvation of souls and the reform of holy Church, which I see to be in such great need. Wretch that I am, I do the very opposite.

But because I do wrong, dearest son, I would not wish you or the others to do it. I long, rather, to see your foundation set on this Rock. The time has come to find out who God's servants are and whether or not they are only seeking themselves for their own sake, God for the private consolation they find in him, and their neighbour for their own satisfaction; also whether we think God is to be found only in one place and not in another. I don't see how this can be. I find, rather, that for a true servant of God every place and every time is just right. It follows that whenever such a man has to give up his own consolation and welcome fatigue for the honour of God, he does so; and whenever he has to come out of the woods for the sake of God's honour, out he comes and appears in public, as did the glorious St Anthony who, in spite of his immense love of solitude, often left it behind in order to comfort and strengthen the Christians.[4] And I could say the same of many other saints.

True servants of God have always come out into the open in times of need and adversity, but fled away in times of prosperity. This is no time to flee away for fear that prosperity will set our hearts scudding before the wind of pride or vainglory, for there is only toil in which to glory![5] We seem to me to have no light; to be so dazzled by our own consolations and our reliance on revelations that, though we may mean well, we find it difficult to see the truth quite clearly. But God, who is supreme and eternal Goodness, gives us true and perfect light. I won't go into this at greater length.

The young man who brings you this letter had told me that you would be coming before Easter; but it now seems, from the letter Brother William sent me, that neither of you will be coming. I do not intend to reply to that letter, but I am very grieved at his foolishness, which is little to God's honour or the edification of others. If it is out of humility and fear of losing his peace that he does not want to come, then let him practise the virtue of humility by meekly and humbly begging leave of Christ's vicar, beseeching his Holiness to allow him to remain in his wood[6] for his greater peace, while being prepared, nonetheless, to abide by his will, as a truly obedient man would; to do this would be more pleasing to God and more profitable to himself. But he seems to me to have done quite the opposite, claiming that when a man is bound by divine obedience, he does not have to obey creatures.[7] I wouldn't mind so much about the others, but that he should disregard Christ's vicar grieves me much, seeing him so forgetful of the truth. Obedience to God never exonerates us from obedience to the holy Father; indeed, the more perfectly we obey God, so much the more perfectly must we obey him. At all times we must submit to and carry out his orders until death. Even though what is required of us may seem to be indiscreet and liable to deprive us of peace and consolation of mind, still we must obey. If we don't, I consider it a grave imperfection and a deceit of the devil.

It seems, from what he writes, that two servants of God have had a great revelation to the effect that both Christ-on-earth and whoever advised him to summon these servants of God,[8] were following human and not divine counsel, and that it was prompted rather by the devil than by God's inspiration, in order to draw his servants away from their peace and consolation; also that if you and the others were to come, you would lose your spirit and so be unable to help by prayer or to be in spirit with the holy Father. Your spirit is easily detached if it can be lost by change of place! On this showing, God is partial to places[9] and is to be found in the woods, but nowhere else in time of need.

What are we to say, then? That we want God's Church reformed, the thorns removed and replaced by sweet-smelling flowers, God's servants; but at the same time we maintain that to send for them and call them away from their peace and quiet of mind so as to come to the aid of the little Ship is a trick of the devil? At least let him speak for himself, but not for other servants of God – since we must not count ourselves among the world's!

This is not how Fra Andrea of Lucca and Fra Paolino have acted.[10] In spite of the effort and inconvenience involved, these splendid servants of God, elderly and in poor health, who had lived all their lives in retirement, set out at once and have come, in obedience to the summons. They are longing to get back to their cells, but they are not seeking to be relieved of the yoke. 'Let what I said be as not said', they say, stifling their own will and personal consolation. Whoever comes to bear the burden, in search not of high office but of the dignity of much toil, with tears, vigils and unceasing prayer, must do the same.

Let's not labour this point any more as there would be much to say. But one thing does astonish me and that is that, although I know the contrary to be the case, I see the opinion being expressed that the Master[11] only came to secure his own promotion. I feel an intolerable anguish of heart when I see God being offended so openly under colour of virtue, in spite of the fact that we can never and must never judge any creature's intention; even if we know of a fault or actually witness it, we must not judge the intention, but bear it with great compassion before God; to do the opposite is to be deceived by our own opinions.[12]

May God in his infinite mercy put us directly on the way of truth and give us true and most perfect light so that we are never in the dark. I beseech you and the Bachelor[13] and God's servants to implore the humble Lamb to send me by his way. I'll say no more.

As to whether you and Brother William come or not, may God's will be done. I hardly expected him to come, but I certainly did not expect him to react so disrespectfully to the obedience laid on him, and in such a foolish way. My greetings to him and to all the others. I beg you and him to pardon me if I have scandalized or grieved you. I confess that I am a scandal to everyone, ignorant and full of defects as I am.

Abide in the sweet and holy love of God. Sweet Jesus. Jesus, Love.

---

[1] *Fra Antonio*, an Augustinian hermit at Lecceto, near Siena, was both a close friend of Bro. William of Flete (see letters 10 & 39) and a disciple of Catherine.

[2] Catherine had just heard that neither hermit intended to respond to Pope Urban VI's appeal – addressed to them and many other religious – to come to Rome in order to provide, there, 'the devout tears and assiduous prayers of the just children of the Church,' See Gardner, pp.293 et seq. for an account of Urban's attempt to implement this idea of Catherine's.

[3] Cf. Matthew 7:24–27.

[4] Catherine chooses the telling example of Fra Antonio's own

patron saint. Traditionally regarded as the first hermit, St Anthony did not hesitate to leave his solitude when necessary, e.g. to instil courage into the persecuted Christians of Alexandria (311 A.D.) and to combat the Arian heresy (335 A.D.).

5   Cf. II Cor. 12:9–10.
6   The hermits lived in a forest of ilex trees, hence the name 'Lecceto'.
7   Cf. Acts 5:29.
8   including Catherine herself.
9   Cf. Acts 10:34.
10   Catherine points to the example of two other hermits who had come to Rome in response to Urban's appeal, one of whom was also a hermit at Lecceto.
11   'Maestro' Giovanni Tantucci; see letter 21, note 1a.
12   See letter 35 for a fuller treatment of this theme.
13   Bro. William.


## LETTER 52   (Gardner VI)

To:   Bartalo Usimbardi and Francesco di Pippino, of Florence.[1]

Date:   (in ms.) May 8 (1379)


Beloved sons in Christ sweet Jesus,

I, Catherine, servant and slave of the servants of Jesus Christ, write to you in his precious blood, desiring to see you grateful and appreciative of the benefits you have received from your Creator, so that the spring of piety may be fed within you.[2] This gratitude will make you eager to practise virtue, for while ingratitude makes a soul lazy and negligent, this sweet gratitude makes it so hungry for time that every hour, every moment, sees it at work. All true virtue comes from this gratitude, for what else but gratitude gives us charity, or makes us humble and patient? Seeing the immense debt it owes to God, the [grateful] soul does its best to live virtuously, knowing that God asks only this. And so, dearest sons, eagerly recall to mind all the gifts you have received from him, so that you may enter into perfect possession of this mother of virtues.

I received your letters in the past few days (one from Bartalo, one from Francesco and one from Monna Agnesa), much to my delight. As regards the cost of the privilege,[3] I reply that Christ's blood paid for everything, so no money is needed; but I want you to pay for it in heartfelt tears and prayer for holy Church and for Christ-on-earth, praying earnestly to God every day for him. I assure you that even if we gave our bodies to be burned,[4] we could never make an adequate return for the very great grace God has given us of being certain of our salvation in this life, provided we have a lively faith and are grateful and appreciative. But our sweet God asks no more from us than we can accomplish. Be virtuous, then, and set about growing fast enough for me to see!

I am sending you the document with the papal Bull by the hand of Fra Jacomo Manni,[5] the bearer of this letter; it is made out to Monna Paola,[6] of the monastery of S. Giorgio, and Monna Andrea her servant, as well as to the four of you, that is, Bartalo and Monna Orsa, Francesco and Monna Agnesa. When you receive it, have your own names duly transferred to a separate document at the bishop's chancellery and give the original to Monna Paola when she returns; at the moment she is here.

So Giannozzo has been taken;[7] I don't know for how long? I am very pleased at your assurance, Francesco, that you will never abandon him. On behalf of Christ crucified, therefore, I order you to visit him often and give him all the consolation and assistance you can. Remember, all God asks of us is to show to our neighbour the love we have for him. I entrust [Giannozzo] especially to you; tell him from me to be a good knight now that God has placed him in the field, and let his 'combat' be true patience, bowing his head humbly to the sweet will of God. Assure him of all comfort and support from me and all the family here, who feel great compassion for him. I will write him a letter when God permits. Tell him to do what he can to get out quickly, and not to be too upset should he not secure full satisfaction. I will say no more.

Abide in the sweet and holy love of God. Bless the children for me. Sweet Jesus. Jesus, Love.

Written on the eighth day of May in Rome.

---

[1]   *Bartalo* and his wife Orsa, Florentine citizens of good standing, were on terms of intimate friendship with the humbler *Francesco*, a tailor, and his wife, Agnese, through their common love for Catherine, whom Francesco and Agnese had sheltered when her life was threatened by the mob in June 1378.

[2]   Cf. letter 47, note 5.

[3]   An official document recording the granting of a plenary indulgence and the conditions for gaining it. Technically, the charge made was to meet the cost of transcription, etc., not for the indulgence itself, but there was much misunderstanding, and even abuse, on this point.

[4]   I Cor. 13:3.

[5]   Not easily identifiable, but cf. letters 9, note 2 and 10, note 9.

[6]   Probably the Abbess of a monastery in Fiesole, near Florence, who was among Catherine's correspondents; cf. Dupré, XXXIV.

[7]   *Giannozzo* Sacchetti, a spendthrift poet who had come under Catherine's influence after a sincere conversion at the beginning of the interdict. Nevertheless, he 'continued to fish in the troubled waters of political intrigue' (Gardner). The imprisonment Catherine refers to here was seemingly for debt, but soon afterwards he got involved in a conspiracy against the Florentine government, was arrested, tortured and finally beheaded as a traitor on 15 October 1379. See Gardner, pp.232, 286 & 326–8.

LETTER 53   (Tommaseo 186; Gigli 276).

*To:*   *Neri dei Pagliaresi, in Perugia (or Naples).*[1]
*Date:*   June/July or September/October 1379.[2]

Beloved and sweetest son in Christ sweet Jesus,
I, Catherine, servant and slave of the servants of Jesus
Christ, write to you in his precious blood, desiring to see
you make the vessel of your heart and soul ready to
receive what God wishes to give you by means of prayer.
And why? Because you couldn't receive it otherwise; for,
as God is always ready to give, so the soul must always be
ready to receive. And how does it make itself ready? With
the original readiness we all received from God when we
were created in his image and likeness. At that moment
we were given a vessel, a ready capacity, along with light:
that is, first memory, which is a storage vessel, then
understanding, into which the light of faith is poured in
holy baptism, and finally the will, pre-disposed and
designed for love, for without love it cannot live. Hence
this capacity to love has come to us from God with our
very being – for we were made for love – and with our
free will we must present and offer to God this being
given to us out of love, and lovingly receive Love in
return; the general love, I mean, that God has for every
rational creature, as well as the special gifts and graces
each soul is aware of receiving. So let us call on God to
flood us with the depth and fire of his inestimable Charity, bringing with it supernatural insight, fullness of grace
and adornment of virtue, and washing the face of our
soul in the precious blood of the humble spotless Lamb.
In its hunger for God's honour and the salvation of souls,
the soul [then] runs to the table of crucified desire and
there eats such quantities of this sweet wholesome food
that it bursts, breaking up the sensual part, and thus
leaving the will quite dead to all self-love and sensual
appetite! Thus does [the soul], as Truth's faithful bridegroom, make ready to die and die again, a thousand times
if it were possible, for that Truth.

Dearest, sweetest son, now is the time for you to give [your life for the Truth];[3] and you will be fit to do so when you are in a permanent state of readiness. I'll say no more.[4] Abide in the sweet and holy love of God. Sweet Jesus. Jesus, Love.

---

[1]   See letter 3, note 5b.

[2]   Neri had accompanied Catherine to Rome. From there she sent him to Perugia in June and to Naples in September, where he continued to work for 'the cause' until her death in April 1380. See Gardner, pp.323 & 325.

[3]   The text reads 'it'.

[4]   Very probably this letter had quite a long personal ending which has been deleted by the early editors – perhaps by Neri himself; cf. letter 6, note 9.

## LETTER 54   (Tommaseo 343; Gigli 236).

*To:*     *Rainaldo of Capua.*[1]

*Date:*   ? September/October 1379.[2]

[Having stated her desire to see in Rainaldo the true light of faith, Catherine outlines the points she proposes to discuss: 'Let us see what may deprive us of this light and what restores it to us; how a soul behaves when thus enlightened, and what fruit it derives from it.' In discussing how the light of faith affects the soul, Catherine says:]

The humble man of faith has no desire to explore the hidden mysteries of God either in himself or in others, in things visible or invisible.[3] His one aim is to know himself, and to know and see in all things the eternal will of God, wherein he savours the fire of his Charity. He has no desire to exalt himself, unlike the proud or presumptuous man who, without knowing self or entering the valley of humility, wants to start investigating the ways of God, thinking and saying to himself: 'Why has God done this? Why not that? Why did he allow this to happen to me and not to him?'[4]

Such a man presumes to lay down the law where by rights he should be acknowledging and pondering on the greatness and goodness of God in all he sees; as the humble man of faith does, who sees and ponders all things within God's infinite greatness, power and goodness. Many who are devoid of humility and make no attempt to know their own defects will nevertheless strain their minds with the effort of peering with their darkened vision into the profundities of sacred scripture, and then want to expound and understand it in their own way. Such people will study the Apocalypse without either humility or the light of faith, and in their faithlessness get themselves so embroiled in things that they can't find a way out, thus deriving death from life and darkness from light. Instead of being filled with God, their minds are crammed with fancies which yield only the fruit of darkness and mental confusion. And all because they have chosen to go upwards before going downwards. Oh, the shame of it, that in doing this we do not even know ourselves yet! I don't keep the law imposed on me, yet here I am wanting to impose a law on God, and to know his secrets. If we really want to be able to see the stars of his mysteries, let us go deep down into the well of true humility.[5] The man of faith does just this, throwing himself on the ground in his search for lowliness. God then raises him aloft. He does not go looking for reasons why this or that should be; his holy faith makes him sure of anything the devil or his own weakness may cause him to doubt. He sees his own reflection in the mirror of unceasing prayer; that is, he sees himself continually reflected in the Truth; from the Truth he derives true and holy desire and with this desire he offers the incense of humble prayer.[6]

Such faith makes a man frank and open-hearted, ready to confess his sins honestly without hiding anything either through shame or for fear of the penance. Hating the fault, he spews out all his dirt in a good confession, hiding nothing on account of some past rebuke, and omitting nothing, for whatever reason. All this is the work of faith.

Now let us look at its fruit: fullness of grace in this life, eternal life in the next. And who has been appointed by God to administer this to us? Hope. By virtue of what? The blood of the humble Lamb. This hope is the humble kind that neither relies on its own virtue nor despairs in the face of any fault one may have fallen into, relying instead on the Blood and driving out despair with the conviction that the divine mercy found in the Blood far exceeds one's own wretchedness. O Hope, sweet sister of Faith, it is you who open the way to eternal life with the keys of the Blood; you who guard the city of the soul from its enemy, confusion. Far from slackening your pace when the devil tries to drive the soul to despair at the deadweight of sins committed, you persevere steadily in virtue, placing the price of the Blood on the scales to restore the balance. It is you who place the crown of victory on the head of perseverance, for it was you who hoped for it by virtue of the Blood. Again, it is you who bind the demon of confusion with the cord of living faith, as it is you who react to a subtle trick he plays in order to keep the soul in a constant state of darkness and affliction.

The trick is that sometimes when a person has in fact confessed his fault honestly, without deceitfully keeping anything back, the devil will try to befuddle his mind and keep him from receiving with glowing heart the fruit of his confession by making him seem not to have confessed his faults properly. 'You didn't confess them all; and you weren't specific enough about the ones you did confess,' he will say, and stir up all sorts of other thoughts and anxieties in the soul. If the soul does not then bestir itself with prudence and hope, it will get bogged down in lukewarmness, in fear and confusion of mind, and in the dark. With the arms of its holy desire thus pinioned and having got itself entangled in the noose of confusion, as I said, the soul is deprived of all joy and becomes unbearable to itself. Is there any way of keeping such a soul from falling into despair? The only way is for it to look into its conscience with the light of faith, where it will see that it had not willingly or culpably omitted to spit out, in confession, the poison of its fault. By all means let it acknowledge in all humility that it had not stressed the gravity of its faults as it might have done, but let this acknowledgement be seasoned with hope in Christ's blood, in the confidence that what the soul lacks, Christ himself will make good.

Another remedy is to consider by this same light how ineffably the soul is loved by God, and to see that his love does not despise the witness of a good conscience; nor could it abide anything contrary to it being left in the soul. Equipped thus with faith, hope and love, let the soul immerse itself in God's mercy, examining itself and making its confession in all simplicity, and then thinking no more about it. Banishing all preoccupation with self, let a man dwell instead on the mercy he has received and goes on receiving from God. And though he may again be assailed by the battle and torment, let him cast it all behind him as far as being afflicted by it goes, but keep it before him in so far as it serves to humble him and lead him to self-knowledge and the fruit of true and perfect hope; confident that to endure, and to journey by the way of the cross, pleases God more than anything else; confident, too, that he will receive the fruit of the Blood in great abundance. It is this, dearest brother, that gives you the eternal Truth and is the remedy for your infirmity.

[Summarizing the substance of the letter, Catherine ends with a characteristic injunction and exhortation:]

Bear in mind that God is more ready to forgive than

you are to commit sin. Hope, then, and be faithful to the
Blood, to holy Church, and to the supreme pontiff, Pope
Urban VI. Abide in the sweet and holy love of God. Sweet
Jesus. Jesus, Love.

---

[1]   The early mss. record only that this man was something of an
intellectual, given to 'investigating the mysteries of God in sacred scripture'; also that he suffered from scruples concerning
confession.

[2]   Fawtier, p.262, suggests that Catherine was put in touch with
her correspondent either through her Neapolitan contacts in
Rome or, more probably, through Neri Pagliaresi in Naples (cf.
letter 53, note 2).

[3]   Cf. Col. 1:16.

[4]   Cf. Dante, *Paradiso*, XXI, 83–102.

[5]   'And some in sorrow's well have seen
In daylight far stars glimmer pale.'
'The Hollow Hill' by Kathleen Raine, in *The Hollow Hill and
other Poems* 1960–1964, London, 1965. And cf. Dante, *Inferno*
XXXIV, 139.

[6]   Psalm 140:2.

LETTER 55   (Tommaseo 353; Gigli 337).

*To:*   *Monna Catella, Monna Cecia Planula and Monna
Caterina Dentice, of Naples.* [1]

*Date:*   May/June 1379. [2]

[Note: Presumably at about the same time, Catherine
sent a substantially identical letter (Tommaseo 26;
Gigli 159) to her niece, Suor Eugenia OP, one of two
daughters of Bartolo and Lisa who had entered the
monastery of S. Agnese at Montepulciano, near Siena
(cf. letters 1 and 36)].

[Urging her correspondents to seek the desire for God

which she describes as the food of angels, Catherine
suggests how to live so that this food alone may become
all important, stressing the need for obedience to God;
deference; prudence and charity in all dealings with
others; and, above all, prayer.]

I say then that when a soul has tasted this angelic food it
sees by the light [of holy faith] that to love and associate
with creatures apart from the Creator is to put an obstacle
between itself and this food. So it makes every effort to
avoid them, and also to love and pursue anything that will
make it grow and abide in virtue. Realizing, too, that this
food is best savoured through prayer based on self-
knowledge, it practises this continually, as it practises all
other ways of drawing closer to God.

There are three ways of praying. The first is that abiding holy desire which prays to God in everything we
creatures do, for it directs all our spiritual and bodily
actions in his honour, and so is called continuous. The
glorious Saint Paul seems to have meant this kind of
prayer when he said: 'Pray without ceasing.'[3] Then there
is vocal prayer, as when the tongue is used in reciting the
Office or other vocal prayers. This is a preparation for
the third kind of prayer, namely mental, which the soul
comes to when it practises vocal prayer prudently and
humbly; that is when, as the tongue prays, the heart is not
far from God.[4]

But one must endeavour to establish the heart firmly in
a love for divine Charity. And whenever one feels God
visiting one's mind, drawing it in some way to think of the
Creator, one should stop praying vocally and rest lovingly in whatever one feels this visitation to be. If there is
still time when this has passed, the soul should resume its
vocal prayer so that the mind will always be full and not
empty. And even if the prayer abounds in battles of all
kinds, in darkness and great confusion of mind, with the
devil suggesting that our prayer is not pleasing to God,
we must not give up prayer on this account, but persist

with fortitude and unfailing perseverance, realizing that this is the devil's way of enticing us away from our mother, prayer; and that God permits this to test in us our fortitude and constancy and also so that, in the struggles and darkness, we may know our own nothingness, while in the good will [that we perceive in ourselves]⁵ we know the goodness of God, who gives and upholds our good and holy desires, and will not refuse this gift to those who ask him.

The soul thus comes to the third and last kind of [fully] mental prayer, in which it receives the fruit of the efforts it has put into the less perfect vocal prayer, for it now savours the milk of fidelity to prayer. It lifts itself above the crude level of feeling and with the mind as of an angel is made one with God by love; by the light of its understanding it sees, knows and is clothed with the Truth. Made now sister to the angels, seated with the Bridegroom at the table of crucified desire, it delights in seeking God's honour and the salvation of souls for which, it now sees clearly, the eternal Bridegroom ran to meet the shameful death of the cross and, in so doing, obeyed his Father's will and achieved our salvation. Such prayer is indeed a mother, conceiving her children, the virtues, in God's love, and giving birth to them in love for others. Where do you find the light that guides you in the way of truth? In prayer. And where do you display love, faith, hope and humility? Again, in prayer. You would not be doing these things unless you loved them, and it is because a creature loves that it seeks to be one with the thing it loves, [that is, with God].⁵ By prayer you ask him for what you need. Knowing yourself – and true prayer is founded on this knowledge – you see you are in great need and feel surrounded by your enemies: the world, with its hurts; the devil, with all his temptations; and the flesh, ever warring against the spirit by rebelling against reason.⁶ You see, too, that of yourself you are not; and since you are not, you cannot help yourself; so you turn, with faith, to him who IS; who knows your needs and can

and will help you in them. You ask with hope, then wait
for his help. This is how we must pray if we are to get what
we desire. No right thing will ever be denied us if we ask
the divine Goodness for it in this way, but we would get
very little benefit from praying in any other.

Where shall we sense the fragrance of obedience, if not
in prayer? Where strip ourselves of the self-love that
makes us impatient when insulted or made to suffer? Or
put on a divine love that will make us patient, and ready
to glory in the cross of Christ crucified? In prayer. And
where shall we sense the sweet perfume of virginity and
purity, and a hunger for martyrdom that will make us
ready to give our lives for the honour of God and the
salvation of souls? In this sweet mother, prayer. She will
make us obey God's holy commandments, and seal her
counsels into our hearts and minds by imprinting on us
the desire to keep them until death. She withdraws us
from the company of creatures and gives us the Creator
as companion. She fills the vessel of our heart with the
blood of the humble spotless Lamb and clothes it in Fire,
for by the fire of Love was it shed.

A soul will of course receive and savour this mother,
prayer, more or less perfectly according as it feeds on the
angelic food of true and holy desire for God, raising itself
up, as I said, to take it from the table of the most sweet
cross. And that is why I said I wanted to see each of you
partaking of this angelic food, for you could not have the
life of grace or be true servants of Christ crucified in any
other way. I will say no more. Abide in the sweet and holy
love of God.

I received a letter from you, which I heard and understood with joy,[7] both because I was hoping for news of
you and because of the good news it brought in a few
words, namely that the light has dawned over that land,[8]
for the heart of Pharaoh has been broken – of the Queen,
that is[9] – that until now has seemed so hard; for in turning
away from her head, Christ-on-earth, and going over to
Antichrist, member of the devil, she persecuted the truth

and exalted a lie. Thanks, thanks to our Saviour who has enlightened her heart – whether by force or by love[10] – and has revealed his wonders to her. Let us now rejoice and exult with heartfelt joy, and with pious practice, as we said, constantly purifying our conscience with frequent confession and receiving communion on every solemn feast so that, made strong in this life of pilgrimage, you may run manfully to the table of the cross by way of the doctrine of the humble Lamb, and there partake of the sweet angelic food; and also so that the stigmata of Christ crucified may glow in you.

Bathe yourselves in his precious Blood. I earnestly recommend myself to you. Sweet Jesus. Jesus, Love.

---

[1]   Little is known about these three women except that they were devoted to Catherine. She acquired a number of disciples in Naples, mainly perhaps through her contacts, in Rome, with emissaries from Queen Joanna and her Court (see note 9 below); but also through Neri dei Pagliaresi (see letters 3, note 5b, and 53), who went to Naples to try and influence the Queen on Catherine's behalf when she finally abandoned the idea of going there herself (cf. letter 57, p.253. and note 20).

[2]   Cf. Fawtier, pp. 302–3 and note 10 below.

[3]   I Thessalonians 5:17.

[4]   Cf. St. Thomas, *Summa theol.* 2a 2ae 83, 13 and 14.

[5]   Phrase in square brackets supplied from Tommaseo 26.

[6]   Romans 7:23.

[7]   Cf. letter 13, note 9.

[8]   the kingdom of Naples; cf. Isaiah 9:2.

[9]   Joanna I of Naples, whose ambiguous character and influential position prompted Catherine to appeal to her repeatedly both to mend her ways and be a loyal daughter of the Church; cf. Dupré letters XXXII, XXXIX & XXXXI urging the Queen to support the crusade and letter 58 below, which is one of a series connected with her repeated tergiversations during the Schism.

[10]   Realizing that the Queen's change of heart had been induced mainly by the victory of Urban's forces at the Battle of Marino, which was followed by a popular uprising in his favour in Naples (cf. Gardner, pp.307–8 & 312–14, and letter 56, note

5), Catherine perhaps already sensed that her conversion would be short-lived; cf. letters 57 and 58.

## LETTER 56   (Tommaseo 351; Gigli 20).

*To:*   *Urban VI*

*Date:*   [in ms.] 30 May 1379.

Most Holy Father,

May the Holy Spirit overshadow your soul, your heart and your feelings with the fire of divine charity.[1] May he so fill your understanding with supernatural light that in your light we little sheep may see light,[2] and that no malicious trick the devil tries to play on you may remain hidden from your Holiness. My desire now, most holy Father, is to see accomplished in you all those things that God's sweet will is asking of you and that I know you yourself greatly desire to accomplish.

My hope is that the sweet fire of the Holy Spirit will be in your heart and soul as it was in the blessed apostles, giving them such strength and power against devils visible and invisible that by [its] power they overthrew the rulers of this world and spread the faith by their endurance. He enlightened them with wisdom to know the truth in respect of the doctrine which Truth himself had left them; whereupon their affections – which follow understanding – were so clothed with the fire of his charity that they lost all servile fear and all desire to please men, devoting themselves entirely to honouring God[3] [and] rescuing souls from the devil, for their one desire was to offer to all men the truth by which they themselves had been enlightened. Only after prolonged vigil, humble unceasing prayer, and the great mental effort of those ten days were they made strong in the Holy Spirit; the effort and the prayerful preparation came first. O most holy Father, they seem to have a lesson for us, and to be instilling courage into your Holiness today by showing us how we too may receive the Holy Spirit.

How then? By remaining in the house of self-knowledge, which always keeps the soul humble so that joy does not [over]-elate it or sorrow make it impatient. No, at all times, it is mature, balanced, and patient, having come to hate its own sensuality. In this house it keeps watch and prays continually, for our understanding must be watching to know the truth of God's sweet will, not sleeping the sleep of self-love. It then receives the gift of continual prayer, that is, holy desire, leading to the practice of virtue, which is a continual prayer. A good man is always praying.[4] Since this is the way to acquire such sweet fortitude, let us follow it with true and holy purposefulness, in so far as we are able.

I said that the apostles encourage you, the true Supreme Pontiff, by their own example; for they overcame the world and dispelled the darkness of infidelity, not by any human means but by the strength, wisdom and charity of God, whose might is undiminished for you, and for all who trust in him. They do indeed, then, instil this strength into you, making you strong, in your bride's hour of need, not in faith alone but in deed. Four weeks ago we saw the power of God achieve marvels by means of sinful creatures,[5] thus showing clearly that he and not human skill achieves the results. Let us then give him the glory, and our thanks.

I rejoice with all my heart, most holy Father, that my eyes have seen God's will accomplished in you in that humble gesture – so long in abeyance – of the holy procession.[6] Oh, how pleasing it was to God – and so displeasing to the devils that they tried to bring scandal out of it, both within and without, but the angels held them in check.

I said just now that I longed to see God accomplish in you his sweet will regarding everything else, and so I remind you that Truth now desires you to devote all your care and concern to progressively establishing rule and order in God's Church, so far as you can in the time available. He will be working through you, giving you strength to accomplish and light to know whatever is required, together with wisdom and prudence in steering his Ship, and the will to do it. He has given you this already, but will now augment it, in his infinite mercy. And so you will overthrow tyrants and dispel the darkness of heresy by his power, for it is he who proclaims, and will proclaim, his truth.

I rejoice, too, that Mary, sweetest of mothers, and sweet Peter, prince of the apostles, have restored you to your place. The eternal Truth now desires you to turn your garden into a servant-of-God garden: while you provide for their temporal needs, they will provide for your spiritual ones. Let their one task be to plead before God for the good estate of holy Church, and for your Holiness. This kind of soldier will bring you complete victory, not only over wicked Christians, those limbs severed from holy obedience, but over infidels. How I long to see the standard of the cross raised above them; they seem already to be inviting us![7]

So let us grow and feed on real solid virtue. Let us withdraw into the house of self-knowledge, and so receive the fullness of the Holy Spirit, as I said. Be comforted, sweetest and most holy Father, for God will give you rest.[8] Great consolation follows great toil, for he is the granter of true and holy desires. Let this be the beginning of a loving and humble demeanour (learnt from the humble Lamb whose vicar you are), with true constancy until death and firm hope in his providence, delighting always in our Creator and in his humble servants. This your Holiness already does, I know, but I mention it because my tongue must obey the outpouring of my heart, though more especially because I feel impelled to it in conscience by the sweet goodness of God. Bear with me for pestering you so much, and pardon my presumption. I am certain that God makes you see the love rather than the words. I humbly ask your blessing. May the sweet and eternal goodness of God, the eternal Trinity, give you his grace and the fullness of the fire of his charity, so that in your hands holy Church may be reformed and you may offer yourself in sacrifice to God.

I will say no more. Abide in the sweet and holy love of God. Rejoice and exult in God's sweet mysteries.[9] If I have offended God or your Holiness in anything, I acknowledge my guilt and beg you to forgive me. I am ready to perform any penance. Sweet Jesus. Jesus, Love.

---

[1]   Catherine was writing at Whitsuntide.

[2]   Cf. Psalm 36:9.

[3]   Cf. Acts 6:2–4.

[4]   lit. 'He does not cease to pray who does not cease to do good', which would seem to be Catherine's rendering of the Benedictine motto *Laborare est orare* (to work is to pray).

[5]   The reference is to the victory at Marino on 29 April, but see Gardner, p.309, note 2, for the use of the word 'creatures' in the plural.

[6]   Before taking up residence at the Vatican, Urban had walked barefoot in a procession, in thanksgiving for his forces' victory at Marino and the capture of the *Castel Sant' Angelo* from his opponents. Cf. Gardner pp.307–314.

[7]   A reference to reports of the massing of Moslem forces, and frequent raids, in eastern Europe.

[8]   Cf. Matthew 11:28.

[9]   The editorial notes in Gigli (vol. II, p.148, note G) suggest that this is Catherine's way of saying 'Happy Feast' for Pentecost Sunday.

LETTER 57   (Tommaseo 344 & VII (Vol. VI);
Gigli 101).

*To:*   *Fra Raimondo of Capua OP, in Genoa.*[1]
*Date:*   Late July/early August 1379.[2]

Dearest father in Christ sweet Jesus,
   I, Catherine, servant and slave of the servants of Jesus
Christ, write to you in his precious blood, desiring to see
in you the light of most holy faith that lights up for us the
way of truth. Without it, nothing we undertake, desire, or
do would bear fruit or achieve the purpose we had in
mind. Rather, everything would be left imperfect and
our love of God and neighbour be remiss; and this, I
think, because our love equals our faith, and vice versa.
He who loves is always faithful to the one he loves, and
serves him faithfully until death. By this I see that I do not
truly love God, or creatures for God, for if I truly loved
him, fidelity would prompt me to expose myself to death
a thousand times a day, if necessary and possible, for the
glory and praise of his name. My faith would not fail
because I would be all set to endure for the love of God, of
virtue, and of holy Church, and hence believe God to be
my help and my shield,[3a] as he was for those glorious
martyrs who went joyfully to the place of martyrdom. If I
had faith, I would have no fear, but be fully convinced
that God is for me as he was for them;[3b] that his power has
not diminished and that he is as ready, able and willing as
ever he was to help me in my need. But as I don't really
love, I don't really trust him, but myself. Sensual fear
shows me that my love is lukewarm and the light of faith
obscured by my lack of confidence in my Creator and my
trust in myself. I confess and do not deny[3c] that this
stump has not yet been rooted up out of my soul, and so
gets in the way of the deeds God requires me either to
perform or to be responsible for, preventing them from
being brought to the glowing and fruitful conclusion he
had envisioned. Alas, alas, Lord, woe is wretched me!

Shall I be like this always, everywhere and in everything? Shall I always bar the way of your providence by my own infidelity? Indeed yes, unless you in your mercy unmake me and make me anew. Unmake me then, Lord; break up my hard heart; don't let me be an instrument that spoils your work!

And I beg you, dearest father, to pray that you and I together may drown ourselves in the blood of the humble Lamb. This will make us strong and faithful. Then we shall feel the fire of divine Charity; his grace will make us doers instead of undoers and spoilers, and so show that we are faithful to God and trust in his help, not in our own wits or those of men.

And with this same faith we shall love creatures, for just as love of neighbour proceeds from love of God, so does faith, in general and in particular; that is, as our love for all men in general is matched by a general faith, so there is a particular faith[4] in the case of those bound together by a closer love – like this of ours which, over and above the general love, has placed a very close and special love between us, and one which is so faithful that it can neither believe nor imagine that the other could want anything but our good, convinced that he presses most earnestly for that good before God and men; that he is forever seeking to bring about in the other the glory of God's name and the good of that soul; forever constraining God to help by giving an increase in fortitude and perseverance to match any increase in the other's burden. The lover is so carried along by this faith that nothing people say, no illusion of the devil, no distance of separation, nothing, can ever make it falter – for to falter is a sign that one is loving God and neighbour imperfectly.

It would seem, from what I have understood by your letter,[5] that you have been struggling with conflicts and thoughts of all kinds occasioned by the devil's wiles and your own hyper-sensitiveness, for you thought the burden was too heavy for you and also that you were not big enough to be measured by my standards. And so you began to wonder whether I loved and cared for you as much as before, without realizing, though you yourself showed it to be so, that my love had grown while yours had diminished, for I love you with the love with which I love myself, and so I firmly believe that what is lacking on your part, God in his goodness will provide! But it did not turn out like that, for you found ways of laying down your burden. And then, so many scraps of excuses to cover over your faithless frailty – but not enough to keep me from seeing a good deal of it, and I can only hope it will be seen by no one else![6] So my love for you is greater than before, not less.

But what am I to say that your foolishness should entertain even the beginning of such thoughts? Could you ever believe I wanted anything other than the life of your soul? Where is the faith you usually have, and ought to have? And the certainty it gave you that anything that is done is seen and determined in the sight of God – not only a really big thing like this, but every little thing? Had you been faithful, you would not have been so vacillating, nor would you have become so mistrustful of God, and of myself; instead, like a faithful and readily obedient son you would have set about doing whatever you could manage to do. And if you could not go upright, you might have gone on all fours; if not as a friar, then as a pilgrim or, if you had no money, as a beggar. Faithful obedience like this would have achieved more in God's sight and in men's hearts than all our human prudence. My sins have prevented me from seeing all this in you.

Nevertheless, I am quite certain that though you were weak, you had and have a good and holy desire to accomplish God's will more perfectly, and that of Christ-on-earth, Pope Urban VI. I would not wish that you had not gone, though; but that you had set out at once by whatever means and whatever route was open to you. Day and night I was being constrained by God concerning many other things too; all of which have come to nothing through lack of earnestness on the part of those who were to accomplish them, but most of all through my own sins, which bar the way to all good. And so, alas, we see ourselves drowning, and offences against God increasing, with countless torments, while I am in torment. May God in his mercy soon take me out of this dark life.

And now this latest disaster in the kingdom of Naples[7] is worse than the first;[8] there is a prospect of so much evil there that God himself must find the remedy. In his mercy he had shown clearly what the ruin would be, and what remedies were needed. But, as I said, my own countless defects impede every good. I shall have much to tell you about all this, unless I am given the very great grace of being taken from this world before I see you again.

All things considered, then, I would have wished you to have gone. I am at peace about it nonetheless, because I am convinced that nothing happens without a purpose[9] and also because I had eased my conscience by doing what I could to get someone sent to the King of France. Now it's up to the graciousness of the Holy Spirit to bring it about. On our own we do a shoddy job.

The holy Father seems to have welcomed the idea of making direct contact with the King of Hungary; he had thought of sending you with some companions. I don't know why he has changed his mind and now wants you to remain where you are and do what good you can there. I beg you to put your heart into it.

Give up all thoughts of self and of your personal pleasure and consolation; let there be great roaring over all these dead[10] to bind the hands of divine Justice – and of the devil and our sensual appetite – with the cords of holy and humble desire. We were offered as dead in the garden of holy Church, and to Christ-on-earth who owns the garden. So let's *be* dead. A dead man neither sees, hears nor feels. Do your best to kill yourself with the knife of hatred and love, so as not to hear the worldly-minded mockery, treachery and reproach the persecutors of holy Church have in store for you. Don't let your eyes see things that can't be done, or trials that may happen!

Instead, by the light of holy faith, let them see that you can do all things in Christ crucified[11a] and that God will not lay on you a burden heavier than you can bear[11b] – though heavy burdens should make us glad, for then God is giving us the gift of fortitude! A loving readiness to endure takes away our hyper-sensitiveness, freeing us to feed in the garden, dead to all else. To see this come about [in you] will be real bliss for my soul. I tell you, sweetest father, today we are being called upon to die, whether we will or no – so stop being alive! End your pains in the pain, but enlarge your holy desire in it; then we can spend our life entirely in anguished desire and willingly give our bodies as food to the wild beasts by willingly, for love of virtue, throwing ourselves into the tongues and hands of beasts of men; like those before us who laboured in this sweet garden, dead to all else, watering it with their blood, but with tears and sweat first. But because I in my wretched life did not first pour out water, I now withhold my blood. No more of this. Let us start afresh and stoke up the fire of desire.

You asked me to implore the divine Goodness to give you something of the fire of Vincent, Laurence and Paul, and of darling John,[12] for then, you say, you will do great things and I shall be glad. In very truth, without this fire, you could achieve nothing, great or small, nor could I be glad. Thinking of this – and having seen proof of it – an impulse has grown within me together with great zeal in God's loving presence. Had you been here with me, I'd have shown you that it is so, and with more than words! I rejoice, and want you to rejoice, for this growing desire is a sign that God wills to fulfill it in you and in me; for he accepts true and holy desires, provided you open the eye of your mind in the light of holy faith in order to know what truly is God's will; knowing it to love it; and loving it to be faithful, with none of the devil's tricks casting a shadow over your heart. Being faithful, you will do all things, and great things, for God – accomplishing perfectly whatever he puts into your hands, there being nothing in you to prevent this. By this same light you will be careful, modest and balanced in speech and conversation, as in all your works and ways; without it, your whole behaviour would be quite the reverse, and everything you undertake would go against you. It is because I yearn for and love you immeasurably for your salvation; because with great desire I desire to see you truly perfect,[13] that I keep goading you with words – though I would rather do it literally! – and reprimanding you, to bring you constantly back to yourself. I have done, and will go on doing, all I can to get you burdened as if you were perfect, for God's honour, and to implore his Goodness to bring you to the ultimate perfection of pouring your blood into holy Church, whether your maidservant, sensuality, likes it or not.[14] Lose yourself in the blood of Christ crucified, and endure patiently my defects and my words. When your own faults are pointed out to you, rejoice, and be thankful to the divine Goodness who has appointed someone to work on you and keep watch for you before him.

You ask me to pray for our Order, and I you, for when I hear how things are, I feel my heart break within me. Generally speaking, our Province is still faithful to Pope Urban and to the Vicar of the Order who, I must say in all truth, is conducting himself very well and being very prudent – for such times as ours – in his dealings within the Order, and with those who wickedly deny the truth. No one who says the opposite – from the little I know about it – has any truth in his mouth.[15] Our most holy Father has ordered him, and given him full authority, to absolve all those Provincials who deny the truth about him. This is not a time for sleep but for earnestly begging our sweet Spaniard[16] to keep watch unceasingly over his Order, the Order that has always proclaimed the faith, but is now contaminating it. This grieves me to death. All I can do is to end my life in weeping and great affliction.

You write that Antichrist and his members are doing their best to get hold of you,[17] but don't worry. God is well able to deprive them of light and strength and so foil their purpose. Reflect, too, that you are not worthy of such a favour, so have no fear! Be sure that sweet Mary, and Truth himself, will always be on your side.

I, too, vile slave, here in the field where blood was shed for love of the Blood[18] (where you left me when you went off with God), will never cease toiling on your behalf. I beg you not to give me cause for tears, or to be ashamed of you before God. You are man enough in promising to do and to endure for God's honour, so don't turn into a woman when it comes to tightening the screw, otherwise I shall have to complain about you to Christ crucified, and to Mary. Take care lest he deal with you as he did with the Abbot of Sant'Antimo.[19] Out of fear and in order not to tempt God, he left Siena and came to Rome, thinking by doing so to avoid prison and be safe. But he *was* put in prison, and punished in the way you know. Thus do the fearful of heart get their deserts! Be a man, then, a real man, and let death come.

I must tell you that I would not be here now had it been safe to go, but it was impossible by either land or sea: you see, it had been decided that I should go to Naples.[20] Pray yourself and get others to pray, asking God and Mary to make whatever is to his honour come about. Fra Bartolomeo, the Master, brother Matteo[21] and the others are all ready to do whatever is needed for God's honour and the good of holy Church, as well as to stretch their own frailty! They and all the others send their greetings. Grandma[22] sends her blessing. And I ask for yours, and beg you to forgive anything I may have said that is not to God's honour or is lacking in respect towards yourself. Let my love be my excuse. I'll say no more. Abide in the sweet and holy love of God. Sweet Jesus. Jesus, Love.

---

[1]   Fra Raimondo had remained in Genoa after twice allowing the anti-Urbanists to foil his attempts to cross into France and so gain access to the French King; cf. letter 50, note 12b and

Gardner pp.316–320.

² See Fawtier p.203.

³ a. cf. Psalm 28:7. b. cf. Romans 8:31. c. cf. John 1:20.

⁴ Cf. Dante, *Inferno*, XI, 63: *fede spezial*.

⁵ Cf. letter 13, note 9.

⁶ Perhaps Pope Urban, who had sent Raimondo on his mission.

⁷ Queen Joanna's second volte-face; cf. letters 55 and 58.

⁸ Cf. Matthew 12:45.

⁹ Italian: *misterio*; cf. letter 25, note 1.

¹⁰ Cf. letter 46, note 4.

¹¹ a. Phil. 4:13. b. Cf. I Cor. 10:13.

¹² These four could be said to have fire in common in that, according to tradition, *Vincent* and *Laurence* were martyred by being roasted on a gridiron, and *John the Evangelist* (the special favourite for whom Catherine always chooses an unusual adjective – cf. letter 21, note 9) was thrown into a cauldron of boiling oil but escaped unharmed (see *Penguin Dictionary of Saints*, pp. 189, 214 & 336). *Paul's* 'If I deliver my body to be burned, but have not love,' etc. (I Cor.13:3) makes him, too, one of the group.

¹³ The Luke 22:15 text is once again used with full emphasis.

¹⁴ Cf. letters 40 and 49.

¹⁵ Cf. John 8:44.

¹⁶ St Dominic, founder of the Order of Preachers.

¹⁷ Cf. note 1.

¹⁸ i.e. Rome.

¹⁹ Fra Giovanni di Gano (see letter 35), who may have shrunk from acting as Urban's ambassador in Siena; cf. Gardner, pp.320–21.

²⁰ Fra Raimondo had himself thwarted an earlier plan to send Catherine with St Catherine of Sweden to Naples to confront the Queen (Raymond, pp.306–307).

²¹ᵃ *Fra Bartolomeo* Dominici, OP; see letters 2 & 7.

²¹ᵇ *'Maestro'* Giovanni Tantucci; see letter 21.

²¹ᶜ Messer *Matteo*, Rector of the *Misericordia* Hospital; see letters 39 & 50.

²² See letter 36, note 2b.

LETTER 58    (Tommaseo 362; Gigli 318).

*To:*    *Queen Joanna I of Naples.*[1]

*Date:*    Early August, 1379.[2]

Dearest and respected mother,
('Dear' you will be to me when I see you being a [real]
daughter, duly subject and obedient to holy Church, and
'respected' in that I shall pay you all due respect once you
have turned away from the darkness of heresy to follow
the light.)

I, Catherine, slave of the servants of Jesus Christ, write
to you in his precious blood, desiring to see in you that
true knowledge of yourself and your Creator which is
necessary for our salvation, for from this blessed knowledge every virtue springs.

Where do we find true humility? In self-knowledge,
for when a soul knows that of itself it is nothing but has its
being from God, it cannot raise its head in pride against
Creator or neighbour, since a thing that of itself is not has
nothing to be proud of. And where does a soul learn the
gravity of its sin? [Again], in self-knowledge, together
with a holy reflection on *who* is offending God and *who* is
the God who is thus offended. We thus see that as human
beings, we are but mud, formed of the slime of the earth,[3]
a stinking sack of filth; subject to many miseries and
needs and finally to death, the death we know will come,
though we know not when. Once having realized, then,
that this bundle of wretchedness is an instrument that
sounds only [the discord of] offence before the supreme
eternal Good (the sweet goodness of God from which it
received its being and every spiritual and temporal grace
that follows from it), the soul comes to loathe its own
frailty; through the graces received from God it recog-
nizes that service, not disservice, is due to him from us.
We are bound to render him glory and honour, and can
serve him in no other way, since he is our God who has no
need of us; though we need him, for without him we can

have nothing. Our offence causes us to lose the life of grace, *and* our dignity, since we thereby lose the light of reason and become mindless animals. Oh, the blindness of men! Can we fall into any state more wretched than that of mere animals? If anyone were to call us a brute beast, we would not tolerate it; indeed we would try to take revenge on whoever said it. Yet such is our frailty that though we turn our own selves into brute beasts we take no revenge on the sensual appetite and self-love that do the turning! And all because we do not know ourselves, and so make light of our sins. And why do we make light of them? Because we do not realize the consequences of our sin and where it is leading us. Did we realize it – by reflecting on the true state of things as I have said – we would get ourselves our of all our vice and disordered living and embrace virtue, thereby rendering honour to God retaining the beauty and dignity of our soul and, by following [him who is] doctrine and truth, ourselves become sons of that same truth.

Sweetest mother, I yearn to see *you* grounded in this truth, which you will follow if you abide in self-knowledge, but not otherwise. That is why I said I longed to see you know yourself. To this truth I invite you, that you may know it and so love it: the truth that God created you for eternal life. Let yourself dwell on the humble Lamb, for he has revealed this truth to you in his blood; for this it was shed and given to us as our ransom; [for this] it was poured into the body of holy Church. What does this Truth promise to one who loves it? That the price of the Blood will bring it eternal life, through a good confession, together with contrition and satisfaction. It promises too, that, every good deed will be rewarded and every sin punished, thus instilling into us a holy fear and love by leading us to fear the sin as we fear the punishment.

Alas,[4] dearest mother, you know that the truth cannot lie. Then why choose to go against it? By going against the truth of holy Church and of Pope Urban VI, you are going against God's truth and losing the fruit of Christ's blood, since it is on this truth that holy Church is founded. Alas,[4] if you are not concerned for your own salvation, show some concern for the peoples entrusted to you, the subjects you have ruled with such diligence and in such peace for so long.[5] Yet now, because you have gone against this truth, you see them at loggerheads, the curse of division setting them at war among themselves, killing one another like animals. Alas, how can you endure to see them torn apart on your account, white rose against red,[6] the truth against a lie, and your heart not burst? Alas, my wretched soul! Do you not see that they were all created by the spotless [white] rose of the eternal will of God and recreated in grace by the glowing red rose of the blood of Christ, which cleansed us from our sin in holy baptism, brought us together as Christians and made us all one in the garden of holy Church? Reflect that they were cleansed and given these glorious roses, not by you or by anyone else, but by our Holy Mother Church alone, through the Supreme Pontiff, Pope Urban VI, who holds the keys of the Blood. How, then, can your soul allow you even to want to take from them something that you cannot give them? And do you not see how cruel you are to yourself? Through their wickedness and lack of unity, you are undermining your own position. Moreover, you will have to account to God for the souls that are perishing because of you. What account can you give? A very bad one. So we shall make a very poor showing before the supreme Judge at the moment of death, which will be upon us any moment.

Alas, if this does not move you, at the very least ought you not be moved by the shame you have incurred before the world? Much more so now, after your conversion, than before. This latest fault is much more serious and displeasing to God and to creatures than the earlier one. After the first one you had acknowledged the truth and confessed your guilt; like a daughter, you had seemed to profess your willingness to return to the mercy and loving-kindness of your Father.[7] Yet after all this, you have behaved even worse than before, either because you were not being sincere and were putting on an act, or because Justice has willed that I should do penance anew for my own old sins, so long persisted in; the penance, that is, of not meriting to see you feed peacefully at the breast of holy Church, who was there waiting to feed you, and to be fed by you – she feeding you with grace in the blood of the Lamb and you helping her with your support. For you saw how widowed she – the Church of Rome, seat and centre[8] of our faith – had become without her husband, and we without our father. Now that she has got him back again, she was looking to you to be a pillar supporting her husband, a shield ready to ward off the blows from him, and hit back at those who seek to wrest him from her. Oh, our ingratitude! Not only is he your father by his dignity, but your son, too,[9] so it is very cruel of you to reverse things [and to present us] with the spectacle of a daughter quarrelling with her own father, a mother with her own son. This grieves me so deeply that I can carry no greater cross in this life. When I think of the letter I received from you, in which you confessed that Pope Urban was truly supreme father and pontiff, and said that you wished to obey him! Yet now I find the opposite. Alas! Round off your confession, for the love of God! What is needed for confession, as I said, is to confess the truth with contrition of heart, and to make satisfaction. Make satisfaction, then, by rendering your debt of obedience, since you have confessed that he is the vicar of Christ on earth. Obey, and so receive the fruit of grace and placate God's wrath towards you. What has happened to the truth normally found in the mouth of a queen, which is usually, which must be, gospel?[10] Nothing that she promises rightly and according to God must ever be taken back. And I see and have proof that you made a promise; that you said you were willing to obey the supreme pontiff, yet now you are doing the opposite, in word and in deed. I am appalled and unbearably grieved to see the eye of your understanding so darkened by the self-love induced by the devil's illusions and evil counsel that you care nothing about your own damnation, the ruination of your people in soul and body, your own physical fate, or your reputation before the world.

Sweetest mother, for the love of Christ crucified, be sweet, and not now bitter, to me. Come back to your senses a little; sleep on no longer in such a slumber, but rouse yourself in the little time you have left. Don't wait for time which does not wait for you. With true knowledge, know yourself and the great goodness of God who *has* waited for you; who, in his great mercy, has not taken time from you in your darkened state. With the desire [we spoke of][11] embrace virtue, put on truth and return to your father, humbled by true knowledge. You will find mercy and kindness in his Holiness, for he is a compassionate father who desires the life of his child. For the love of Christ crucified, do not lie on in death of soul, lest this shameful and wretched disgrace live on after your death – for bodily death is at your heels, yours and everyone else's, but more especially at the heels of those whose youth is already behind them.[12] No one, however great or powerful, has power or might enough to fend off death. It is a sentence passed on us the moment we are conceived in the womb, and one from which none can escape. And we are not animals! Once dead, an animal is no more. But *we* are rational creatures, created to the image and likeness of God, so that when the body dies, the soul, in its being, does not, though it certainly dies to grace, through sin, if one dies in mortal sin. So let sheer necessity drive you; be merciful, not cruel, to your own self. Respond to God who calls to you with his clemency and compassion, and don't be slow to respond. Do so resolutely, lest you should have addressed to you those harsh words: 'You did not think of me during your life, so I do not think of you at your death'[13] – that is, you did not respond when I called to you while you still had time; now time for you is past, and you have no other way out.

I am relying on the infinite goodness of God to give you the grace to force yourself to respond with great eagerness and prompt obedience to holy Church and to Pope Urban VI. God will not despise all the many prayers and tears that have been and are being poured out by his servants for your salvation. Be grateful and appreciative for such a gift, that the spring of filial piety may well up within you.[14] I will say no more.

Abide in the sweet and holy love of God. Sweet Jesus. Jesus, Love.

---

[1]   See letter 55, note 9.

[2]   The letter was prompted by the news that the Queen had again deserted Urban's cause; cf. Gardner, pp.312–316, and letter 57.

[3]   Cf. Genesis 2:7.

[4]   Ital. *'Doh!'* – an untranslatable ejaculation conveying a blend of compassion and reproach.

[5]   33 years. Apart from a war of defence against Louis of Hungary (who sought to avenge the murder of his brother, Andrew, the Queen's first husband), peace had prevailed in the kingdom of Naples throughout Joanna's reign.

[6]   Only Catherine mentions this detail. An early commentator adduces grounds for supposing that Urban's coat of arms included six red roses and argues from this that the anti-Urbanists had chosen a white rose as their emblem. (Cf. Gigli, Vol.III, pp.581–2, note D, where it is further suggested that the emblems which gave their names to the Wars of the Roses were brought back to England by English soldiers of fortune who were scattered and eventually driven out of Italy after the death of John Hawkwood; see letter 8. But this is pure speculation.)

[7]   Cf. letter 47 note 20.

[8]   Ital. *principato*.

[9]   A Neapolitan by birth, Urban had been one of Joanna's subjects.

[10]   This may be an allusion to a saying attributed to the Queen's cousin, King John of France, to the effect that even if fidelity and truth were to be banished from the world, they should nevertheless find a sure refuge in the mouths of kings. (Gigli, Vol. III, p.583, note H).

[11]   lit. with *this* desire. Catherine seems to pick up here the

theme of the earlier part of the letter.

[12] The Queen was already in her middle fifties, having been born in 1324.

[13] Cf. Matthew 7:21–23.

[14] For this expression, cf. letters 45, 47 & 52, and also the Sequence *Dies irae*

> *Rex tremendae majestatis*
> *Qui salvandos salvas gratis*
> *Salva me, fons pietatis.*
>> (King of majesty tremendous,
>> Who dost free salvation send us,
>> Fount of pity, then befriend us.)

## LETTER 59   (Tommaseo 358; Gigli 212).

*To:*   *Andrea di ser Vanni.*[1]

*Date:*  September/October 1379.[2]

Dearest son in Christ sweet Jesus,

I, Catherine, servant and slave of the servants of Jesus Christ, write to you in his precious blood, desiring to see you a just good ruler, that God's honour may be accomplished in you, and also your own desire for good that I know God in his mercy has given you. But I see no way of ruling well over others unless we first rule over ourselves. A soul that rules itself, rules others in the same way, for it gives to its neighbour the same love it gives to itself. As perfect love for God generates perfect love for others, so a man will rule his subjects as perfectly as he rules himself.

How does one who fears God rule over himself? With what kind of justice? Here is my answer. Such a man will direct the three powers of his soul by the light of reason, maintaining thereby a right order in all aspects of his life, whether spiritual or physical; when, how, and wherever legitimate circumstances may place him. Thus, he directs his memory to retain God's benefits and his own offences against the supreme Goodness. He directs his mind to see the love with which God has poured out his grace and to know the doctrine of his truth. Similarly, he directs his will to love God's infinite goodness, which he has seen and known by the light of his mind. And because he has known that we creatures of God must love him with all our heart, with all our soul and with all our strength, he ascends the seat of conscience to keep a grip on this sweet and glorious order when he sees sensuality wanting to disrupt it. And if some trick of the devil or his own frailty should damage or disrupt the perfection resulting from this order, he metes out an enlightened justice that gives each his due.[3] Hence, if his sensuality hurls a deadly blow, it is itself done to death, for his own perverse will is beheaded with the axe of hatred of vice and love of virtue!

Moreover, according to the gravity of the offence, justice disciplines the soul's disordered affections by exacting from it the penalty prescribed by divine Justice. What penalty, and how is it exacted? I will tell you . The sensual appetite that seeks worldly status, honours and wealth, is required by right reason to desire and embrace disgrace, to despise honour and to seek abasement. It is required, too, to give up its wealth voluntarily and be wedded to poverty, to trust in God and not in such fickle and unstable things as self and worldly status. And should this perverse appetite seek the stench of unchastity, justice has a grip on it and forces it to seek and delight in purity. If it goes for pride, it is given humility; if infidelity, faithfulness; if avarice, the largesse of charity. Hatred and dislike of others are replaced by benevolence, imprudence by prudence. Thus all the virtues are the bans and penalties to which the judge on the seat of conscience sentences the soul's affections in order to punish its sensual appetite and destroy its love of vice by beheading its self-will, as I said. Thus does a man uphold reason in his soul, rendering to it its due of virtue, reason being mistress and sensuality the maidservant. Thus, too, does he render due honour to God and the love of charity to his neighbour.[4]

Such a man's place is the house of knowledge of self, and of God's goodness within him, measuring out to others the measure by which he himself hopes to be measured,[5] frequently washing every mark of sin from the face of his soul in Christ's blood by means of a good and holy confession, and nourishing it with the food of angels; that is, with the sweet sacrament of the body and blood of Jesus Christ, wholly God and wholly Man, which every faithful Christian must receive at least once a year. Anyone who wishes to receive it more often may do so, but not less; and under no pretext must a man refrain, be he righteous or a sinner. If a sinner is not well-disposed, he must make himself so; and a just man must not refrain through humility, saying: 'I am not worthy of so great a mystery. When I feel more worthy I will make my communion'. This he must not do, but rather reflect that however just he may be, he never could be worthy. And the moment he considered himself worthy, he would indeed be unworthy, wrapping his pride in the cloak of humility. But God is worthy to make us worthy, and so it is in his worthiness that we must receive communion. And receive it in two ways: in actual fact, and with an attentive mind, that is with holy, true, and burning desire, a desire that is not confined to the moment of receiving communion but accompanies us always and everywhere, as food we take to give the life of grace to the soul.

All this, dictated by holy justice, proceeds from the order established and maintained among the three powers of his soul by a man acting according to right reason. Possessing this order himself, he is able to dispense it to his neighbour by prayer, exhortation, and a good and holy life. And if he has to rule over others, the fact that he observes the law within himself makes him desire his subjects to observe it too; and to make them zealous in observing it, he punishes those who do not. Hence, as he punished in himself the sensuality that sought to rebel against the divine law, so, when required to rule over the bodies of his subjects, he seeks to punish them when they fail to observe the civil law and the other statutes and good ordinances enacted by those in lawful authority, making his punishments mild or severe as the order of justice and the dictates of reason require.

This justice must not be contaminated or whittled away by fear of suffering or bodily death; by threats or flattery; by any desire to please creatures or secure material gain. It must not barter men's honour, or their flesh, for money, as unjust men do who live without order or the light of reason. The just man clings to justice, come what may, observing it himself to the best of his ability; seeking in all his deeds and actions to promote God's honour, the salvation of his own soul and the overall good of every man; giving good straightforward advice; and making the truth known in so far as he can. This he must do if he wishes to keep himself and his city in peace, and to preserve holy justice. Lack of justice alone accounts for the many evils that have happened and are happening.

Desiring, therefore, to see this justice in you and [to see you] preserving it in our city, ruling and governing it in due order, I stated my desire to see you a true and just ruler, for unless a man begins by observing this justice in himself, as I said, he could never observe it in regard to others, whatever his position. So I invite you and desire you to be most earnest in keeping your own self in order, as I said, so that you may successfully accomplish the task you have now been set by divine Goodness. In true humility, keep God always before your eyes in everything you have to do, that God may be glorified in you.

Abide in the sweet and holy love of God. Sweet Jesus. Jesus, Love.

---

[1]   This 'virile painter . . . and loyal and conscientious politician' (Gardner) – to whom an early portrait of Catherine is attributed and who was often sent on important embassies by those in

power in Siena – probably came to know Catherine through his friendship with Ser Cristofano Guidini (see letter 12), though he does not seem to have been a disciple in the strict sense.

2    This is one of several letters Catherine wrote to Andrea while he was 'Captain of the People' in Siena; see Gardner, p.90.

3    Cf. Romans 13:7.

4    Cf. letter 1, note 6.

5    Cf. Matthew 7:2.

# LETTER 60[1]    (a. Tommaseo 373; Gigli 102)
(b. Tommaseo 371; Gigli 103)

a. *To: Fra Raimondo of Capua, OP, in Genoa.*

*Date:*  [in ms.] 15 February 1379 (i.e. 1380; cf. letter 49, note 2).

Beloved and sweetest father in Christ sweet Jesus, I, Catherine, servant and slave of the servants of Jesus Christ, write to you in his precious blood, desiring to see you a pillar embedded once again in the garden of holy Church, to serve as the faithful bridegroom of truth you ought to be. Then indeed I shall account my soul blessed. So I want you never to let adversity or persecution make you look back, but rather to glory in it, since by our endurance alone we manifest our love and constancy and give glory to God's name.

Now is the time, dearest father, to lose one's whole self, not to think of self at all, like those glorious labourers[2] who prepared to give their lives with such eager love and longing, watering this garden with blood, together with humble unceasing prayer, and perseverance until death. Beware lest I see you timid, frightened by your own shadow. Rather, be a stout warrior and never withdraw from the yoke of the obedience the Supreme Pontiff has laid on you.[3] In the Order, too, undertake whatever you see to be to God's honour. His great Goodness requires this of us; for this alone has he put us here.

Look at the great need we see in holy Church, for we see her left utterly alone. And Truth revealed this to be so, as I write to you in another letter.[4] And as the bride has been left alone, so too has her bridegroom.[5] O sweetest father, I will not keep God's great mysteries from you, but will describe them to you as briefly as possible, so far as my poor tongue can express them in words. I will also tell you what I want you to do. But do not be grieved by what I have to say, for I do not know what the divine Goodness will do with me, whether he will leave me here or call me to himself.

Father! Father and sweetest son! Stupendous mysteries has God accomplished since the Feast of the Circumcision,[6] such that the tongue alone cannot tell of them. But passing over all that period, let us come to Sexagesima Sunday,[7] for it was then those mysteries occurred that you will hear of in the brief account I am giving you,[4] quite unlike anything I have ever experienced. So intense was the pain in my heart that my tunic was torn through my clutching at as much of it as I could while I writhed in the chapel like one convulsed. Had anyone tried to hold me, he would surely have robbed me of life.

Coming now to the evening of Monday, I felt the urge to write to Christ-on-earth and to three cardinals, so I had myself helped into the study. When I had finished writing to Christ-on-earth[8] I could write no more, so intense became the pains in my body. After a while, the demons began terrorizing me to such an extent that I was absolutely stunned; they seemed to be raging against me as if a worm like me had been responsible for snatching from them what had long been theirs in holy Church. Such was the terror, and the physical pain, that I wanted to flee from the study and take refuge in the chapel, almost as if the study itself were responsible for my agony. So I rose up and, being unable to move on my own, leaned on my son Barduccio.[9] But I was immediately thrown down and, once down, my soul seemed to have left the body – not in the same way as when it did leave it,[10] for on that occasion my soul tasted the good the immortals enjoy, for it received the supreme Good together with them. But this time it seemed like a thing apart: I no longer seemed to be in the body, but saw my body as if I had been someone else. And when my soul perceived my companion's distress, it sought to discover whether I was in any way connected with that body, in order to say to him: 'Don't be afraid, son.' But I saw that I could not move its tongue or any other part of it in any way, except as one would move a lifeless corpse. So I left the body alone, just as it was, while my understanding remained fixed in the abyss of the Trinity. My memory was filled with the thought of the needs of holy Church and of all Christians, and I cried out in [God's] presence, asking with confidence for divine help, offering him my desires and constraining him by the blood of the Lamb and by all the suffering that had been endured.[11] So resolutely did I ask this that I felt certain he would not refuse that petition. I then pressed for all your needs, begging him to accomplish in you his will and my desires. Then I asked him to preserve me from eternal damnation.

I remained thus for so long that the family were mourning me as dead; and meanwhile the terror of the demons had ceased. Then the humble Lamb became present to my soul, saying: 'Fear not, for I will accomplish your own desires and those of my other servants. I want you to see that I am a skilled Master Potter, reworking and remodelling vessels as he pleases.[12] I know how to rework and remodel these vessels of mine, and that is why I am now taking the vessel of your body and refashioning it in the garden of holy Church in quite a new way.' And as that Truth held me close with most winning ways and words which I here pass over, my body began once again to breathe a little and to show that the soul had returned to its vessel. Then I was filled with wonder, while there remained such a pain in my heart that I have it still. From that moment, every delight, every respite, every food, was taken from me and when, later, they carried me upstairs, the room seemed full of devils who launched into a fresh attack, the most terrible I have ever endured, in an attempt to make me believe and see that it was not I myself in my body, but an unclean spirit. But I pleaded pitifully for divine help, though I did not refuse the trial but said: 'O God, come to my aid. O Lord, make haste to help me,[13] [for] you have left me to fight this battle alone, without the consolation of the father of my soul,[14] who has been taken from me because of my ingratitude.'

For two nights and two days these storms went on. It is true that my mind and my desire suffered no hurt but remained ever fixed on their Object, but my body seemed almost to have collapsed. Then on the Feast of Mary's Purification[15] I wanted to hear Mass. All the mysteries were then renewed, as God revealed the great need that there was – as later became apparent, for Rome has been on the verge of revolt, buzzing with slanderous and irreverent talk, but God put ointment on their hearts and I believe all will end well.[16] Then God laid on me this obedience: that throughout the holy [season of] Lent I was to have the whole family's desires offered in sacrifice, and [Mass] celebrated before him for this one intention, that is for holy Church; also that I should myself hear a Mass every morning at sunrise, which as you know for me is impossible,[17] but under his obedience everything has been possible. And this desire[18] has become so much a part of me that memory retains, understanding sees, and will can desire nothing else. And not only does my soul turn away from things here below for this one thing; even while conversing with the true citizens [of heaven] it is neither able nor willing to share their delight but only the hunger[19] that they have now, as they had while still pilgrims and wanderers in this life.

In this and in many other ways which I cannot describe, my life is being consumed and distilled into this sweet Bride – I in this way and the glorious martyrs by their blood. I implore the divine Goodness to grant that I may soon see the redemption of his people. When it is time for Terce[20] and I get up from Mass, you would see a dead woman going to St Peter's, where I take up again my toil in the barque of holy Church. And there I remain until it is nearly time for Vespers,[21] nor would I ever wish to leave that place, night or day, until I see this people a little more firmly established [in peace] with their father. My body is without food of any kind, not even a drop of water, with more sweet bodily torments than I have ever had to endure, so much so that my life hangs by a thread. I simply do not know what the divine Goodness will choose to do with me but, judging by what I feel – though I don't mean that I can actually feel what he may choose to do with me – but judging by how my body feels, it seems to me that I must seal all this period with a fresh martyrdom in my soul's beloved,[22] that is, in holy Church. Then, perhaps, he will raise me up to be with him and so put an end to my agony and to my anguished desires. Or else he will again gird my body round, as he has done in the past. I have begged, and do beg him in his mercy to accomplish his will in me and not to leave you or the others orphans[23] but to keep you always in the way of Truth's doctrine, with true and most perfect light, as I am sure he will.

And now I implore and constrain you, father and son given to me by that most sweet mother Mary.[24] If you hear that God is turning the eye of his mercy towards me,[25] [this means that] he wants to renew your life; so throw yourself, like one dead to all sensual feeling, into this barque of holy Church. Always be guarded in your speech with others. You will not often be able to keep to your actual cell, but I want you always to have the cell of your heart and to take it everywhere with you, for you know that as long as we keep ourselves locked in there, our enemies cannot harm us. Then everything you undertake will be directed and ordered according to God. Moreover, I beg you to bring your heart to maturity

with true and holy prudence and to make your own life
an example to men of the world by never conforming to
its ways. Also, let that bounty towards the poor and voluntary poverty you have always had be renewed and
freshened within you, with true and perfect humility; no
matter what position of honour God may give you,[26]
never grow slack about this, but penetrate ever more
deeply into the valley of humility; seeking your delight on
the table of the cross, where you partake of the food of
souls, and embracing your mother – humble faithful and
unceasing prayer – with holy vigils, and celebrating Mass
every day unless absolutely prevented. Fly from frivolous
idle chatter. Be, and show yourself to be, mature in what
you say and in all you do. Cast away all self-indulgence
and servile fear, for sweet Church has no need of such
people but only of those who are harsh with themselves
and merciful to her. These are the things I beg you to try
to observe.

I ask you too, as regards the book[27] and any other
writing of mine you find – you and Fra Bartolomeo and
Fra Tomaso and the Master – to go through them[28] and
to do with them whatever you see to be most to God's
honour, together with Messer Tommaso;[29] it all gave me
some relief. Furthermore, I ask you, in so far as you can,
to be shepherd and ruler, and as a father, to this family,
and so keep them in the love of charity and in perfect
union, lest they be, or be left, scattered like sheep without
a shepherd.[30] And I believe I shall do more for them and
for you after my death than during my life. I shall
beseech the eternal Truth to allow whatever fullness of
grace, whatever gifts he may have given to my soul to
overflow on you all, that you may be as lamps set on the
lampstand.[31] I implore you to implore the eternal Bridegroom to make me accomplish manfully the obedience
he has laid on me, and to forgive my many iniquities. And
I beg you yourself to forgive every act of disobedience,
lack of reverence and ingratitude I may have committed
towards you, every pain or bitterness I may have caused

you, and my lack of zeal for our salvation. I ask, too, for your blessing.

Pray earnestly for me and get others to pray, for the love of Christ crucified. Forgive me for writing distressing words to you. I do not write them to distress you[32] but because I am uncertain, and I do not know what the goodness of God means to do with me. I want to have done my duty.

Do not grieve because I am physically separated from you and you from me for, although your presence would have been an immense consolation for me, it gives me even greater consolation and joy to see the fruit you are bearing in holy Church. Now I urge you to strive even harder, for she has never been in greater need. Christ-on-earth and Messer Tommaso[33] are sending you tools that will enable you to work effectively. And no matter what persecution you may have to endure, go nowhere else without permission from our lord [the Pope]. Courage, courage, in Christ sweet Jesus, and no regrets. I will say no more.[34]

Abide in the sweet and holy love of God. Sweet Jesus. Jesus, Love.

---

[1]   This letter is in two parts. No 60a is Catherine's last letter to Fra Raimondo, in which she describes an intense experience that affected both soul and body. With it she enclosed a separate account of the profound mystical aspects of her experience. The two form a unity and there is no question of no. 60b having been addressed to Pope Urban VI, as suggested by Tommaseo in his heading and notes to his no. CCCLXXI.

[2]   the martyrs.

[3]   The reference is to Raimondo's mission in Genoa; cf. letters 50 (note 12b) and 57.

[4]   No. 60b.

[5]   the Pope.

[6]   1 January.

[7]   The second of three Sundays immediately preceding Lent. In 1380, Sexagesima Sunday would have fallen on 29 January.

[8]   Urban VI. This letter does not seem to be extant.

[9]   *Barduccio* Canigiani; see letter 48, note 7.

[10]   Catherine here recalls an earlier occasion when she had been in a trance for so long that she was thought to have died. Cf. Raymond, pp.191–196.

[11]   i.e. Christ's own sufferings as well as those of all other faithful Christians, including Catherine herself.

[12]   Cf. Romans 9:21 and Jeremiah 18:1–5.

[13]   These opening words of each 'Hour' of the Divine Office were a favourite invocation of Catherine's.

[14]   Fra Raimondo.

[15]   2 February.

[16]   For details of this episode, see Gardner, p.332.

[17]   Cf. Raymond, p.318: 'Because of the pains in her sides and her other complaints, she was in the habit of waiting until Terce to hear Mass.'

[18]   to obey.

[19]   for God's honour and the salvation of souls.

[20]   One of the 'Little Hours' of the Divine Office, which would have been recited fairly early in the morning.

[21]   Evensong.

[22]   Ital. *nella dolcezza dell'anima mia*; see letter 9, p.73. for a parallel use of this expression.

[23]   Cf. John 14:18.

[24]   Cf. letter 22, note 6.

[25]   by taking her to himself in death.

[26]   Less than a month after Catherine's death (29 April 1380), Fra Raimondo was elected Master General of the section of the Dominican Order that had remained faithful to Urban.

[27]   The *Dialogue*.

[28]   i.e. the writings. The phrase is ambiguous and could also mean either 'get' or simply 'keep' the writings together, but we accept the view expressed by B.R. Motzo in 'Per una edizione critica delle opere di S. Caterina da Siena,' in *Annali della Facoltà di Filosofia e Lettere della R. Università di Cagliari*, Rome, 1931, p.112.

[29]   a. *Fra Bartolomeo* Dominici OP; see letters 2 & 7. b. *Fra Tomaso* della Fonte OP; see letters 1, 36 and 38. c. *'Maestro'* Giovanni Tantucci; see letter 21. d. *Messer Tommaso*. This might be *Tommaso* Buonconti of Pisa who, like his brother Gherardo (see letter 6, note 8), was a long-standing disciple and had accompanied Catherine to Avignon; however, it is more likely to be *Tommaso* Petra, one of Urban's secretaries whom Catherine had first met in Avignon. Like Fra Raimondo, he too had been on intimate terms with Cardinal Pedro de Luna (cf.

letter 40 & note 4), as he grew to be with Catherine herself while she was in Rome.
[30]   Cf. Matthew 26:31.
[31]   Matthew 5:15.
[32]   Cf. II Corinthians 2:4 ff.
[33]   This is certainly *Tommaso* Petra (see note 29d.). The 'tools' are presumably papal briefs authorizing Fra Raimondo to act on the Pope's behalf.
[34]   The translation of this last paragraph is based on the fuller text given in Cod. Casanatense (Rome) no. 292, as cited by B.R. Motzo, art cit. p.111, note 2.

b.[1] . . .[2] I was panting with grief on account of the anguished desire which had once again been conceived in me in the sight of God; for the light of understanding had seen itself reflected in the eternal Trinity, and had perceived in that Abyss the dignity of the rational creature, the wretchedness into which man falls through mortal sin, and the need of holy Church, which God revealed within her;[3] perceived, too, how no one can return to taste the beauty of God in the abyss of the Trinity except by way of this sweet Bride (for we pass through the door of Christ crucified[4] and only in holy Church is this door to be found) and that this Bride was offering life, for she has within her so much life that no one can kill it; that she was a source of fortitude and light; that no one can weaken her strength or darken her light, in their essence, and that her fruit never fails but is ever on the increase.

Then God eternal said: 'All this dignity which your intellect could never comprehend is given you by me. Gaze, then, in grief and bitterness, and you will see that people approach this Bride merely for her outer shell, that is, for her temporal substance, while she is quite empty of any who seek her marrow, that is, the fruit of the Blood. Unless a man brings with him the price, which is charity, with true humility and the light of holy faith, he will eat death in this fruit, not life; for like a thief, he will be taking what is not his. The fruit of the Blood is for those who bring the purchase price, love, since she[5] was founded on love and is Love. And it is my will (said God eternal) that each one's gift to her should be prompted by love, according as I entrust it[6] to my servants to minister in various ways as they have themselves received it. But I am grieved, for I find no one who will minister to her. Indeed, all seem to have abandoned her. But I shall myself be the Healer.'

And as her sorrow and the fire of her desire increased, she cried out before God, saying: 'What can I do, O inestimable Fire?' And his Graciousness replied: 'Offer your life once more, and never let yourself rest. This was the task I set you, and now set you again, you and all who follow you, now and in the future. Take care, then, all of you[7], never to relax but always to increase your desires, for I here wait lovingly to uphold you, in body and spirit, with my grace. And that your minds may not be distracted by other things, I have made provision by kindling a new ardour in her whom I have set to rule over you,[8] using mysteries and new ways to draw her on and set her to this task, so that she may serve my Church with her temporal substance[9] while the rest of you [do so] with faithful, humble and unceasing prayer; together with whatever tasks are required, as my Goodness exacts them – from you[10] and from them, each according to his capacity. So entrust your life, your heart, and your affections entirely to this Bride, for my sake and with no thought of self.

Gaze into me and there behold the Bride's groom, that is the supreme pontiff, and see his good and holy purpose, untrammelled by reserve or restraint; [see, too,] how, as the Bride is alone, so too is her groom [and how] I am allowing him, with his unrestrained way of doing things, and through the fear he instils into his subjects, to sweep holy Church clean. Then another will come who will accompany and fill her with love. The Bride's experience will be that of the soul: at first fear enters in and strips it of vice,[11] then Love fills it and clothes it with virtue. All this will come about through sweet endurance, sweet and wholesome to those who choose to feed in truth at her breast. But do this: Tell my vicar to make peace in so far as he can, and to grant peace to anyone willing to receive it. And to the pillars of holy Church[12] say that if they really wish to repair all the damage, then let them do this: let them come together and make themselves into a cloak to cover over what seem to be faults in their father's methods.[13] Let them adopt an ordered way of life, alongside those who fear and love me, and let them all be together, throwing self to the ground. If they do this, I, who am Light, will give them the light holy Church needs. And when they have seen among themselves what is to be done, with true unity of purpose, let them propose it promptly, boldly and after much deliberation to my vicar, who will thus be constrained not to stand out against their goodwill, since he too is animated by a good and holy purpose.'

The tongue alone cannot recount such mysteries, or describe what I saw in my mind and felt in my heart.[14] And having passed the day full of wonder, it came to evening, when I felt my heart being so drawn by Love that I could not resist the urge to go to my place of prayer. I also began to feel as I had felt at the time of my death,[15] so I prostrated myself with intense self-reproach for having served Christ's Bride with so much indifference and negligence, and for having been the cause of others doing likewise. When I arose, with all that I have said impressed on my inward understanding, God placed me before him – though I am always present to him since he contains in himself all things[16] – but [now] in a new way, as if memory, understanding and will had nothing whatever to do with my body. And his Truth became so luminously clear that in that abyss the mysteries of holy Church were renewed, as were all the graces past and present I have received throughout my life, including the day on which my soul was espoused into him.[17] But all of this was driven into oblivion for me by the growing intensity of the fire, and I paid heed only to what could be done, which was to offer myself in sacrifice to God for the sake of holy Church and in order to remove the ignorance and negligence of those whom God has put into my hands. Then the devils began yelling destruction at me, trying with their terrors to hinder and diminish the ardour of my free and burning desire. But while they were striking at the shell of the body, my desire burned ever hotter and I cried out: 'O eternal God, receive the sacrifice of my life into this mystical body of holy Church.[18] I have nothing to give except what you have given me, so take my heart and squeeze it out over the face of the Bride.'[19] Then, turning [to me] the eye of his Loving-kindness, God eternal plucked out my heart and squeezed it out into holy Church. And such was the force with which he had drawn it to himself that had he not immediately (not wishing the vessel of my body to be broken) girded it with his might, my life would have ended there and then.

At that the demons began yelling all the more, as if they felt some intolerable pain, doing their utmost to instil terror into me and threatening me that they were able to prevent me from carrying out my task. But since hell is no match for the virtue of humility with the light of most holy faith, [my soul] became more and more at one and worked away with tools of fire, at the same time hearing most winning words in the presence of the divine Majesty, with promises that brought joy. Indeed, my spirit was plunged in a mystery so deep that my tongue is now quite unable to speak of it.

Now I say:[20] 'Thanks, thanks be to the most high eternal God, who has placed us as knights on the battlefield to do combat for his Bride with the shield of most holy faith.' The field is ours. The very power and might that defeated the demon who had mankind in his grip – for he was defeated not by Christ's humanity alone but by virtue of his Godhead – shall again work his ruin; that is, he will be defeated, not by what our bodies suffer, but by virtue of the glowing measureless Charity of God. Amen. Sweet Jesus. Jesus, Love.

---

[1]   Fra Tommaso Caffarini OP, a devoted disciple and admirer of Catherine as well as one of the early editors and author of a 'Supplement' to Raymond's life, declares that she herself penned this account of her last mystical experiences, which she enclosed with her farewell letter to Fra Raimondo (letter 60a). If so, we can only guess at what cost, bearing in mind the intensity of her experience, as well as her physical condition and relative lack of skill in the physical act of writing (cf. letter 13, note 9).

[2]   The account begins thus abruptly in the mss.

[3]   Catherine herself – but the very intensity of the experience soon forces her to adopt the more personal 'I'.

[4]   Cf. John 10:7.

[5]   the Church.

[6]   the fruit of the Blood.

[7]   The sense of this obscure passage hinges largely on the meaning given to the pronouns used. The plural 'you' at this point suggests that God is here conceived of as addressing all Catherine's disciples.

[8]   Probably Catherine herself.

[9]   This seems to mean Catherine's own body, which was being 'poured out' into the Church. Cf. letters 14, p.89 and 20, p.111 for a similar expression and the rest of this letter for its elucidation.

[10]   The singular intimate '*tu*' reappears at this point.

[11]   Ital. 'spogli*a*ta'. We read 'spogi*a*la' here.

[12]   the Cardinals.

[13]   Cf. Genesis 9:23.

[14]   lit. 'what the understanding saw and the affections conceived'; cf. I Cor. 2:9.

[15]   Cf. letter 60a, note 10.

[16]   Cf. Colossians 1:15.

[17]   Fra Raimondo has described this earlier vision; cf. Raymond, pp.99–100.

[18]   Cf. Dialogue p.285 and note 24, p.300.

[19]   In an earlier vision (circa 1370), it had seemed to Catherine that Christ exchanged her heart for his own. Commenting on her account of this experience, Fra Raimondo records that she never afterwards felt able to say: 'Lord, I give you my heart.' (cf. Raymond, pp.165–66). In drawing attention to this parallel,

Mother Drane stresses the profound significance of the phrase
'I have nothing to give except what you have given me.' (cf.
Drane, p.549, n.1).

[20]   Translation of this paragraph based on text of Cod.
Casanatense no. 292 as cited by B.R. Motzo, art.cit. p.124.

# Extract from: *The Dialogue of Divine Providence* or *Book of Divine Doctrine*

[While Catherine and her companions were on their peace-making mission in the Val d'Orcia,[1] the heightening tension between the Pope and his adversaries prompted her to send Fra Raimondo to Rome 'with a number of suggestions which, if properly implemented, would have been of benefit to the Church.'[2] His report of the situation in Rome was disturbing; as Catherine reflected on it while absorbed in prayer after holy communion she was caught up to God and given a profound insight into his ways and purposes, an experience of which she tried to give some account in a letter she wrote to her confessor early in October 1377.[3]

This insight forms the basis of *The Dialogue of Divine Providence*, Catherine's only book. It consists of a series of interchanges between herself and God the Father, each of which develops out of a central core which is itself a short and complete 'dialogue'. It is this 'dialogue', together with the book's Prologue – both of which incorporate long extracts from the letter in question, more or less verbatim – which has been chosen for inclusion in this selection.

Our translation is based on the text as edited by Giuliana Cavallini, who shows clearly in her Introduction[4] how the traditional sub-division of the text into treatises and chapters has tended to obscure the book's basic unity of structure.[5]]

## [PROLOGUE]⁶

In the name of Christ crucified and of sweet Mary.

I

A⁶ soul that yearns with great desire for God's honour and the salvation of souls, having trained itself for some time in the practice of virtue, and grown accustomed to dwell in the cell of self-knowledge, so as better to know the goodness of God in itself, is then led by love – since love is the consequence of knowledge – to seek the truth and to be clothed in it.

The sweet taste and light of this truth can in no way be approached so directly as through humble and unceasing prayer (based on knowledge of self and of God), for such prayer makes a soul one with God through following in the footsteps of Christ crucified, so that by ardent yearning and loving union the soul makes God to be its other self. Such seems to be Christ's teaching when he says: 'To him who loves me and keeps my words I will manifest myself, and he shall become one with me and I with him.'⁷ And in several places we find similar words which reveal to us the truth that through loving him the soul becomes another him.

And to make this clearer, I remember hearing from a servant of God⁸ that once when her mind was wholly wrapt in prayer, God did not conceal from her inward eye the love he bears to his servants; rather, he revealed it to her, saying among other things: 'Open the eye of your understanding and gaze into me and there perceive the dignity and beauty of my creature endowed with reason. And in the midst of the beauty I have bestowed on the soul by creating it to my own image and likeness, see especially that of those who are clothed in the bridal dress of charity, adorned with many true virtues. They are made one with me by love. And so I tell you that were you to ask me who they are, I would reply (said the sweet loving Word): "They are another me", for they have lost and drowned their own wills and have united and conformed themselves with mine.'

So it is true that the soul is made one with God by love. Hence the soul I speak of, desiring more earnestly to follow this truth, stirred up in herself that primary desire which aims at the soul's own good, for she well knew that no soul can be of benefit to others, by teaching and example and prayer, unless it has first been of benefit to itself by the acquiring of virtue; and she addressed four petitions to the eternal Father.

The first was for herself; the second for the reform of holy Church; the third for the world at large; and in particular for the reconciliation of those Christians who are in rebellion against holy Church and impiously maltreating her.[9] The fourth petition was to beseech divine Providence to provide for all things, and particularly as regards one matter that had arisen.[10]

## II

Her desire was intense and continual but it greatly increased when the First Truth showed her the world in its need and how storm-tossed it was, and how much it was offending God. Moreover, she had had read to her a letter she had received from the father of her soul,[11] in which he described his pain and intolerable grief at the offences committed against God, the harm being done to souls, and the persecution of holy Church. All this kindled in her a fire of holy desire, her grief at the offences being lightened by the hope that God would find a remedy for so much evil.

And since it is in communion that the soul seems most sweetly to cling to God, and to know him best – for then the soul is in God and God in the soul, as a fish is in the sea and the sea in the fish, – she longed for morning to come so that she might hear Mass. When morning came – it was

Mary's Day[12] – and the time for Mass, she was present at it with eager longing and great self-knowledge; and with such shame at her own imperfections, which seemed to her to be the cause of the evil being perpetrated all over the world, that she conceived a just and holy hatred and loathing for herself; and with this knowledge and hatred and justice she purified her soul of the stains of guilt that seemed to her to be, and were, in it, saying:

'O eternal Father, I lay a charge against myself before you, and beg you to punish my sins in this world of time. And because I, through my sins, am the cause of the penalties that others have to bear, I beseech you, in your loving-kindness, to inflict them all on me.'

(omissis: pp 5–33).

## [DIALOGUE: MERCY ON GOD'S PEOPLE][13]

### XIII

Then that soul, panting and on fire with intense desire, was filled, in God's goodness, with ineffable love through having experienced the immense charity with which he had so sweetly condescended to grant her petition and, by giving her hope, to ease the bitterness engendered in her by the offence to God, the harm done to holy Church and the realization of her own wretchedness. Her bitterness was thus both diminished and intensified, for in showing her the way of perfection, the supreme eternal Father made her see once again the offence against him and the harm done to souls, in the way I shall now describe.

It is through self-knowledge that the soul comes to know God better, through knowing his goodness in itself; and so, in the sweet mirror of God it knows its own dignity and lack of it: the dignity of having been created in the image of God – and this by pure gift, not as something due to it;[14] the lack of it inasmuch as, in the same mirror of God's goodness, it sees the indignity of having fallen into sin by its own fault. As a man is better able to see the dirt on his face when he looks into a mirror, so when the soul in true self-knowledge raises itself by desire to gaze with the eye of the mind at its reflection in the sweet mirror of God, the purity it sees in him makes it more keenly aware of the stains in itself.[15]

This increase in light and knowledge caused a sweet bitterness to grow in her and the [unalloyed] bitterness to fade, through the hope which the First Truth gave her. As a fire blazes up when it is fed with fuel, so the fire blazed in her so fiercely that no human body could have endured it and lived. Only the strength of him who is supremely strong encircling her kept her in life.

Purified by the fire of divine love which she found in the knowledge of herself and of God, and her hunger growing with her hope for the salvation of the whole world and for the reform of holy Church, she rose up with confidence before the supreme Father, who had shown her the leprosy of holy Church and the wretchedness of the world, and she said, as if with the words of Moses:[16] 'O my Lord, turn the eyes of your mercy on your people and on the mystical body of holy Church,[17] for you will be the more glorified by pardoning so many creatures and giving them light and knowledge – since all would praise you when they see themselves escape through your infinite goodness from the darkness of mortal sin and from eternal damnation – than if you were to pardon only me who have so much offended you and am the cause and instrument of all this evil. Therefore I beseech you, divine eternal Love, to be avenged on me but to show mercy to your people. Never will I leave your presence until I see you have mercy on them. How would I feel to see myself having eternal life, and your people death?[18] And [to see] darkness well up in your Bride – who in herself is all light – chiefly on account of my sins, and other people's? I desire you then, by your grace I beseech you, to have mercy on your people, by that same uncreated love which moved you to create man to your own image and likeness, as you declared: 'Let us make man to our image and likeness.' And this you did, O eternal Trinity, that man might share in all that you are. For this you gave him memory to recall your benefits, by which gift he participates in your power, eternal Father; understanding with which to know and see your goodness, and so share in the wisdom of your only-begotten Son; and will, that he might love what his mind has seen and known of your truth, thus participating in the loving-kindness of the Holy Spirit.

What made you establish man in such dignity? Only that measureless love with which, gazing within yourself at your creature, you fell in love with him, and out of this love created him and gave him being so that he should experience your own supreme eternal Goodness.

I see that through sin he lost this dignity; that by rebelling against you he fell into a state of war against your Loving-kindness,[19] and so we became your enemies.

But you, moved by the same fire with which you created us, willed to provide a means of reconciliation for the human race which had plunged into this great war with you, so that out of war might come great peace; and you gave us the Word, your only-begotten Son, to be the mediator between us and you.[20] He was our justice,[21] punishing in himself our injustices; carrying out the obedience that you, eternal Father, laid on him when you clothed him in our humanity and he took on our human likeness and nature.

O abyss of Love! What heart would not break to see such sublimity descend to such lowliness?[22] We are your image, and you are now ours, through the union you have made in man, veiling the eternal Godhead in the cloud of wretchedness and corrupted clay of Adam. What made you do this? Love. You, God, have become man, and man has become God.[23] By this ineffable love, then, I constrain, I implore you to show mercy to your creatures.'

## XIV

Then God, looking mercifully on her, yielding to her tears and letting himself be bound by the bond of her holy desire, answered, grieving: 'Sweetest daughter, your tears constrain me – since in them is my charity and they fall for love of me – and your anguished desires hold me fast. But look and see how my Bride has soiled her face, has become leprous with impurity and self-love, and swollen with the pride and avarice of those who feed at her breast, namely the whole Christian community, comprising the general body of holy Church and also her mystical body, by which I mean my ministers, those who not only feed at her breasts themselves but are required to feed and hold to those breasts the whole body of believers, together with any others who may choose to leave the darkness of paganism and join themselves as members to my Church.[24]

See with what ignorance, darkness and ingratitude, and with what filthy hands, the glorious milk and blood of my Bride are administered, and with what presumption and irreverence received! Hence what is in itself life-giving, on account of their defects often brings them death – I mean the precious blood of my Son which, having banished death and darkness, gave light and truth and confounded falsehood. His Blood provided and accomplished everything needed for the salvation and full perfection of any man who disposes himself properly to receive it. Nevertheless, as it gives life and every grace in proportion to the disposition and affection of the receiver, so it brings death, not life, to the wicked if they receive it unworthily, in the darkness of mortal sin. And this not through any defect in the Blood, nor in the one who administers it – supposing him to be in a like evil state, or a worse one – for no defect in him can spoil or defile the Blood or diminish its grace and power, nor will he harm the one to whom he administers it, but only himself by his sin, for which he will be punished unless he corrects himself with true contrition and repentance.

I say, then, that one who receives it unworthily suffers harm, not through any defect in the Blood or in the one who administers it, but through his own bad disposition and defects; through having heaped so much filth and wretchedness on soul and body and been so cruel towards himself and his neighbour – towards himself by depriving himself of grace and trampling with the feet of his affections on the fruit of the Blood that was his in holy baptism, once that Blood had removed the stain of original sin he incurred at his conception.

I gave my Word, my only-begotten Son, because the whole mass of mankind had been corrupted by the sin of the first man, Adam, rendering all of you, as vessels formed from this clay, corrupt and unfit for eternal life. For this reason I united my sublimity with the lowness of your humanity – in order to remedy its corruption and death and restore it to the grace it had lost though sin.

In myself I cannot suffer, and yet my injustice requires suffering as a consequence of sin. And of himself alone man could not make adequate satisfaction, for even if a man were in part to do this, he would only do it for himself alone, not for other rational creatures; and in any case the supposition is impossible, for what is involved is sin committed against me, who am infinite Goodness.[25] Therefore, as it was nonetheless my will to restore mankind – enfeebled as it was and incapabale, as I have said, of making satisfaction – I sent my Word, my own Son, clothed in your very nature, that of Adam's corrupt clay, so that he might suffer in the self-same nature that had offended and, by thus suffering in his body, even to the shameful death of the cross, appease my anger.

In this way I appeased my justice and also satisfied that divine mercy which had chosen to make amends for man's sin and dispose him to that good for which I had created him. And so human nature, joined with the divine, did suffice to satisfy for the whole human race, not merely through the pain endured in the finite nature, that is, in the clay of Adam, but by virtue of the eternal Godhead, the infinite divine nature. The two natures thus united, I received and accepted the sacrifice of my Son's blood, mixed and kneaded with his divinity by the fire of my divine Love, which was the bond that held him fixed and nailed to the cross.

Human nature thus sufficed to satisfy for sin, but only by virtue of the divinity. Thus, too, was removed the corruption caused by Adam's sin, leaving only its mark – a propensity to sin, and all bodily defects – as a scar remains when a wound has healed. So it was with Adam's sin that had caused the deadly rot: when my Son, the great Doctor, came, he cured the patient by drinking on man's behalf the bitter medicine that man was too weak to drink; like a wet-nurse who takes a medicine on the baby's behalf because she is big and strong and can bear its bitterness, whereas the baby cannot.[26] And so he, your Wet-nurse, by the greatness and strength of his Godhead when conjoined with your nature, endured the bitter medicine of the cruel death on the cross in order to heal and give life to all you sin-enfeebled children.

There remained only the mark of the original sin you inherited from your father and mother at your conception, and that mark is taken away, though not entirely, at baptism, which is empowered to give the life of grace by virtue of this glorious and precious Blood. At the moment of baptism, original sin is banished from the soul and grace infused into it. The inclination to sin, too, that scar left by original sin, is weakened, and the soul can hold it in check if it wishes.

The vessel of the soul is now ready to receive and accumulate more or less grace according as one chooses to dispose oneself, in one's affections, to love and serve me, though one is equally free to dispose oneself to evil, in spite of having received grace in holy baptism. So when the age of discretion comes, with free will one can freely choose either good or evil as one pleases. The freedom men have is such, and has been so strengthened by the

glorious Blood, that no devil or other creature can force a
man to commit the slightest sin against his will. He has
been delivered from serfdom and made free, that he may
be master of his own sensuality and attain to the end for
which he was created.

O wretched man, wallowing in the mire like a beast and
failing to recognize the marvellous gift he has received
from me – the greatest he could possibly have received,
poor ignorant wretch!

## XV

I want you to know, daughter, that when men do not
acknowledge the grace they received through my recreat-
ing them in the blood of my only-begotten Son and
restoring mankind to grace as I said, but go on from bad
to worse and from sin to sin; when they go on persecuting
me[27] with their many offences and set so little store by the
graces I bestowed, and bestow, on them that not only do
they not consider them graces but sometimes even feel I
am doing them an injury – almost as if I were wanting
something other than their sanctification! – their lot, I
say, will be all the harder, their punishment all the more
severe. All the more so now after their redemption by the
blood of my Son than before it, before the corruption of
Adam's sin had been removed.

It is right that he who receives more should render
more, be the more indebted to his benefactor. Man was
already heavily in debt to me for the being I had given
him, creating him to my image and likeness. He owed me
glory, but chose to withhold it and to glorify himself
instead; thus disregarding the obedience I had laid on
him and becoming my enemy. Then with humility I
destroyed his pride, humbling myself and taking your
human nature; releasing you from the devil's service, I
made you free. And that is not all, for if you reflect you
will see that man has [now] become God and God man, by
the union of the divine and human natures.

Such is the debt men have incurred, the treasure of the

Blood in which they are recreated to grace. See then how much more they owe me after the redemption than before. How their duty is to render me glory and praise by following in the steps of the Word incarnate, my only-begotten Son, and so to pay their debt by loving me and their neighbour with true genuine virtues, as I have said. If they fail to do this, their offence is the greater because of the greater love they owe me, and therefore my divine justice requires that I punish them the more severely, namely with eternal damnation. Hence a false Christian is more severely punished than a pagan. By divine justice he is ever, yet never, consumed, that is, afflicted, in the fire; and being afflicted, he feels himself consumed by the worm of conscience,[28] but he never is, for the damned do not lose their being whatever torments they suffer. I tell you, they ask for death and cannot have it, for they cannot lose their being. The being that was theirs by grace they lost through their own fault, but not their [natural] being. Hence sin is more severely punished after being redeemed by the Blood than before, because of the greater gift received; yet sinners do not seem to perceive this, nor be aware of their evil state. They have made themselves my enemies after I had reconciled them through the blood of my Son.

Nevertheless there is a remedy, a way of appeasing my anger, and it takes effect through my servants, if they are eager to constrain me by their tears and bind me with the bond of desire. You see that you yourself have bound me with this bond, the bond I gave you because I wanted to have mercy on the world. This is why I give my servants a hunger and desire for my honour and the salvation of souls, so that, constrained by their tears, I may mitigate the fury of my justice. So let you and my other servants take your tears and your sweat, drawn from the fountain of my divine Charity, and use them to wash the face of my Bride. I promise you that by this means her beauty will be restored. Not by the sword nor in other cruel ways, but peacefully, by the humble and unceasing prayer of my servants, by the sweat and tears they shed with burning desire.

And thus I shall fulfill your desire with much suffering while your patience sheds light on the darkness of men's wickedness. And fear not the world's persecutions, for I shall be with you, caring for you in my never-failing Providence.'

## XVI

Then rising up with deeper knowledge, and filled in God's presence with joyous confidence in the divine Mercy and delight in his Love on perceiving that, in his loving desire to have mercy on mankind, though they were his enemies, God had given his servants the means to constrain his goodness and appease his wrath, that soul was filled with joy. She lost all fear of the world and its persecutions, seeing that God was with her. And holy desire flaming more strongly within her, she could not rest satisfied but pleaded with holy confidence on behalf of the whole world. And although her second petition – for the reform of holy Church – had already included both Christians and unbelievers, she now extended her prayer (as God himself prompted her to do) to embrace the whole wide world, crying:

'Eternal God, show mercy to your sheep! Be indeed the good shepherd! Delay no longer in having mercy on the world which seems already to be almost at its last gasp, seemingly utterly bereft of unifying charity, of any love for you, eternal Truth, or any mutual love of men for one another grounded on love for you.'

## XVII

Then God, as though drunk with love for our salva-tion, contrived to kindle still greater love and sorrow in that soul, showing with what love he had created man (about which something was said above) and saying: 'And now do you not see how they all strike at me, though I created them with such burning love and gave them grace and almost an infinity of gifts, and all freely and not as in payment of a debt? Yet see how they strike at me with sins of every sort, and especially with their miserable hateful self-love, the root of all evil. With this love they have poisoned the whole world; for as love of me contains every virtue that comes to birth between a man and his neighbour – as I have explained – so carnal self-love, since it arises from pride, as my love does from Charity,[29] contains in itself all evil. And they do this by means of each other, being out of charity with their neighbour through not having loved me and not loving one another, for these two loves go together. This is why I told you that all good and all evil is done by means of one's neighbour.

I have much cause to complain of man who from me has received nothing but good and in return hates me, doing every kind of evil. But I have said that on account of the tears of my servants I will mitigate my anger at this; so now I repeat: Let you, my servants, range yourselves in front of them with many prayers, burning desires and sorrow for the offence to me and damnation to themselves; then I will mitigate the wrath of my judgement.

## XVIII

Know that no one can fall out of my hands, because I am he who is[30] and you of yourselves are not, except in so far as you have been made by me who am Creator of all that participates in being, that is of everything except sin, which has no being and so is not of my making. And because sin is not in me, it is not lovable. Herein lies the offence committed by my creatures; they love sin, which ought not to be loved, and hate me whom they are under an obligation to love – me, who am supreme Goodness and who gave them being with such flaming love. But they cannot get away from me! Either I hold them with my justice because of their sins, or I hold them with my mercy.[31] Open, then, the eye of your mind and look into my hand; you will see the truth of what I say.'

So she, raising her eyes in obedience to the supreme Father, saw the whole wide world in the hollow of his hand.

Then God said: 'My daughter, see and understand that no one can be taken from me. All men are there, either for justice or for mercy, as I said, for all are mine, are my creation, and I love them ineffably. And therefore in spite of their wickedness, I will have mercy on them by means of my servants, and will grant the petition you have put to me with such love and sorrow.'

## XIX
. . . [omissis, pp 47–48].

*[Catherine is almost carried out of herself by the fire of her desire to worship God and plead for sinners, to the extent of yearning to sweat blood in reparation,[32] so much so that . . .]*

Spurred on by holy desire she raised herself yet higher as she opened her inward eye and gazed into the divine Love where she saw and savoured how much we are obliged to love, and to seek, the praise and glory of God's name in the salvation of souls. And she saw that God's servants are summoned to this task, and in a special way the father of her own soul whom she now brought before the divine Goodness, begging God to enlighten him with grace that he might in truth follow the Truth.

## XX
Then in response to her third petition, her hunger for the salvation of this soul, God said: 'Daughter, this is my

will: let him seek to please me, the Truth, by hunger and zeal for the salvation of souls. But this neither he nor anyone can do – as I have told you – without suffering persecutions, according as I bestow them. To the extent, then, that you wish to see me honoured in holy Church, you must conceive a desire to suffer with true patience. This will prove to me that he and you and all my servants seek to honour me in earnest. Then he will be a very dear son to me, and will take his rest, he and the others, on the breast of my only-begotten Son; whom I have made into a bridge over which you can all pass to your last end, to receive the fruit of all the toil you have endured for my sake. Endure, then, manfully.

## XXI

I said I had made a bridge of the Word who is my Son, as indeed I have, and now I want you to know, my children, that the road was so badly broken by the sin and disobedience of Adam that no one could lay hold of immortality, nor did men glorify me as they should, since they had no share in the good for which I had created them, and their not having it left my truth unfulfilled – the truth that I had made man to my image and likeness that he might possess eternal life, partake of me, and enjoy my supreme eternal sweetness and goodness. Sin put this end out of man's reach and left my truth unfulfilled, for it was sin that had barred heaven and the doors of my mercy against him.

This same sin germinated thorns and tribulations of every kind, and my creature found he was at war with himself; no sooner had he rebelled against me than he rebelled against himself too. At once his flesh rebelled against his spirit so that man lost his state of innocence and became an unclean animal. Moreover, all created things now rebelled against him, which would have obeyed him had he remained in the state in which I had placed him. By not remaining therein, he transgressed my law and merited eternal death in soul and body. And no sooner had he sinned than a stormy torrent began to flow that ever buffets him with its waves, bringing him weariness and trouble from his own self, from the devil, and from the world. And you were all drowned in it because none of you, however just, could get through it to eternal life.

And so, wishing to remedy your great evils, I have given you my Son as a bridge, that you may not drown in, but pass over, the flood – the stormy sea of this dark life. See then how indebted my creature is to me, and how foolhardy it is to persist in drowning rather than accept my remedy.

## XXII

Open the eye of your understanding and see the blind and ignorant; see, too, the imperfect, and also the perfect who truly follow me, that you may grieve over the damnation of the ignorant and rejoice at the perfection of my beloved children. You shall also see the divergent paths followed by those who walk in the light and by those who walk in darkness. But first I want you to consider the bridge that is my Son, and to see how its great span reaches from heaven to earth; see, that is, how it links the grandeur of the Godhead with the clay of your humanity. By that span of it is meant the union I have made with man.

It had to be so in order to remake the road that had been broken – as I said – and so enable you to pass over the bitterness of the world and attain to life. Yet no heaping up of earth alone could ever have sufficed to make a bridge great enough to span the torrent and open the way to eternal life;[33] that is, human nature by itself could not satisfy for sin and remove the corruption generated by Adam's fall, which had contaminated the whole human race and made it stink, as I have already said. So your nature had to be joined with the sublimity of mine, the eternal Godhead, that it might suffice to make amends for all men – the human nature suffering the punishment for sin, and the divine nature, united with it, accepting the sacrifice of my Son offered to me on your behalf to save you from death and give you life.

So my sublimity stooped to the earth of your humanity and together they made a bridge and remade the road. And why? So that you might indeed come to the joy of the angels. But it would be no use my Son's having become your bridge to life if you do not use it.'

## XXIII

Here the eternal Truth was showing that while he had created us without our consent he will not save us without it. Rather, he wants us to bring our free will into operation, freely, responsibly, and with genuine virtues using the time given us. So he went on:

'You must all keep to this bridge by seeking the praise and glory of my name in the salvation of souls and by painfully enduring many trials as you follow in the footsteps of the sweet loving Word, for you can come to me in no other way.

You are my labourers, for I have sent you to work in the vineyard of holy Church.[34] You are labouring in the general body of Christian people, where I set you, by grace, when I gave you the light of holy baptism which, in turn, you received in the mystical body of holy Church at the hands of my ministers, whom I have set working along with you. You are in the general body, they in the mystical body; their task being to nourish your souls with the Blood administered in the sacraments which you receive from holy Church, and to draw out the thorns of mortal sin and plant grace in your souls. They are my labourers in the vineyard of your souls. They form a unity in the vineyard of holy Church.[35]

Every rational creature has his own vineyard, his soul, the will being the labourer appointed to work in it with freedom of choice, and in time, that is, for as long as he lives. Once this time is past he can work no more, whether well or ill, but while he lives he can work at this vineyard of his in which I had placed him. And this labourer in the soul has been given a strength no devil or any other creature can take from him unless he chooses; for his baptism made him strong and equipped him with a knife of love of virtue and hatred of sin. This love and hatred he finds in the Blood, for it was out of love for you and hatred for sin that my only-begotten Son gave his blood and died; and it was through this Blood that you received life at baptism. You have this knife, then, to be used with your free will while you have time, to cut out the thorns of mortal sin and put in the virtues; otherwise you cannot hope to receive the fruit of the Blood from those labourers I have placed in holy Church who, as I said, remove mortal sin from the soul's vineyard and dispense grace in the Blood they administer to you in the sacraments of holy Church.

The first thing to do, then, is to bestir yourself with heartfelt contrition, with sorrow for sin and love of virtue. This done, you will receive the fruit of the Blood. You could not do so otherwise, not if you neglect to prepare yourselves, on your side, as branches of the vine of my Son who said: "I am the true vine and you are the branches, and my Father is the vinedresser."[36] For so it is. I am the Vinedresser, since all that has being comes from me. My power is measureless and with it I rule the universe; nothing is made or ruled except through me. And it was I who planted the true vine of my only-begotten Son in the earth of humanity, in order that you, as branches abiding in the vine, should bear fruit.

Therefore, whoever bears no fruit of good and holy works will be cut away from the vine and wither. Having no longer any life of grace from the vine, he will be thrown into the eternal fire, as a sterile vine-shoot is cut off and thrown on the fire because it is no use for anything else. Similarly, men like these, being cut off from grace because of their sins, and dying in mortal sin, are good for nothing, and divine Justice throws them into the fire that burns for ever. Such people have not cultivated their vineyard, but rather destroyed it; and not only their own but their neighbour's too. Not only have they not planted any good shoots of virtue, they have even dug up the seeds of grace they received in baptism, when they shared in the blood of my Son which was the wine given you by this true Vine. But they have taken the seed and fed it to beasts,[37] that is, to all kinds of sins, trampling on it with the feet of disordered affections, thus offending me and doing harm to themselves and their neighbour.

But not so my servants – and you should imitate them by remaining united and grafted into the Vine, for then you will bear much fruit through sharing its sap. By abiding in the Word of my Son, you abide in me, for I am one with him and he with me. Abiding in him you will follow his teaching, and following it you will come to share in the Word's own substance, that is, to share in the eternal Godhead united with humanity, and draw therefrom a divine love which intoxicates the soul. This is what I mean by saying that you share in the substance of the vine.

## XXIV

And do you know what I do, once my servants are united in following the doctrine of the sweet loving Word? I prune them, that they may bear more fruit, and their fruit be tested and not turn into wild fruit. As a man prunes the shoots of his vine so as to get better and more wine from them, cutting off the barren shoots and burning them, so do I, the true Vinedresser, with my vine, pruning with much suffering my servants who abide in me, that they may bear more fruit and better fruit, and their virtues be tested. But the barren ones are cut off and thrown into the fire, as I have said.

The true labourers toil away at their souls, uprooting all self-love and turning over in me the earth of their affections. They nurture and foster the growth of the seed of grace they received in holy baptism. And as they work their own vineyard, they work their neighbour's too, since the two go together – as you remember, I have explained that all evil and all good are done by way of one's neighbour; that you are my labourers who have come forth from me, the supreme eternal Labourer[38], and that by the union I have made with you I have oned and grafted you into the Vine.

Bear in mind that every rational creature has his own vineyard, and that this is joined to his neighbour's without anything in between. All are so joined together that no one can do any good to himself without benefiting his neighbour, nor any evil to himself without harming his neighbour. And all of you together form one great vineyard which is the whole body of Christians, united in the vineyard of the mystical body of holy Church, whence you draw your life. And within this vineyard is planted the vine of my only-begotten Son, into which you must be grafted – otherwise you at once become rebels against holy Church and are like limbs that are cut off from the body and immediately decay.

Even so, while you have time you can get up out of the stench of sin with true repentance, and have recourse to my ministers, the labourers who hold the keys of the wine, that is of the Blood, that has flowed from that Vine, a blood so perfect that no defect in its ministers can deprive you of its fruit.

It is the bond of charity that binds [my servants], together with true humility acquired through knowledge of self and of me. So you see, I have made you all my labourers. And now I call on you again, because the world is already at its last gasp, so much have thorns multiplied and smothered the seed that it will not produce any fruit of grace. I want you then to be true labourers, zealously helping to tend souls in the mystical body of holy Church. For this I have chosen you, for it is my will to have mercy on the world, the world for which you pray to me so earnestly.'

## XXV

Then that soul exclaimed with ardent love:

'O inestimable sweetest Charity! Who would not be set on fire by such love? What heart can keep from melting at such tenderness? O abyss of Charity, you seem to be mad with love for your creatures, as though you could not live without them, and yet you are our God and have no need of us. The good we do adds nothing to your greatness, for you are beyond all change. Nor does our evil do you any harm, for you are supreme and eternal Goodness. What is it that moves you to show such mercy? Love alone, and not any debt you owe us or any need you have of us, for we are the guilty ones, we the wicked debtors.

If I understand aright, O supreme eternal Truth, though I am the thief, you have been hanged in my place; for I see the Word, your Son, fastened and nailed to the cross, made into a bridge for me, as you have shown me, your wretched servant. And therefore my heart is bursting, yet cannot burst, with the hunger and desire it has conceived for you.' . . .

---

1   See Introduction, p.26 and letters 33–37.
2   Raymond, p. 377.
3   Tommaseo 272.
4   op. cit. pp. XXI et seq.
5   In the earliest mss, an occasional large capital at key points constituted the only guide, apart from paragraph signs, as to how the text was to be sub-divided. A similar large capital has been used at these points in our translation; the bracketed sub-headings are taken from Cavallini's edition and the chapter numbering of earlier editions is indicated by a Roman numeral in the margin.
6   See note 5.
7   John 14:23.
8   Catherine herself.

[9]   The Florentines and their allies; cf. letters 19, 20, 24, etc.
[10]   The circumstances that prompted this fourth petition remain obscure.
[11]   Fra Raimondo of Capua OP – see letter 9, note 1; also letter 13, note 9.
[12]   Saturday, traditionally regarded as specially dedicated to our Lady.
[13]   See note 5.
[14]   Romans 4:4–5.
[15]   Cf. II Corinthians 3:18.
[16]   Cf. Exodus 32:11–14.
[17]   See infra p.285 & note 24.
[18]   Cf. Exodus 32:31–32.
[19]   Italian: *clemenzia*, personified here and elsewhere by Catherine as the characteristic attribute of the Holy Spirit; cf. line 18 above.
[20]   I Timothy 2:5.
[21]   Cf. I Corinthians 1:30.
[22]   Cf. letters 13 and 34.
[23]   Cf. II Peter 1:4.
[24]   Catherine here clarifies her distinction between the 'general' body of holy Church and the 'mystical' body of the hierarchy. This rather strange idea may have been current among preachers of her day. It does not seem to derive from any of the great masters (St Paul, St Augustine, St Bernard and St Thomas) on whom Catherine draws so often.
[25]   Cf. St Thomas, *Summa theol.* 3a 1, 2 ad 2 & 46, 1 ad 3.
[26]   This would have been an accepted – and necessary – practice in Catherine's day.
[27]   Cf. Acts 9:5.
[28]   Cf. Mark 9:48.
[29]   Cf. letter 1, note 6.
[30]   Cf. Exodus 3:14.
[31]   Cf. Tobit 13:2, 5.
[32]   Cf. letter 40, p.181.
[33]   Cf. Genesis 11:1–9.
[34]   Cf. Matthew 20:1–16.
[35]   See note 24.
[36]   John 15:1–10.
[37]   Cf. Matthew 7:6.
[38]   John 15:1.

# Index of Addressees

*(The numbers refer
to Letters)*

# Index of Names*

* See Bibliography for scholars
mentioned in the notes.